Understanding older homeless people
Their circumstances, problems and needs

MAUREEN CRANE

OPEN UNIVERSITY PRESS
Buckingham · Philadelphia

Open University Press
Celtic Court
22 Ballmoor
Buckingham
MK18 1XW

email: enquiries@openup.co.uk
world wide web: http://www.openup.co.uk

and

325 Chestnut Street
Philadelphia, PA 19106, USA

First Published 1999

A catalogue record of this book is available from the British Library

ISBN 0 335 20186 5 (pbk)   0 335 20187 3 (hbk)

Library of Congress Cataloging-in-Publication Data

Crane, Maureen.
    Understanding older homeless people: their circumstances, problems and needs/
Maureen Crane.
      p. cm.
    Includes bibliographical references and index.
    ISBN 0 335 20187 3 (hbk)   ISBN 0 335 20186 5 (pbk)
    1. Homeless aged—Services for—Great Britain.   2. Homeless aged—Great Britain
    —Social conditions.   3. Homeless aged—Care—Great Britain.   I. Title.
HV4545.A4C73   1999
362.5'086'942—dc21   98-45150
                                                                                     CIP

Typeset by Type Study, Scarborough
Printed in Great Britain by Biddles Limited, Guildford and Kings Lynn

Understanding older homeless people

RETHINKING AGEING SERIES

Series editor: Brian Gearing
                School of Health and Social Welfare
                The Open University

The rapid growth in ageing populations in Britain and other countries has greatly increased academic and professional interest in gerontology. Since the mid-1970s there has been a marked increase in published research studies which have stimulated new ideas and approaches to understanding old age. However such knowledge has not been widely disseminated. There continues to be concern about the education and training in gerontology of professional workers and whether research findings about ageing reach professionals and the general public.

The *Rethinking Ageing* series aims to fill this need for accessible, up-to-date studies of important issues in gerontology. Each book is intended to review and enhance understanding of a major topic in ageing, and to have particular relevance for those involved in age care, whether as researchers, service providers or carers. All the books in the series address two fundamental questions. What is known about this topic? And what are the policy and practice implications of this knowledge? At the same time, authors are encouraged to *rethink* their subject area by developing their own ideas, drawing on case material and their research and experience. Most of the books are multi-disciplinary and all are written in clear, non-technical language which appeals to a broad range of students, academics and professionals with a common interest in ageing and age care. The very positive response from readers and reviewers to the books published so far has encouraged us to extend the series with new titles while retaining this approach.

Current and forthcoming titles:
Simon Biggs *et al.*: **Elder abuse in perspective**
Ken Blakemore and Margaret Boneham: **Age, race and ethnicity**
Joanna Bornat (ed.): **Reminiscence reviewed**
Bill Bytheway: **Ageism**
Maureen Crane: **Homeless people in later life**
Andrew Dunning: **Advocacy and older people**
Mike Hepworth: **Stories of Ageing**
Frances Heywood and Robin Means: **Housing and home in later life**
Beverley Hughes: **Older people and community care**
Tom Kitwood: **Dementia reconsidered**
Eric Midwinter: **Pensioned off**
Sheila Peace *et al.*: **Re-evaluating residential care**
Moyra Sidell: **Health in old age**
Robert Slater: **The psychology of growing old**
John Vincent: **Politics, power and old age**
Alan Walker and Tony Maltby: **Ageing Europe**
Alan Walker and Gerhard Naegele (eds): **The politics of old age in Europe**

Contents

List of tables and figures		vii
Series editor's preface		ix
Acknowledgements		xi
1	Studying older homeless people and their needs	1
2	Homelessness: a history of concepts and theories	9
Part I	**Biographies and pathways into homelessness**	27
3	The prevalence and profiles of homelessness among older people	29
4	The breakdown of family households	43
5	Itinerant working lives	60
6	Mental illness and stressful events	71
7	The aetiology of homelessness among older people: a synthesis	84
Part II	**Meeting the needs of older homeless people**	95
8	The circumstances of older homeless people	97
9	Psychological and physical health problems	122
10	Sub-groups of older homeless people and their problems	140
11	British policies and services to address homelessness	146
12	Resettling older homeless people	168
	Appendix A: Glossary	183
	Appendix B: The methodology of the empirical studies	185
	References	189
	Index	206

List of tables and figures

Table 3.1   Households accepted as homeless and vulnerable due to old age by local authorities   33

Table 3.2   An estimate of the number of people aged 50 years and over in England and Wales who are unofficially homeless, mid-1990s   35

Table 3.3   The age when the Four-City Study subjects first became homeless   39

Table 3.4   Duration of the Four-City Study subjects' current episode of homelessness   41

Table 6.1   The Four-City Study subjects' self-reports of mental health problems before becoming homeless   74

Table 7.1   The accommodation of the Four-City Study subjects before first becoming homeless   85

Table 7.2   States and events in the life course that antecede homelessness in old age   86

Table 8.1   Interviewers' ratings of the appearance of homeless people, Chicago (percentages)   98

Table 8.2   The Four-City Study subjects' use of soup kitchens and day centres by type of accommodation   106

Table 8.3   Family and social contacts among homeless people, Chicago (percentages)   114

Table 8.4   Housed and homeless older people's marital status (percentages)   114

Table 8.5   The Four-City Study subjects' contact with relatives   115

Table 8.6   Housed and homeless older people's frequency of contact with relatives (percentages)   116

Table 9.1   Drinking patterns of the Four-City Study subjects   128

Table 9.2   Mental health of the Four-City Study subjects at the
             time of interview   129
Table 9.3   Mental health of the Four-City Study subjects by
             type of accommodation   130
Table 9.4   Standardized morbidity rates of health problems among
             homeless people   133
Table 10.1   Dominant sub-groups of older homeless people   142
Table 10.2   The frequency of older male and female homeless
             sub-groups   143
Table 11.1   Examples of dedicated services for older homeless people,
             Great Britain, 1990s   164

Figure 3.1   Movement of the Four-City Study subjects between
             housing and homelessness   40
Figure 8.1   The daily routine of a homeless person and a housed
             person   112
Figure 8.2   The contact with services over 24 hours by a homeless
             person and a housed person   113
Figure 12.1 Pathways from the streets to resettlement, the Lancefield
             Street Centre, London   171

Series editor's preface

The 'Rethinking Ageing' series has largely featured books on issues which are already prominent on the map of ageing studies. It seems important, however, to extend the ambit of the series to include topics of significance which have been neglected and whose importance to gerontology has not been widely appreciated. Homelessness in later life is a good example of this. Research into the causes and needs of the older homeless population has been scant; and in social policy and in journalistic writings *older* homeless persons have hardly been considered, there having been a tendency to associate homelessness with young people. Maureen Crane's *Understanding Older Homeless People* should do much to change these perceptions. It greatly deepens our understanding of the phenomenon of homelessness, which includes both older persons who become homeless as youths or young adults and those who have become homeless for the first time in old age.

Maureen Crane emphasizes the complexities and multi-dimensionality of homelessness. She is clear that the causes of homelessness are not what they are often assumed to be, and, as in other areas affecting later life, myths and misconceptions abound. For example, far from homelessness being the result of, on the one hand, a simple lack of accommodation, or, on the other, some lifelong personality malfunction, a number of people become homeless in later life after having held down long-term jobs, or having lived for years in houses and relationships with others.

A major theme of the book is that homelessness is an issue which cannot be simply explained by economic and structural factors, like lack of access to housing or poverty: personal and biographical factors play an important role. Drawing on her own research involving first-hand observations of people living in temporary shelters and hostels and sleeping rough on the streets of London and the North of England, and on other studies, Maureen Crane examines the histories of older homeless persons and the stages at which they became homeless. Through the case studies included in the book, she demonstrates that the origins of the phenomenon are deep rooted and that they are intricately related to social and psychological factors, including mental illness. While arguing that there is no single cause or theory which can account for homelessness, she does identify two common pathways: 'vulnerability interacting with stress and leading to social disconnection and homelessness; and traumatic and stressful events leading to alienation and homelessness' (Chapter 7).

In the second half of the book, Maureen Crane draws on the experiences of older homeless individuals to bring out the many different factors required to understand their circumstances, problems and needs. She indicates key points in the stages of homelessness where intervention may be helpful, introduces sub-groups of older homeless people with different problems and needs, and discusses practical measures of support and rehabilitation.

Understanding Older Homeless People deserves to gain recognition as an important book. Drawing on the author's extensive research and involvement with this marginalized and vulnerable group, it is as deeply felt as it is clear headed and well-written. We are delighted to include it in the 'Rethinking Ageing' series.

Brian Gearing

Acknowledgements

I thank particularly the older homeless people with whom I have been in contact for their trust, support and cooperation. Without their willingness to recollect and share sometimes painful memories, this book would not have been possible.

I would like to thank the staff working with homeless people who have supported and assisted my work. I send particular thanks to Andy, Terry, Nancy, Vicky, Allan, Phil, Owein, Charmaine, Sarah, Jeanette, David Devoy, Charles Fraser, Sam Parnaby and the other St Mungo's staff who have developed the Lancefield Street Centre into a model which successfully helps older homeless people, and have assisted in the monitoring and evaluation study at the Centre. I send particular thanks to Maggie and her colleagues at the Over 55s Accommodation Project in Leeds; Denni, Jacquie and staff at the former women's hostel at 59 Greek Street; Claire, Tina and colleagues at St Martin-in-the-Fields; Anthony and staff at St Mungo's hostel, Hilldrop Road; Sue and her colleagues at the former Woodhouse Resettlement Unit; Janice and her colleagues at the former West Bar Probation Day Centre; and the staff at Parker Street Hostel, Queen Mary's Hostel, The Hollies, the St Mungo's hostel in Harrow Road and their former hostel in Hatton Garden, the Resettlement Unit in Leeds, St Botolph's Crypt in London and St George's Crypt in Leeds, St Wilfrid's and St Anne's Day Centres (Sheffield and Leeds), Minshull Street Probation Day Centre in Manchester, and the Passage Day Centre in London.

I send special thanks to Tony Warnes at the Centre for Ageing and Rehabilitation Studies, University of Sheffield, who supervised my doctoral thesis and has continued to work with me and assist me in developing my research career. The depth of his support, encouragement and guidance has been invaluable. Innumerable hours have been spent, in a multitude of places, discussing ideas and broadening and channelling my thoughts and understanding ever further. Through his support and encouragement, opportunities for more intense research on homelessness continue to develop. I am also grateful to him for his encouragement, comments and assistance with this book.

I am extremely grateful to the Economic and Social Research Council which awarded me a studentship (Award No. R00429354084) and supported me through the doctoral study. It was commenced at the Age Concern Institute of Gerontology, King's College, University of London, and completed at the Centre for Ageing and Rehabilitation Studies, University of Sheffield. I would like to thank Anthea Tinker and the staff at the Age Concern Institute of Gerontology for their help and support with my work in its early years.

I would like to thank Virginia Graham and the Trustees of the Henry Smith (Kensington Estate) Charity for believing in my work and steadfastly supporting the development of the Lancefield Street Centre in London through many hurdles in the planning stage, and subsequently. I thank the King Edward's Hospital Fund for London and the Sir Halley Stewart Trust for providing funds to enable me to conduct further research into the problems and needs of older homeless people, and to establish a longitudinal study of the resettlement of older homeless people. The book draws on the findings of this research.

I would also like to thank Michael Sosin, Paul Koegel and the other researchers in America with whom I have been in contact. I send particular thanks to Carl Cohen for his help with and support for my work over many years.

Lastly, I am grateful to Ralph McTell for allowing me to use his song 'Streets of London', as an introduction to this book.

Streets of London

Words and music by Ralph McTell

Have you seen the old man in the closed down market,
Kicking up the papers with his worn out shoes?
In his eyes you see no pride, and held loosely at his side,
Yesterday's paper telling yesterday's news.

  Chorus
  So how can you tell me you're lonely
  And say for you that the sun don't shine?
  Let me take you by the hand and lead you through the streets of London.
  I'll show you something to make you change your mind.

Have you seen the old girl who walks the streets of London,
Dirt in her hair and her clothes in rags?
She's no time for talkin', She just keeps right on walkin',
Carrying her home in two carrier bags.

In the all night café at a quarter past eleven
Same old man sitting there on his own.
Looking at the world over the rim of his tea-cup.
Each tea lasts an hour and he wanders home alone.

Have you seen the old man outside the seaman's mission,
Memory fading with the medal ribbons that he wears?
In our winter city the rain cries a little pity
For one more forgotten hero and a world that doesn't care.

1

Studying older homeless people and their needs

This homeless experience is the most fearful thing that has ever happened to me. I have had a hard life caring for my sick husband and bringing up three children on my own, but I have always come through it. Ending up homeless has knocked me for six; my nerves have gone to pieces.

(Betty, who first became homeless in her late sixties)

Homelessness is a timeless, universal phenomenon. It affects men and women of all ages, and involves single people, married couples and those with families. It is an international problem and currently a matter of welfare concern in countries such as Britain, Germany, Italy, Spain, the Netherlands, the United States of America, Canada, Australia, Brazil and Japan (Sahlin 1997; Taschner and Rabinovich 1997; Daly 1996; Avramov 1995; Giamo 1994). The problem has increased over the last twenty years in many countries. Among 11 European countries in the early 1990s, the United Kingdom was reported to have the second highest proportion of homeless people, with a rate of 12.2 homeless people per 1,000 of the total population (Daly 1993). Only Germany had a higher rate of 12.8 per 1,000. Concern about the increasing problem led to the first European seminar on homelessness in Ireland in 1985, and the United Nations declared 1987 as the International Year of Shelter for the Homeless (Daly 1992; Drake 1989).

Homelessness in Britain is controversial and an issue for politicians, statutory and voluntary agencies, the media and the public. Ignorance about the problems and behaviours of homeless people leads to distorted images and stereotypes, and over the years has generated policies of both restraint and assistance. There is real concern about the situation of homeless people, and efforts are made to help and support them. Since the 1990s, the government has invested large sums in accommodation, **out-reach workers** and **resettlement** schemes. There is public support for homeless people, at least through buying *The Big Issue*, the magazine they sell. At the same time, homeless people are publicly attacked. Assumptions are made that people are homeless through choice, and leading politicians have made critical remarks about those **sleeping rough**[1] and beggars (Leppard 1994; Middleton 1994). Local authorities and businesses 'move' homeless people from public areas, such as London's Lincoln's Inn Fields, prevent loitering at railway stations, and ban drinking alcohol in public (Leppard 1994; Cavell 1993). Plans for shelters and services for homeless people are often opposed by local residents and businesses.

This chapter discusses conceptions of homelessness as a social and welfare problem and as a sociological and psychological phenomenon, and describes the situation of older homeless people in contemporary society. It makes clear the applied and academic reasons for raising understanding of the problems of homelessness among older people, and describes the sources of information and the structure of the book.

Homelessness as a social problem and an academic challenge

Homelessness, particularly sleeping rough, is an extreme and deviant behaviour in contemporary society. Most people fulfil social roles and responsibilities and conform to conventional norms. They live in traditional housing, sustain employment, form intimate relationships, raise families and develop community ties. But homeless people have withdrawn or 'retreated' from conventional lives and responsibilities. Most do not work regularly or participate in family relationships, nor do they live in customary housing. A former

The bandstand in Lincoln's Inn Fields where homeless people used to sleep

concert pianist has lived in an old car for 12 years in Chiswick, west London, after being evicted from her house on the street (Inside Housing 1998). The most profound form of retreatism is exemplified by three elderly men: one, since release from prison, has lived alone in woods on the outskirts of London for 30 years; another has spent the last 20 years travelling around Britain, sleeping in bushes, and never staying in a town for more than a few days; and the third, aged 69, has his own house yet chooses to sleep in a doorway. In New York City, to give a contrasting example, there are around 5,000 people living underground in secluded tunnels beneath Manhattan – they have been labelled 'the mole people' (Toth 1993). Some have inhabited the tunnels for at least 12 years, live seven levels below the streets, and reports suggest that if they came to the surface their eyes would have problems adjusting to sunlight. One 72-year-old man is in the tunnels; a second man, in his fifties, has not been above ground for three years.

Homelessness, particularly of these extreme and **entrenched** kinds, is difficult to understand. It has been studied mainly from two perspectives. It is recognized as a social and welfare problem of interest to politicians, policy-makers, and housing, health and social welfare organizations. From this perspective, research concentrates on the circumstances, problems and needs of homeless people, and the types of interventions and services which manage the problem. Homelessness has also aroused academic interest, particularly in the United States and to a lesser extent in Britain. Sociologists and psychologists have theorized and conducted empirical research to increase our understanding of deviancy, marginality, the psychopathology of homeless people, and the reasons why people adopt and maintain **homelessness behaviours**.

Older homeless people in contemporary society

The stereotypical images of a homeless person used to be of a tramp wandering from town to town, of an old alcoholic man on a park bench, or of an elderly **bag lady** pushing a trolley laden with garbage. Nowadays, homelessness is more often seen as a problem among young people and, from the visibility of those who sleep or loiter in shop doorways, town centres and on busy streets, it is sometimes misleadingly equated with sleeping rough. Yet rough sleepers are far outnumbered by 'hidden' homeless people who stay in hostels, bed-and-breakfast hotels, squats, or sleep on the floor of friends' accommodation. In Britain, the problems and needs of young homeless people have received attention in many studies and through services such as Centrepoint and The London Connection (Craig *et al.* 1996; Downing-Orr 1996; Hutson and Liddiard 1994; Kirby 1994). In comparison, acknowledgements that older homeless people exist are rare. They are seldom mentioned in the media, few services are targeted at their needs, and only a handful of studies have examined their circumstances.

With the institution of 'safety nets' and community care by statutory services, it may seem inconceivable that homelessness among elderly people is a problem in an affluent society. Yet many older people stay in hostels and night-shelters, and sleep rough. Some have lived on the streets for more than

20 years. While young rough sleepers tend to congregate in busy shopping areas and to be easily visible, older rough sleepers often stay hidden away from town centres. They have been found sleeping at night in old cars, public toilets, phone booths, derelict buildings, sheds, coal-cellars, rubbish skips, bushes and woods. In the novels *Cannery Row* [1945] and *Tortilla Flat* [1935], John Steinbeck (1995) portrayed makeshift sleeping places in the rusty pipes leading from a cannery, in a boiler, and in a chicken-house. That some older citizens actually live in such obscure places is a political and welfare embarrassment.

Older homeless people are diverse. The traditional tramps, alcoholics and bag ladies of 30 years ago still exist. But others do not fit these stereotypes. A few display exceptional and idiosyncratic behaviours, become recognized as 'characters', and gain the attention of the general public, the media and various establishments. A 76-year-old man died on the streets of London on Christmas Day 1997. He had fought at Dunkirk, served in the RAF as a radar and electronics engineer, and taught for a few years at a London college. Latterly, he had attended the House of Commons daily for more than 30 years and was known by most politicians. When he left the House of Commons each evening, he returned to his home, a doorway in central London. In an obituary, he was described as the 'Hobo of the House' (Cobain 1998).

The behaviour of the majority of older homeless people is, however, mundane and undistinguished and they do not attract attention. Feelings of demoralization, depression, hopelessness, shame and rejection deter them from making their circumstances known and seeking help. One man was a London taxi-driver for more than 25 years until he was mugged and sustained serious head injuries, epilepsy and confusion. He was unable to work, his long-standing marriage ended in divorce, his wife claimed possession of their house, and he became homeless when he was in his fifties. He slept rough for more than ten years until out-reach workers found him and encouraged him to move to a hostel. Another man became homeless in his forties after his mother died. He slept rough for more than 15 years in an isolated spot in London. He claimed no benefits, was unknown to services, and survived by eating food from litter bins.

The purpose of this book is to understand how and why people are homeless in old age and the measures which are needed to prevent and alleviate the problem. From a theoretical perspective, it deepens the current understanding of the reasons why some older people are homeless by examining their histories, the processes and pathways which lead to homelessness, and their experiences once homeless. From a social policy perspective, it presents a balanced picture of the diverse circumstances, attitudes, problems and needs of older homeless people. The book has a strong applied purpose, and by reviewing policy and service developments, it makes recommendations of the types of interventions, services and programmes which are required to meet their needs and make a difference to their lives.

The book is about older homeless people who sleep rough or stay in hostels and night-shelters. This group are particularly isolated and neglected, and there has been little research into their situation. Although it is about *older* people, it involves both those who became homeless as youths or early adults

Many older homeless people do not attract attention

and thus became elderly while sleeping rough or staying in hostels, and those who became homeless for the first time in old age. There is no consensus among British and American researchers and service providers as to the age at which 'older' homelessness begins, and they have applied variously 50, 55 and 60 years as the cut-off age (Crane and Warnes 1997a). In America, Cohen and Sokolovsky (1989: 26) argued for the benchmark to be 50 years, as homeless men of that age had physical disabilities and health problems comparable to the housed population 10–20 years older, and because, psychologically, 'many viewed their lives as over'.

Sources of information

The author's interest in homelessness dates back to 1988 when a preliminary investigation examined the services which were available to elderly people sleeping rough in central London (Crane 1990).[2] This was the first British study to focus on older rough sleepers. Visits were made to hostels, night-shelters, day centres and soup kitchens. It was followed in 1990 by an investigation of elderly homeless people who were sleeping on the streets in central London which collected information about their histories (Crane 1993).[3]

The main source of information for this book is an ethnographic field study of 225 homeless people aged 55 years and over in London, Sheffield, Leeds and Manchester which was conducted for a doctoral thesis (the Four-City Study).[4] The study had two aims: (i) to investigate the antecedents and pathways which lead to homelessness among older people, and increase the understanding of the aetiology of homelessness; and (ii) to identify the problems and needs of older homeless people with a view to informing welfare policy and practice. It concentrated on an isolated group of older homeless people who were sleeping rough or living in hostels and night-shelters and who were neither in contact with local authority housing departments nor officially registered as homeless (Crane 1997). Intensive field-work was conducted for 15 months from June 1994, and over 1,500 hours were spent on the streets and at day centres, soup kitchens and hostels.

Through extended interviewing, partial life histories were collected from the subjects about their family and social relationships, accommodation and work experiences, and their pathways into homelessness were traced. Wherever possible, the subjects were interviewed on several occasions. This allowed checks for reliability, discrepancies to be verified, and subjects to be revisited for more precise information. This was particularly important as the study relied on retrospective information which, in most instances, could not be corroborated. Most subjects had no contact with relatives, their histories were generally unknown to service providers, and some had mental health problems which affected their ability to provide accurate information. The study design and methodology are detailed in Appendix B.

The book also draws on recent primary research of services working with older homeless people. The Lancefield Street Centre Study started in February 1997 at an experimental 24-hour drop-in centre and 33-bed hostel for older homeless people, in Lancefield Street, west London (Crane and Warnes 1998). The research has two elements. It combines a monitoring study of the Lancefield Street Centre residents with a longitudinal study of the resettlement of older homeless people. The monitoring study has collected histories from 70 residents and information about interventions and services received while at the project, and changes in their health, morale, social contacts and self-reliance. The longitudinal study of resettlement monitors the progress of older people who are rehoused in permanent accommodation from the Lancefield Street Centre, from St Martin-in-the-Fields, central London, and from the Over 55s Accommodation Project in Leeds. By August 1998, there were 36 subjects in the study. This study's methodology is also described in Appendix B.

Evidence gathered for two recently commissioned investigations of older homeless people and services is also used. In late 1996, an exploratory survey was carried out for Help the Aged and Crisis of the extent of homelessness among older people in Liverpool and Glasgow, and of services for this client group in London, Leeds, Liverpool and Glasgow (Crane and

Warnes 1997a). A further study was commissioned by Help the Aged in 1997 of innovative services working with older homeless people throughout Britain, and 16 services were described fully in a manual (Crane and Warnes 1997b).

Other sources include the author's ten years' experience of working voluntarily at soup kitchens for homeless people; innumerable discussions with staff working with homeless people at hostels and day centres; and study trips in 1991 and 1993 to New York, Chicago, Milwaukee and San Francisco to visit services for older homeless people and to meet with researchers involved in this field. The book draws on empirical studies, theoretical contributions, and literature reviews about homelessness in Britain, Europe and the United States.[5] Knowledge is drawn from the fields of the sociology and psychology of deviance, urban anthropology, psychiatry, housing studies, social policy and social history.

The structure of the book

The next chapter discusses the history of concepts and theories of homelessness, following which the book is divided into two parts. Part I has five chapters and presents evidence on the pathways into homelessness for older people. An introductory chapter (Chapter 3) outlines the prevalence and patterns of homelessness among older people, and then three chapters examine individual pathways, being successively the breakdown of family households, itinerant working lives, and mental illness and stressful events. The final chapter of Part I (Chapter 7) synthesizes the material and relates the evidence to current theories of homelessness. It challenges the predominant assumption that homelessness is the outcome of structural and economic change, and demonstrates how early American sociological theories and hypotheses can be developed to understand contemporary homelessness.

Part II, consisting of five chapters, describes the circumstances and problems of older homeless people, and proposes a typology of the group. This is followed by a chapter (Chapter 11) which summarizes British policies and services for homeless people, with a brief historical review but concentrating on developments since the 1980s. It examines the extent to which present services are meeting the needs of older homeless people, and identifies pioneering projects for the group in Britain and elsewhere. The book concludes with a chapter on resettling older homeless people, and makes recommendations for service development. The appendices provide a glossary of specialist and colloquial terms (these appear in bold on first mention in the text), and detail the methodology of the empirical studies.

Notes

1 People whose primary night-time residence is in the streets, in doorways, train stations and bus terminals, or secluded or hidden locations, such as abandoned buildings, disused cars, subway tunnels and barns.
2 Conducted for the Diploma in Gerontology at Birkbeck College, University of London.

3 Undertaken as part of the M.Sc. in Gerontology at King's College, University of London.
4 Doctorate awarded in 1997 by the University of Sheffield.
5 The author has had to rely on the English-language literature but, as already stated, homelessness is common in many countries.

2

Homelessness: a history of concepts and theories

To understand why a person becomes homeless you cannot look simply at that person's life history; in my situation you have to trace it back to my grandmother and look at her relationship with men.

(Jean, 62 years old and sleeping rough in London)

There is no universally accepted definition of 'homelessness'. It is defined differently by policy-makers, service providers, researchers, media reporters and the general public. This inconsistency affects the scale of the problem, the people it includes and our understanding. When definitions are examined, confusions and paradoxes emerge. In Britain, the statutory or legal definitions associate homelessness mainly with a lack of accommodation. But when examined closely, homelessness is found to be a more complex state. The age-old condition of vagrancy survives in British legislation and debate as a synonym for homelessness, and sociological and psychological concepts and markers have a bearing on the condition.

This chapter examines the concepts, attributes, hypotheses and theories of homelessness which are encountered in everyday discourse, social welfare debates and academic analyses. First, early concepts and hypotheses relating to vagrancy, hoboism and social detachment are described. These are followed by discussions of attributes, propositions and theories of contemporary homelessness, and further demonstrate the complications and disparate ideas which arise in our understanding of the problem. Lastly, studies, hypotheses and theories specifically of older people are examined.

The age-old condition of vagrancy

Homelessness has been associated with vagrancy and vagabondage in Britain since AD 368 and in the United States since at least the early nineteenth century (Clement 1984; Ribton Turner 1887). A **vagrant** is a person without a settled home or regular work, and the rare derivatives 'divagate' (to stray from one place to another), and 'noctivagant' (wandering by night), emphasize the 'wandering' aspect of vagrancy (*Shorter Oxford English Dictionary*, 1973). In its extreme form, vagrancy becomes pathological dromomania, 'the desire to travel pushed to the point of abnormality, an obsession for roaming', and drapetomania, 'an insane or uncontrollable impulsion to wander away from home' (Allsop 1967: 29–30). Other synonyms have also been applied to homeless people which indicate unsettledness and movement from place to place, including 'vagabond' and 'tramp'. In England and Wales, the Vagrancy Act 1824 recognized three groups of vagrants: idle and disorderly persons, for example pedlars who were trading without a licence, and beggars in public places; rogues and vagabonds, that is to say, 'every person wandering abroad and lodging in any barn or out-house, or in any deserted building, or in the open air, or under a tent, or in any cart or waggon, and not giving a good account of himself or herself'; and incorrigible rogues, such as persons who have escaped from a place of legal confinement (Home Office 1974: 2).

Vagrancy is believed to exist to some extent within all highly developed civilizations but, as a mass phenomenon, to arise in a period of rapid economic and social disorganization (Caplow 1940; Gillin 1929). In the fourteenth century, the problem increased in Britain and was associated with the disestablishment of the monasteries and the Black Death. In America, vagrancy and the development of **skid rows**[1] have been linked to the Civil War, the large number of European immigrants, and to the economic crisis in the 1870s (Cohen and Sokolovsky 1989).

Early twentieth-century hoboism

By the early twentieth century, the 'homeless' population who were using casual wards[2] in Britain and skid rows in America included migratory or itinerant workers who worked casually and seasonally on farms or on construction sites (described in Chapter 5). They were single men, known as 'hoboes', derived from 'hoe boys' (Cohen and Sokolovsky 1989). Hoboes were distinguished from vagrants: whereas vagrants rarely worked but wandered and scavenged, hoboes 'worked and wandered' (Wallace 1968). Hoboes had their own songs and traditions, were active in organizations such as the Industrial Workers of the World, and a Hobo College was developed in Chicago. Skid row became known as 'hobohemia', and camps erected by the men on the outskirts of a city as 'hobo jungles' (Anderson 1923).

American sociologists at the time associated the aetiology of homelessness with economic and industrial changes, particularly periods of recession and advances in technology whereby unskilled jobs became scarce or obsolete (Anderson 1923; Solenberger 1911). Men in mercantile and manufacturing industries lost their jobs and left home to seek unskilled work. Because the work was often seasonal, irregular and low-paid, they had to move from place to place and could only afford to live in cheap lodging houses in skid rows. By continuously moving around, they lost contact with their family, became unsettled and demoralized, and ended up as vagrants when they eventually could not find work. Anderson (1923) noted, however, that many unemployed men would return to work once an economic depression had passed, without experiencing disorganization and homelessness.

Sutherland and Locke (1936) acknowledged a link between industrialization, technological changes, unemployment and homelessness, but highlighted that such a theory did not explain why some men in the 1930s remained employed while others became unemployed and homeless. They offered three explanations which they believed differentiated unemployed men who became homeless from those who remained settled. Their hypotheses were that men who became homeless were incompetent and unable to sustain work which would support them; or that they were reared in economically deprived homes as children and had been compelled to abandon school and accept jobs which had few opportunities; or that such men had personalities which favoured mobility and the homeless lifestyle. Hence, the early American sociologists proposed that, although economic factors and unemployment played a contributory part in causing homelesness, individual and personality factors were critical factors differentiating unemployed men who became homeless from those who remained settled.

Early sociological concepts and hypotheses

As early as 1911, Alice Solenberger associated homelessness with the absence of social relationships rather than with a lack of accommodation. She recognized a homeless man as one who had no family group, and included in her definition those who lived in hotels and boarding-houses. This theme was developed between the 1950s and 1970s by American sociologists who recognized the abnormal social states of skid row residents, the majority of whom were men. Many residents were single and had never married, were estranged from their relatives and had few friends, and many were heavy drinkers and were unemployed or worked in semi-skilled and unskilled jobs (Bahr and Caplow 1974; Bogue 1963; Blumberg *et al.* 1960).

Undersocialization and institutionalization

Undersocialization was related to homelessness by Straus (1946) and Pittman and Gordon (1958) who recognized the limited social experiences of homeless men. Many had come from broken childhood homes, had never had close friends, had either remained single or experienced broken marriages, and had often drifted between jobs with no sense of responsibility or continuity. Socialization is a life-long process through which people learn roles, norms and values, and develop social skills and self-identity (Parsons 1951). It is normally achieved within primary close-knit family and peer groups, and through work and marriage. Some people are undersocialized, having been 'deprived of the opportunity of sharing experiences with others, of belonging to social groups, and of participating in social activities' (Straus 1946: 363). Children and adolescents who are undersocialized may become delinquents or feel isolated and lonely, and enter adulthood feeling insecure, unable to manage social relationships and responsibilities, and avoid commitments such as marriage, family-raising and regular employment (McCord 1990; Erikson 1982; Rutter 1971; Straus 1946).

The American researchers proposed that men who are poorly socialized and dependent leave their childhood homes when adult, and move into semi-protective, institutional environments which relieve them 'of responsibility for coping with problems of food, housing and related needs' (Pittman and Gordon 1958: 128–9; Straus 1946). They secure an institutional lifestyle by joining the armed forces or merchant navy whereby accommodation is provided in barracks; or by working as labourers and in railroad gangs and living in work-camps, or obtaining live-in jobs in hotels and hospitals. They become dependent on this lifestyle, isolated from conventional society, and use hostels and shelters and drift into homelessness when they are no longer working.

Several reasons for undersocialization and homelessness were proposed. It was hypothesized that men who became homeless were dependent on their mothers and did not receive training to assume responsibilities. Once adult, they were unable to make decisions and relied on others to guide them (Bogue 1963; Blumberg et al. 1960; Pittman and Gordon 1958). It was also hypothesized that undersocialization may have generational links. Homans proposed that poor socialization was passed through generations, and that men who were poorly affiliated reared children of 'lowered social capacity' (Bahr and Caplow 1974). Only tentative support for this proposition was found among homeless men in New York.

Institutional living was also associated with homelessness. According to Bahr and Caplow (1974: 65), 'prolonged association with total institutions or other environments, that provide the necessities of life with a minimum of individual initiative, may incapacitate inmates for life in more demanding contexts. They may establish patterns of behavior incompatible with the outside'. Institutional living occurred in the military service, hospitals, prisons, orphanages, among railroad gangs and in work-camps. It was reported to result in dependency and 'disculturation' as people lose learned skills and the responsibilities needed for independent living. People generally sleep, work and pursue leisure activities in different places and with different co-participants. According to Goffman (1961: 18), institutions break down the barriers which normally separate these three spheres of life as 'inmates typically live in the institution and have restricted contact with the world outside the walls'. Institutional living thus engenders isolation from family and friends, and in environments such as army barracks and work-camps for labourers it may foster heavy drinking (Bahr and Caplow 1974; Pittman and Gordon 1958).

Social change leading to disaffiliation, alienation and retreatism

People normally maintain social relationships and ties through associations with their family, work, church, neighbourhood and local community. Howard Bahr and his colleagues perceived homelessness as a state of *disaffiliation*, a 'detachment from society characterized by the absence or attenuation of the affiliative bonds that link settled persons to a network of interconnected social structures' (Caplow et al. 1968: 494). Skid row men were seen to be detached from mainstream society and many were poorly affiliated with one another (Caplow et al. 1968). Merton (1968: 209) noted that tramps and vagrants 'may gravitate toward centers where they come into contact with other deviants and although they may come to share in the subculture of these deviant groups, their adaptations are largely private and isolated rather than unified under the aegis of a new cultural code'.

Homelessness was also associated with a state of *alienation* and estrangement from conventional family and social groups (Bahr 1967; Wallace 1965). Whereas disaffiliation may indicate mere apathy, alienation implies repulsion. An alienated person feels separated from a group or community, has no sense of involvement in society, and is 'estranged from, [or has been] made unfriendly toward his society and the culture it carries' (Nettler 1957: 672; Fischer 1976). The sense of alienation is that a person is alienated *from* something or someone (Keniston 1972). Merton associated vagrants, tramps and chronic drunkards as being *retreatists*, describing them as being '*in* the society but not *of* it' (Merton 1968: 207). The term 'retreat' means a withdrawal or retirement from a situation which is difficult or disagreeable, and connotes coming out of circulation, drawing back, or relinquishing a position (Bahr and Caplow 1974).

Merton (1968) proposed that when people experience social change and become 'exempt' from roles through, for example, retirement or widowhood, they experience an abrupt disruption of norms and social relationships. They lose established patterns of behaviour, have no structure in their lives or clearly defined values or goals, and this can produce a state of *anomie*, that is, 'an acute disjunction between the cultural norms and goals and the socially structured capacities of members of the group to act in accord with them' (Merton 1968: 215–16). They react by 'retreating' from society and becoming homeless. It particularly occurs 'in response to acute anomie . . . when it appears to individuals subjected to it that the condition will continue indefinitely' (Merton 1968: 242).

Durkheim (1984), writing in 1893, originally associated anomie with the division of labour in society. According to him, equilibrium was maintained in society and a state of anomie was prevented if 'organs solidly linked to one another are in sufficient contact . . . being adjacent to one another, they are easily alerted in every situation to the need of one another and consequently they experience a keen, continuous feeling of mutual dependence . . . they regulate themselves' (Durkheim 1984: 304). Once some 'blocking environment is interposed between them', a person is no longer controlled by rules or limits, sees no purposes or goals, and a state of anomie arises. Parsons (1951: 39) described anomie as 'the polar antithesis of full institutionalization'.

Concepts and attributes of contemporary homelessness

From the early understanding of homelessness, a number of terms, definitions and concepts have been acquired. Homelessness has become officially recognized in many countries. The United Kingdom Housing (Homeless Persons) Act, which was passed in 1977 and consolidated into Part III of the Housing Act 1985, states that a person is homeless if:

- they have no accommodation they are entitled to occupy;
- they have a home but are in danger of violence from someone living there;

- they are living in accommodation meant only for an emergency or crisis, such as a night-shelter;
- they are a family who are normally together but are living in separate houses because they have nowhere to live together;
- their accommodation is movable, for example a caravan, and they have nowhere to place it (Audit Commission 1989).

A person is threatened with homelessness if 'it is likely that he will become homeless within 28 days' (Housing Act 1985, Section 58.4). This definition has been maintained in the Housing Act 1996.

The creation of statutory and unofficial homeless groups as a response to legislation

Before the Housing (Homeless Persons) Act 1977 was passed, local authorities provided housing to people deemed to be (most) 'in need' (Malpass and Murie 1994). The 1977 Act imposed statutory duties upon local authorities to house groups of people who were considered to be 'homeless' or 'threatened with homelessness', provided that they were in 'priority need', had not made themselves intentionally homeless, and had a 'local connection' with the area covered by the local authority (Audit Commission 1989). Those in 'priority need' included people with dependent children; pregnant women; people who became homeless following a fire, flood or similar emergency; and those who were vulnerable because of old age, mental illness or physical disability.

By imposing duties on local authorities to rehouse homeless people who meet specific criteria, the 1977 Act created two groups of homeless people: the officially registered and those who are homeless but unrecognized as such. Only the former are included in official statistics of homelessness. People who are unofficially homeless include those who have never made their homeless circumstances known to local authorities, and those whose application has been rejected because they are not considered to be in priority need or are deemed to have made themselves intentionally homeless. People who are *de facto* or unofficially homeless fall into two sub-groups. The first, *hidden* homeless people, are accommodated by relatives or friends, and their homeless situation is concealed and may only become apparent if other people can no longer accommodate them (Watson and Austerberry 1986). The second sub-group have no access to housing which they can rightfully or by invitation occupy, and are thus **indigent**, that is to say, 'lacking in what is requisite . . . lacking the necessaries of life' (*Shorter Oxford English Dictionary*, 1973). They 'live' in public places such as doorways, abandoned buildings, railway stations, under bridges, or stay in temporary hostels and night-shelters. The extent to which the problem is overt depends on whether people conceal themselves or sleep in doorways or other visible locations.

The application of the concepts of **statutory** and unofficial homelessness can be complicated. Occasionally an individual or household is accepted as statutorily homeless even when they are housed (Currie and Pawson 1996; O'Callaghan *et al.* 1996; Niner 1989). They are included in statistics of homelessness yet they have never actually been without accommodation. At the other extreme, some people sleeping on the streets are elderly or mentally ill, and meet the criteria of 'priority need' but are unknown to local authorities. The official response to homelessness relies on individuals to declare their homeless state, and thus assumes that all homeless people are competent to initiate a housing application and 'manage the system'. Yet homelessness is sometimes indicative of poor competence in everyday affairs.

A lack of secure accommodation

The Housing Act 1985 uses the lack of accommodation as the prime attribute of homelessness, and the definition is often used in studies of homelessness. Ambiguities over the housed or homeless status of some people inevitably arise. At one extreme are owner-occupiers and people with tenancies who have secure accommodation and are presumed to be housed. At the other extreme are people who 'sleep rough' and are unequivocally homeless. But there are many intermediate and paradoxical states. There is no consensus about whether people in marginal housing such as lodgings, 'digs' and hostels are housed or homeless. Early twentieth-century American sociologists recognized people living in rooming houses and lodgings as homeless, but since the 1970s homelessness has become more narrowly defined and often means an absolute lack of accommodation or 'rooflessness' (Veness 1992; Rossi 1990).

Another equivocal situation is when people with no accommodation are 'housed' temporarily in prisons, hospitals, army barracks, work-camps or tied accommodation. They have little security and no control or rights over the accommodation. Their length of stay is dependent on detainment in prison, treatment in hospital, or the duration of employment. Building labourers who live in work-camps, or merchant seamen who are accommodated on ships, are sometimes employed for only a few months at a time. For them, homelessness is in abeyance while they are temporarily accommodated. According to the *Homelessness Code of Guidance for Local Authorities* in England and Wales, people are homeless if they are living in accommodation which is 'not designed to be lived in long-term', indicating that people in bed-and-breakfast hotels, hostels, hospitals and prisons, or those employed and accommodated for just a few months, should be regarded as homeless if they have no alternative housing (Department of the Environment (DoE) *et al.* 1994, Section 5.8c).

The definition of what constitutes a 'home' is also unclear; it has environmental and psychological attributes. It is perceived to be a physical structure providing roots and a central point for departure and return; a source of identity offering familiarity, security and a sense of belonging; and a place of regeneration where people can acquire warmth, stimulation and emotional well-being (Porteous 1976; Hayward 1975). In rural Delaware, a 76-year-old woman lived in two dilapidated mobile homes and a hut (Veness 1993). She slept in one, cooked in another, and stored personal belongings in the third. Although some considered her homeless, she regarded this arrangement as home. In contrast, there are people with tenancies who sleep on the streets each night (Crane 1993; Lamb and Lamb 1990). Some have paranoid ideas about neighbours and fear harm if they return home, while others are lonely and prefer to be with people on the streets. By their very behaviour, they would be regarded as homeless (and included in street counts of homeless people), yet while they have a tenancy, they are not legally homeless. Homelessness is therefore associated with certain behaviours and not all cases are captured in terms of access to accommodation.

Overt and unconventional 'homelessness behaviours'

Vagrancy and hoboism are not common features of contemporary homelessness. There is little demand nowadays for migratory and seasonal workers and therefore hoboism is no longer a way of life. Only a small proportion of indigent homeless people demonstrate vagrant behaviours and wander from place to place (Rahimian *et al.* 1992). Nevertheless, some homeless people display unconventional homelessness behaviours which are distinctive, sometimes highly visible, and often individualistic and 'massless'. Indigent homelessness is a state which, by its very nature, leads people to 'live' in public places, behave in unconventional and sometimes extremely deviant ways, and engage in activities which people normally conduct in the privacy of their homes. Homelessness behaviours attract public attention, distinguish homeless people from others on the streets, and encourage stereotyping.

Homelessness behaviours include lingering and sleeping on the streets; sitting on cardboard in shop doorways; carrying all one's possessions; walking aimlessly around the streets; drinking alcohol alone or in groups in places not licensed for the purpose, as in doorways or in parks; and congregating at soup kitchens or at street handouts where free food and clothing are distributed. The deviancy of homelessness behaviour varies considerably, the most bizarre and abnormal manifestations being associated with destitution, deteriorating mental health, and personal neglect. More extreme and deviant behaviours include picking up cigarette butts from the pavements; begging; scavenging in litter bins for food; hoarding rubbish in carrier bags or shopping-trolleys; drunkenness and causing a disturbance; lying on the pavement; muttering or shouting; and urinating in public places. Such people may be even more noticeable by their ill-fitting or old, defective clothing, and personal filthiness and odour.

But not all homeless people display homelessness behaviours, nor are all who behave in this way homeless. The behaviour characterizes many indigent homeless people but generally not statutory homeless people. The latter are in contact with housing and welfare services who are obliged to help them, and their homelessness is not usually evident to the general public. They are temporarily housed, usually have access to eating and washing facilities, and receive state benefits or earnings. They therefore do not need to beg, scavenge, or rely on soup kitchens. On the contrary, some people who have conventional housing congregate regularly for long periods with homeless people on the streets, use street handouts and soup kitchens, and return to their accommodation for just a few hours at night. A few remain on the streets all night. Although they have secure accommodation, they display homelessness behaviours.

Disaffiliation, alienation and contemporary homelessness

Disaffiliation and alienation remain features of contemporary homelessness. Affiliation describes a person's relationship with society. Disaffiliation is a matter of degree. People may be totally disaffiliated or detached only from particular groups. Although members of delinquent gangs, hippies and gypsies are sometimes detached from conventional society, they are affiliated within 'subcultural groups' and work towards collective goals (Okely 1983; Fine and Kleinman 1979; Cloward and Ohlin 1960). Many indigent homeless people not only are detached from mainstream society, but also have minimal social interaction with one another (described in Chapter 8).

By participating in social and community groups, people normally fulfil roles, accept responsibilities, meet obligations, and develop recognition, status and prestige. Disaffiliation and homelessness therefore imply a state of near-rolelessness. Homeless people have to occupy themselves with basic survival, such as acquiring food and finding shelter. But they have few other social roles, commitments or responsibilities. However, homelessness also implies downward social mobility, being on the 'skids'. Many homeless people have owned property or sustained tenancies, worked for many years, and married and raised children. They have had relationships, roles and responsibilities, and presumably earned recognition and social standing. For them, becoming homeless has meant a loss of roles, commitments and status. They have lost their social position, their home and material possessions which normally convey economic worth, status and social identity (Dittmar 1992; Goffman 1959), and are thus ascribed low status and social marginality (Wallace 1965).

Alienation may occur because a person deliberately rejects and retreats from society, or society may withdraw and exclude an individual either deliberately as a result of stigmatization, or accidentally as the result of an event such as widowhood which destroys a person's only support links. Deviant behaviours elicit negative sanctions and lead to stigmatization and rejection (Rubington and Weinberg 1978). The extent to which deviant behaviour is stigmatized depends on its visibility, and the status of the potentially 'marked' person (Schur 1979; Goffman 1963). Deviants who are unassertive and powerless are more likely to be stigmatized and alienated than those who are socially and economically advantaged (Jones *et al.* 1984; Snyder *et al.* 1977; Seeman 1975). In relation to homelessness, alienation can be seen as self-perpetuating, as a result of both the deviant behaviours of homeless people and their stigmatization and rejection by conventional society. As homeless people become entrenched in homelessness and their behaviours deviate further, they become increasingly isolated from families and social groups. They have no rights to accommodation, few social roles, and are unproductive, powerless, yet visible members of society. These factors are likely to intensify alienation.

Hypotheses and theories of contemporary homelessness

Natural disasters and catastrophic events, such as house fires, floods, wars or earthquakes, can result in sudden homelessness for individuals, families and communities. Caplow *et al.* (1968: 496) refer to victims of such disasters as 'refugees', and they include 'persons compelled to abandon their homes because of events for which they cannot be held responsible'. 'Refugees' are distinguished from other homeless people because they usually retain or renew affiliations and they are generally resettled in a community, although it is acknowledged that some may become permanent refugees who are dis-affiliated and not resettled.

Lay commentators, politicians and a few academics have argued that some people become homeless through choice or 'wanderlust', that is to say, an urge to roam and encounter new places and experiences (Anderson 1923; Solenberger 1911). Studies have found this to be rare: fewer than one in ten homeless people admit that they have 'chosen' the homeless lifestyle (Snow and Anderson 1993; Roth *et al.* 1985; Digby 1976). Diverse theories have been developed to explain the reasons for homelessness from structural, economic, sociological and psychological perspectives. Most are American in origin. British contributions have focused on structural and economic reasons rather than sociological and psychological causes.

Economic and structural changes

Contemporary researchers in Britain, Europe and America frequently associ-ate the root causes of homelessness with a shortage of low-cost rented housing, unemployment and poverty (Avramov 1995; Wolch and Dear 1993; Rossi 1989; Ropers 1988). Greve (1991: 18) proposed that homelessness in Britain was principally caused by 'a critical shortage of affordable rented housing', a problem which has been reinforced since 1979 by a sharp reduc-tion in council house building, a substantial decrease in finances for new building, and a government programme to encourage local authorities to sell council houses to tenants. He claimed that employment opportunities, wage and income levels, demographic changes, the rate at which new households are being formed, and policies relating to social security and housing benefit contribute to homelessness in that 'people are unable to find or retain housing at rents or prices they can afford and with security of tenure' when faced with crises such as unemployment or relationship breakdown (Greve 1991: 23).

Ropers (1988) proposed that homelessness in America has its roots in eco-nomic and structural factors, but his hypotheses differed to those of John Greve. Whereas Greve claimed that a shortage of affordable rented housing was the crucial factor contributing to homelessness, Ropers suggested that its origins stem from economic displacement and unemployment. He theorized that economic depressions and technological innovations lead to job dis-placement and unemployment, people become disaffiliated from the job and housing market, and they lose a work role and its associated income and social integration. This adversely affects their self-esteem and self-identity and they become socially and psychologically estranged. This can be likened to the works of the early American sociologists who associated unemployment and homelessness with personal disorganization.

There has been little advance on the early theoretical propositions about the significance of economic and structural factors in the causation and progression of homelessness, and few theories and models have been developed and empirically tested which explain why only a minority of unemployed people become homeless. In America in the mid-1980s, when the economic recession receded and unemployment decreased, it was noted that the number of homeless people continued to increase (Jencks 1994; Morse 1992). It was suggested that 'a direct, linear relationship does not necessarily exist between homelessness and the health of the national economy, including employment rates' (Morse 1992: 6). Recent analyses comparing poverty, housing, unemployment and homelessness in American cities have found that rates of poverty and unemployment in areas had *no* significant effect on rates of homelessness (Burt 1992; Elliott and Krivo 1991). Cities with relatively favourable housing and employment conditions still had a problem of homelessness.

Advances on early hypotheses of undersocialization and institutional living

There has been little advance since the 1950s and 1960s on hypotheses of the relationship between undersocialization, institutional living and homelessness. Studies still report that a high proportion of homeless people have experienced broken childhood homes, have remained single or experienced broken marriages, and have irregular employment histories and few social relationships. An increase in the number of young homeless people in the 1990s has generated new hypotheses. The belief is that some who become homeless are raised in dysfunctional and problematic family homes, and experience disruptions, abuse and rejection. As a result, they become alienated from their family, are not taught the necessary skills to live independently, and become homeless when family relationships deteriorate (Downing-Orr 1996; Snow and Anderson 1993). It is also hypothesized that some people have not received adequate preparation to cope independently when they leave a supported environment or the military service (Kirby 1994; Randall and Brown 1994a; Rosenthal 1994; Cohen and Sokolovsky 1989). But living in an institution is sometimes an intermediate step between personal or social problems and homelessness. People may join the army or merchant navy because of family problems (Hutson and Liddiard 1994; Sosin *et al.* 1988).

The social histories of homeless people have rarely been examined, making it impossible to advance early propositions of undersocialization leading to homelessness. Some men are reported to become homeless in middle age following the death of their parents with whom they have always lived (Walker *et al.* 1993; National Assistance Board 1966). Yet reasons for this have not been examined. There is little evidence which demonstrates whether people who become homeless after leaving institutions are managing independently before entering an institution and lose their coping skills while in the setting, or whether they are dependent and unable to cope and these factors necessitated their being in an institution.

Advances on early hypotheses of social change leading to homelessness

It is proposed that social change, such as the breakdown of family or social relationships, can cause strain and conflict and lead to homelessness (Snow and Anderson 1993; Wright 1989; Sosin *et al.* 1988). Events such as widowhood and retirement typically require a person to make substantial readjustments, adapt to new role demands, change routine behaviours and adapt to financial constraints (Holmes and Rahe 1967). People may be unable to cope with new roles, norms and goals which are forced upon them. They may lack the necessary psychological, social or material resources to make the changes, or they may find them contentious.

People cope with stresses and changes in different ways. Some confront a problem and seek ways of solving it, while others use avoidance tactics such as escapism and denial (Hooker *et al.* 1994; Lazarus 1993). Some people are particularly vulnerable to stress, for example those who are mentally ill (Miller and Miller 1991; Kahana *et al.* 1990). Those who are socially and economically advantaged are often in a better position to manage changes than people who have financial difficulties, low self-esteem and who lack social support (Norris and Murrell 1984; Thoits 1982; Pearlin and Schooler 1978). But there is little understanding as to why only a minority of people adopt the *extreme* behaviour of retreatism and abandon their homes and conventional lifestyles at a time of change and upheaval.

Personal incompetencies: mental illness and alcoholism

Mental illness and alcoholism have been associated with the aetiology of homelessness (Snow and Anderson 1993; Cohen and Sokolovsky 1989). Some people are vulnerable and have high levels of personal disability and few resources. They are supported materially and emotionally by their family or relatives. Eventually their family's ability to help is eroded either financially or psychologically, frictions occur at home and their support system is destroyed. Because they cannot cope on their own, they become homeless (Rossi 1989; Wright 1989; Sosin *et al.* 1988). But little is known about the aetiology of mental illness and alcoholism in people who become homeless. Stressful events during adulthood, such as widowhood or marital breakdown, may incite heavy drinking or mental health problems which progress to homelessness (Crockett and Spicker 1994; Calsyn and Morse 1991).

These pathologies may also have deep-rooted origins. The onset of paraphrenia, that is, late-onset schizophrenia, has been associated with long-standing difficulties of socialization (Gurland and Fogel 1992; Kay and Roth 1961; Jaco 1954). Some behaviours may be replicated in future generations, and alcoholism, for example, may stem from parental experiences. Associations have been made between broken childhood homes, parental conflict, heavy drinking by fathers, and alcoholism in adulthood (McCord and McCord 1962; Park 1962; Robins *et al.* 1962). A relationship has been found between heavy drinking among homeless men and a similar drinking pattern by their fathers (Welte and Barnes 1992; Bogue 1963). For some people, mental illness and alcohol abuse may originate from experiences in childhood or adolescence of parental difficulties, while for others the origins may lie in adulthood and be associated with stressful life events.

Holistic explanations of homelessness

Since the late 1980s, American researchers have developed syntheses of why people become homeless (Rosenthal 1994; Snow and Anderson 1993; Wright 1989; Sosin *et al.* 1988; Wolch *et al.* 1988). Structural and economic conditions, namely poverty, unemployment and insufficient low-cost rented housing, are believed to influence the social and financial situation of people over time. Individuals who lack informal and formal sources of help are vulnerable. Particularly at risk are those who have disabilities such as mental illness or alcohol problems, and those who have been discharged from institutions such as mental hospitals or prison. A crisis or stressful event, such as marital breakdown, redundancy or eviction, may result in homelessness among those who are vulnerable. But few theorists have systematically integrated and analysed structural, social and psychological factors. The 'propositions' often deal with covariations which encompass most situations, and generally involve little explanatory theory.

Analyses have attempted to identify risk factors for homelessness, by examining the prevalence of factors such as disruptive childhood, mental illness and substance abuse in the histories of people before they became homeless (North *et al.* 1998; Herman *et al.* 1997; Koegel *et al.* 1995; Susser *et al.* 1993). But the interactions between a disturbed childhood, other factors, and homelessness are unknown. A broken childhood home may immediately lead to homelessness for some people, while others may experience a disruptive childhood home but only become homeless in middle or old age when other factors trigger the problem. Holistic theoretical propositions tend to lack richness and refinement in understanding the processes leading to homelessness.

Studies, hypotheses and theories specifically of older people

Older people have been included in British and American investigations of homeless people since the early 1900s, but few studies specifically of this population have been conducted, most since the late 1980s. An exploratory study of older homeless people sleeping rough in London in 1990 found that some of the 54 male subjects and 21 female subjects had only recently become homeless, but others had been on the streets for years (Crane 1993). The dominant expressed reasons for becoming homeless were widowhood, marital breakdown, eviction, redundancy and mental illness. Apart from the recent Four-City and Lancefield Street Centre studies, and the commissioned reports of older homeless people and services (described in Chapter 1), the only other substantial British investigation was conducted on elderly homeless people in contact with local authorities in four areas of Scotland (Wilson 1995; 1997a). The majority of the respondents were less than 65 years old, many were living in secure accommodation or with adult children, and only a small proportion were homeless and living in hostels or sleeping rough.

Common reasons for homelessness were marital breakdown, family disputes, eviction from privately rented accommodation, and the loss of tied accommodation on retirement.

The most penetrating and influential American investigations of older homeless men have been conducted in New York City (Cohen and Sokolovsky 1989; 1983). An in-depth, qualitative study was conducted on 281 homeless men over the age of 50 years who in 1982–83 were living on the Bowery, the skid row area of New York City (Cohen and Sokolovsky 1989). Eighty-six men were sleeping rough, 177 lived in **flop-houses**, and 18 in dilapidated tenements. They had been living on the Bowery from a few days to 63 years. Several attributes recurred in their histories. These were disrupted childhoods, poor education, low-skilled jobs as in casual labouring which brought contact with the Bowery, moderate to heavy alcohol consumption, mental and physical health problems which prevented employment, and emotional distress following widowhood or relationship breakdowns.

The case files of 157 elderly homeless people referred to emergency shelter services in Chicago in 1986–87 were examined (Kutza 1987). The reasons for homelessness could be determined for only 43 per cent of the sample. The majority had become homeless within the previous year and eviction, family disputes or mental health problems were contributory factors (Kutza 1987). A further 13 per cent, while not homeless, were living in poor conditions deemed to be a health or safety risk. The emergency services had been alerted to their circumstances by a landlord, a neighbour or the police. Another study examined the records of 475 people aged 60 years and over in Chicago who were homeless or living in deplorable housing conditions, and who were in contact with the Chicago Department of Human Emergency Services homeless programme (Keigher *et al.* 1989). Many had been homeless for only a short time, and were people who had lived alone and were evicted for forgetting or refusing to pay rent, generally associated with mental illness, dementia and alcoholism (Keigher *et al.* 1989). Homelessness also occurred following the loss of support from a spouse or carer, the loss of income, or through a self-initiated move due to paranoid fears.

Homeless older people (68 men and 17 women) in Detroit were the subject of a brief investigation in the late 1980s. Their pathways into homelessness were associated with 'life-long difficulties with other people, lack of a supporting family, poor education and lack of job skills, and personal problems such as alcohol abuse and criminal behavior' (Douglass *et al.* 1988: 51). In association with these factors, poverty was identified as the critical cause of homelessness. There was no report, however, that life histories had been examined, and the conclusions appear impressionistic. Other brief surveys have been conducted on older homeless people in New York City shelters (Ladner 1992), and in Tampa Bay, Florida (Rich *et al.* 1995).

Overall there is a dearth of information about older homeless people in Britain and America, for only a scatter of mostly small-scale and short-term studies have been carried out. The few existing studies have identified common features among the group, including isolation, estranged family relationships, and high rates of mental and physical illnesses, but have rarely distinguished between those who have been homeless for years and those who became homeless for the first time in old age (Chapters 8 and 9). The New York and Detroit studies concluded that homelessness among older people is often the result of long-standing problems of family and social relationships, work difficulties, mental illness and alcoholism (Cohen and Sokolovsky 1989; Douglass *et al.* 1988). The Chicago studies suggested that eviction or poor living conditions arising from mental illness and inadequate coping are crucial factors leading to homelessness in later life (Keigher *et al.* 1989; Kutza 1987).

Many and often conflicting biological, sociological and psychological theories of ageing have been proposed over the years, although none have been related to homelessness, and the indications are that there is only a tenuous link between ageing and homelessness. Role theorists such as Parsons (1942) proposed that the loss of roles associated with retirement, for example, produces demoralization and reduced self-esteem, and people

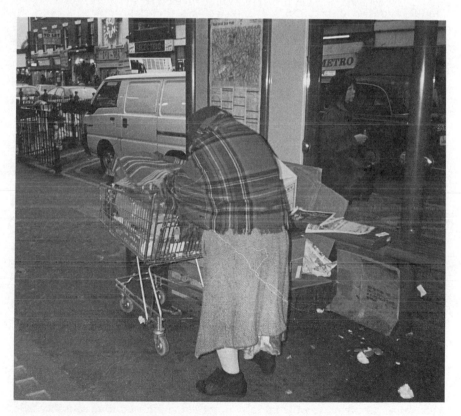

Little is known about the backgrounds of older homeless people

become pessimistic about their abilities and are unable to make changes (Fennell *et al.* 1988). Although homelessness is sometimes associated with the loss of roles, many people become homeless when they are faced with additional roles and responsibilities with which they are ill prepared to cope. Psychological theories of ageing are associated with development throughout the life course. Erikson (1965) identified eight developmental stages from childhood to old age, proposing that difficulties at one stage influenced subsequent behaviour. Although failure to develop at any stage of the life course can leave a person vulnerable and unprepared to face changes and demands as they arise, additional factors and problems are needed in the equation before homelessness will ensue.

Cumming and Henry's (1961) disengagement theory asserted that the successful adjustment to old age was by means of a rational and deliberate withdrawal from society in preparation for the ultimate disengagement through incapacitating disease and death. It was discounted by many theorists only a few years after its introduction (Bengston *et al.* 1997; Maddox 1964), and was challenged by the activity theory which proposed that successful ageing and life satisfaction were achieved by maintaining activity patterns and values of middle age (Havighurst 1963). Disengagement theory proposes that the disengaged person has a sense of psychological well-being and high life satisfaction (Neugarten 1996). Yet homelessness among older homeless people is typically a state characterized by depression, low self-esteem and demoralization (Crane 1993; Cohen and Sokolovsky 1989; Douglass *et al.* 1988). Furthermore, homelessness is generally related to long-standing social and personal difficulties or to sudden losses and stresses, and is not usually an intentional move unrelated to life events and changes.

Conclusions

This chapter has highlighted the complexities of understanding homelessness. The phenomenon is complicated and multi-dimensional, with legal, housing, sociological and psychological connotations. Legally, homelessness is defined in terms of access to housing. From a sociological perspective, it is a person's relationship with society, homelessness representing maladjustment. Behaviourally, it is a set of deviant responses to society's norms. Its main attributes include a lack of secure, conventional accommodation; disaffiliation and alienation; and several overt and non-conventional behaviours. Yet not one of these in isolation captures the phenomenon of homelessness. Many contemporary British and American policy-makers and researchers recognize homelessness as a lack of shelter, yet this single criterion oversimplifies the complexity of the problem.

Understanding of the reasons for homelessness remains simplistic. As recently as 1993, American investigators noted that 'good research about causality is conspicuous by its absence in the literature on homelessness; virtually no one has engaged in inquiry that specifically examines the factors that cause people to become literally homeless . . . most derive causality from their own politically oriented perspectives' (Baum and Burnes 1993: 133). Likewise, in 1997 an Australian investigator documented that 'much of the literature on homelessness remains atheoretical and anecdotal' (Hallebone 1997: 24). Contemporary theorists lack consensus, and the literature contains disparate ideas about the causes of homelessness. The problem is sometimes seen to be rooted within the structure of society, and structural and economic circumstances are emphasized. At other times, the focus is on sociological and psychological features, and homelessness is associated with personal events, circumstances and disabilities. British analysts have generally focused on the former, while American investigators are divided between the two.

Early American theories of social change, undersocialization and institutional living were developed to account for a wide range of deviant and antisocial behaviours, and applied to homeless people. Although factors such as dependency, poor social relationships and vulnerability are still ascribed to homeless people, there has been little advance on the early theories. Fifty years ago it was identified that the pathway leading to homelessness 'involves a combination of several social factors together with certain personality characteristics of the individual' (Straus 1946: 365), and that studies were needed to determine why some people become homeless while others under the same social conditions remain housed (Sutherland and Locke 1936; Anderson 1923). Yet there has been little advance in understanding why a relationship breakdown causes vulnerability for some people but displacement for others.

Most works relating to homelessness consist of either theoretical propositions or empirical investigations, yet rarely have these been combined. Sociologists, such as Merton and Parsons, recognized deviancy and retreatism as problems construed within the social system. Yet neither proved these hypotheses through empirical evidence (Glaser and Strauss 1967). Some theorists have used secondary statistical data or information from other studies to explain causes of homelessness without generating empirical proof. Others have proposed reasons for homelessness, combining structural and economic reasons with those of sociological and psychological factors, yet have neither conducted analyses nor developed theories to demonstrate these relationships. Because of the diversity and unrelatedness of factors, holistic propositions lack the richness and fullness of the early sociological theories, and carry little weight and meaning.

Since the early 1980s, American research into homelessness by sociologists, psychiatrists and social policy analysts has burgeoned, and the methods employed have diversified and become more penetrating. Rich qualitative material has been collected and analysed through prolonged observations, in-depth semi-structured interviewing, ethnographic studies over many months, the tracking of respondents through time, and comparative studies of homeless and non-homeless groups. This information has increased our knowledge of the lifestyles and problems of homeless people. Although often based on cross-sectional and retrospective data rather than longitudinal evidence, models have been constructed to explain the progression of homelessness, and to advance knowledge of the reasons why people remain homeless. There is, however, limited information about the entry into and exit from the state.

British research has focused on statutory homeless people, with only occasional studies of homeless people sleeping rough or in hostels. British sociology has neglected the population, and the themes of research have been set by housing management and medical concerns. Most British studies have relied on single survey methods, and in-depth investigations have been few. To advance understanding of homelessness, theories need to be developed and supported by models and explanations generated from rigorously analysed, empirical evidence which differentiate between necessary and sufficient conditions, identify the interactions between events and states and the processes leading to homelessness, and gauge thresholds, supports and resources which advance or prevent homelessness.

Notes

1 The areas of cities predominantly inhabited by homeless men which offered cheap lodgings in missions, flop-houses (lodging houses made up of small cubicles), single-room occupancy (SRO) hotels (originally designed as accommodation for migratory workers), and services such as cheap bars and cafés, second-hand clothing stores, and pawnshops (Hoch 1991; Cohen and Sokolovsky 1989).
2 Casual wards originated from the Poor Law system, were attached to workhouses, and provided free food and shelter to vagrants. They were also known as 'spikes', the term deriving from the splitting iron used in stone-breaking. They became the responsibility of the National Assistance Board in 1948 as reception centres (described in Chapter 11).

PART I

Biographies and pathways into homelessness

The following five chapters are concerned with the diversity and classification of biographies and pathways into homeless for older people in the Four-City and Lancefield Street Centre studies. Single incidents, such as bereavement or eviction, are often cited as the immediate causes of homelessness. This part of the book extends beyond simplistic reportage by drawing on partial life histories, records of observations, and supplementary information from case files and from service providers working with older homeless people. The interactions between events and states are examined, their progression into homelessness is described, and interpretations are made and hypotheses proposed of the reasons why and how older people became homeless. The emphasis therefore is not on single reasons for homelessness, but on describing and understanding the processes involved.

The respondents in the Four-City and the Lancefield Street Centre studies were interviewed and asked for reasons why they became homeless. In many instances they cited a single event, such as widowhood, as the cause of homelessness. This was usually an incident which had occurred immediately before they became homeless. But they were often unable to conceive how earlier events, such as broken childhood homes, and less direct states, such as long-standing mental health problems, may have created vulnerability and contributed to the problem. They often could not explain or articulate why they behaved in a certain way, for example, why they abandoned their homes after becoming widowed, or why they remained in an abusive marital relationship for years. Possibly they were unaware of a reason for their behaviour. In order to understand the transition into homelessness, it was necessary to examine their histories and recognize possible contributory factors.

From the details that the subjects provided, it was possible to identify incidents or situations which preceded and triggered homelessness. Commonly reported or identified triggers were broken and disturbed childhood homes, the death of a parent or a spouse, the breakdown of marital relationships, itinerant working lives, retirement from the armed forces or from work settings with tied accommodation such as hotels and hospitals, and mental illness. Taking each theme in turn, it was then possible to reconstruct the states and events which preceded homelessness, and identify recurrent patterns of experience and ways in which situations interacted with other events and states in their histories. The analyses examined: (i) the subjects' circumstances when they were housed and the factors that maintained stability; (ii) events which upset this stability, and how their circumstances changed; (iii) why and how such changes were likely to have had an influence on particular subjects; and (iv) how these changes progressed to homelessness. This methodology is detailed elsewhere (Lofland and Lofland 1984; Plummer 1983).

Chapter 3 introduces Part I by summarizing our current knowledge of the prevalence of homelessness among older people in Britain, and describing their profiles of homelessness. The next three chapters examine common themes and pathways leading to later-life homelessness. Each chapter focuses on one situation. Different pathways into homelessness are identified for each situation, and the events are thus divided into sub-groups. The characteristics of the subjects in each sub-group are described, their histories are examined in detail, and the states and events which contibuted to homelessness are identified. Case studies are used to assist with explanations and interpretations. Pseudonyms are used to protect the identity of the subjects, and some details have been withheld to prevent recognition.

Chapter 4 examines the breakdown of family households, including broken childhood homes, the death of parents, widowhood and marital breakdown. Chapter 5 focuses on itinerant work histories, with reference also to people who become homeless in later life following retirement or redundancy. Chapter 6 examines the role of mental illness and stressful events in leading to homelessness. Chapter 7 concludes with a synthesis of pathways into homelessness for older people and the ways in which the findings advance our knowledge of the aetiology of homelessness.

3

The prevalence and profiles of homelessness among older people

I was born for this way of life. In a hostel you get your meals; you don't get that in a flat on your own. Housing is seen to be the solution to homelessness but I'll tell you what happens. People are put in houses, they stay behind the four walls with a bottle of cider, and come out from their houses one year later as alcoholics.

(Fred, rehoused after 15 years' homelessness)

This chapter discusses the prevalence and profiles of homelessness among older people in Britain. Little is known about the number of older people who are homeless as few counts or estimates have been made. Homelessness may be a problem which first presents in old age or it may be a long-standing problem among people who become elderly while homeless. In order to develop effective services, it is necessary to understand the problem, and have knowledge of its extent, onset and duration. This chapter first describes ways in which enumerations of homeless people in Britain have been undertaken and the difficulties which arise. Statistics about the number of older people who are homeless are presented, followed by an exercise which estimates the number of homeless older people in England and Wales. The second section describes the demographic details of older homeless people, namely sex and age distributions and place of birth. Finally, profiles of homelessness among the group are discussed, including age of onset, number of episodes, and duration.

The prevalence of homelessness among older people in Britain

Difficulties of identifying and enumerating homeless people

Homelessness is generally a problem of large towns and cities, although it does exist to a lesser extent in some small British towns and rural areas (Bramley 1994; Lambert *et al.* 1992). In Boston, a small Lincolnshire market town and river port with approximately 25,000 people, there were 459 homeless people over six months, including 65 sleeping rough (Wright and Everitt 1995). But there are no accurate figures (or reliable estimates) of the number of people who are homeless in Britain. Official statistics only exist for people who are accepted by local housing authorities as statutorily homeless. These indicate a substantial increase since the late 1970s, from 53,100 homeless households in England in 1978 to 138,740 by 1992, and 103,340 in 1997 (Department of the Environment, Transport and the Regions (DETR) 1998; Bramley *et al.* 1988). No reliable figures exist of the number of people who are unofficially homeless, but indications are that this number might be considerable. Estimates of the number of people sleeping rough or living in hostels, squats and hotels in London range from 37,600 to 75,000, and of 'hidden' single homeless people from 32,000 to 53,000 (Moore *et al.* 1995; Single Homelessness in London (SHiL) 1995).

Attempts have been made in Britain to enumerate homeless people sleeping rough and staying in hostels and shelters. Both the 1971 and 1981 population censuses endeavoured to count people sleeping rough, but the results were unreliable and not published (Thompson 1995). The 1991 Census took a new approach to the enumeration of rough sleepers. The **street sites** used at night by people sleeping rough were listed with the help of local authorities, voluntary organizations and churches, and special enumerators were recruited from groups working with homeless people. The census findings have, however, been contradicted. Six rough sleepers over pensionable age were found by the census enumerators in inner London (Office of Population Censuses and Surveys (OPCS) 1993a: 90, Table 5). Yet six months earlier, an intensive street investigation in the area over three months found 130 rough sleepers over the age of 60 years (Crane 1993). In Birmingham, no rough sleepers were found on Census night, yet shortly afterwards another single-night count found 61 people sleeping rough (Oldman and Hooton 1993).

The Census is believed to be flawed because insufficient time was spent developing links with local organizations working with homeless people and preparing for the count, and in some areas there were inadequate resources to complete the count. Some cities, such as Bristol and Leeds, have conducted single-night counts since the Census. In parts of central London, six-monthly street counts have been carried out since March 1992 to monitor the effects of the **Rough Sleepers Initiative**.[1] The counts are coordinated by Homeless Network,[2] undertaken by street out-reach workers who work with homeless people, and supplemented by enumerations of homeless people in emergency hostels and night-shelters on the same night.

There are several methodological weaknesses with single-night counts. Homelessness is not a persistent state but there is a constant flow of people of all ages becoming homeless and being rehoused. A single-night count provides little indication of the scale of homelessness over a period. A telephone survey of 1,507 households in the United States found that 14 per cent of the respondents had been homeless at some time in their lives, almost 5 per cent within the five years prior to contact (Link *et al.* 1995). Similarly, 4.3 per cent of almost 10,000 heads of household in England surveyed in 1994–95 reported that they had been homeless in the preceding ten years (Burrows 1997). Evidence suggests that the annual homeless population, the number destined to be homeless at least once during a year, is three to five times greater than the number homeless on any given night (Wright and Devine 1995). In the year ending September 1996, the Over 55s Accommodation Project in Leeds, rehoused 70 older homeless people but also received 87 new referrals of older homeless people (Crane and Warnes 1997a). Hence, at just one project in one British city, many older people presented as homeless and were resettled in just one year.

It is extremely difficult to locate and include all homeless people in a single-night survey. When 'capture-recapture' techniques[3] were used to make contact with homeless people in Westminster, it was asserted that only one-third of homeless people would be located in a study which relied on simple survey methods (Fisher *et al.* 1994). A count of homeless people in Kentucky over a two-month period found that, had it relied on information collected on the first day, virtually all homeless people in rural areas and many in urban areas would have been excluded (Burt 1995). Analyses of a street and shelter night count, conducted in the United States in conjunction with the 1990 Census, suggested that only 28 per cent of street people had been enumerated (Wright and Devine 1995). Likewise, in the City and east London, 63 people sleeping rough were counted on one night, but enumerators were unable to locate another 17 people (21 per cent) who were known to sleep rough locally (Homeless Network 1995).

Assessing the number of homeless older people is particularly difficult. Many sleep in hidden sites, yet for safety reasons, enumerators and investigators often do not search in isolated and dangerous spots such as derelict buildings, squats, parks or underground tunnels (Homeless Network 1996; Moore *et al.* 1995; OPCS 1991b). The problem may be most severe in rural areas, where it is easy for rough sleepers to hide in woods and barns, and where there are few soup kitchens or other services to attract them. Some older homeless people ride on buses at night which is a time when enumerations are usually conducted, while some frequently move around towns and because of their **transience** are equally difficult to locate (see Chapter 8). An accurate enumeration would involve intensive searching in all areas which would be time-consuming and would require innumerable investigators. Furthermore, it would have to be undertaken regularly to identify changes in the homeless population.

Reliable identifications of older homeless people are also difficult. Some are easily recognized because they are seen on the streets for long periods during the day and night, they are dirty and unkempt, and have distinct behaviours. But others are well groomed, carry few possessions, their behaviour betrays no sign of disorder, and it is not apparent from a single observation that they are homeless. This only becomes evident when they are seen *regularly* on the streets or in doorways at night. Some deny that they are homeless to avoid being questioned, to preserve anonymity, or because they are distrustful and fearful. In the Four-City Study, an older man in London was contacted several times. He was always clean and smartly dressed, stayed in a café each night until it closed at 2 a.m., and regularly used soup kitchens. He denied that he was homeless and his housed or homeless state was never determined. While conducting the six-monthly street counts in London, enumerators have found that many homeless people wander around the streets at night and are excluded from counts (Homeless Network 1995).

Statistics of homeless older people in Britain

No counts (or even reliable estimates) exist of the number of older people who are homeless in Britain. They are often not known to 'officialdom': many are not registered with a general practitioner, or on electoral rolls or official housing and social services departments' lists, and some are not in receipt of benefits and are therefore unknown to the Department of Social Security. Some even avoid centres and shelters designated for homeless people. According to official statistics in the early 1990s, between 6,700 and 7,400 households were accepted by local authority housing departments in England, Scotland and Wales as statutorily homeless and vulnerable on the grounds of old age (Table 3.1). This amounted to 4–5 per cent of all acceptances in England, and 3 per cent in Scotland and Wales.

Official statistics are, however, ambiguous. Some local authorities accept as homeless and vulnerable men and women aged 60 years and over, while others only include men when they reach the age of 65 years; some elderly people who are homeless or threatened with homelessness are housed by local authorities without the applications being processed through the homelessness channels; and some elderly people living in unsuitable housing are registered as homeless although they have never been without permanent accommodation (Wilson 1995; Niner 1989). Furthermore, official statistics represent the number of households accepted as homeless, and some households may consist of two or more elderly people. Statistics for Scotland indicate that 800–900 *households* each year are accepted as homeless and vulnerable due to old age, but Wilson (1995) estimated that 1,600–1,800 elderly *people* present each year as homeless to Scottish local authorities.

Official figures for the number of older people who are homeless offer little indication of the scale of the problem. They exclude those sleeping rough, or in hostels and bed-and-breakfast hotels who are not registered as homeless with local authority housing departments. No reliable figures exist as to the number of older people who are unofficially homeless, and there is no comprehensive central register. In February 1996, a survey of 49 **direct-access hostels** in London found that 362 residents (14 per cent) were over the age of 60 years (Harrison 1996). An enumeration of people over the age of 55 years who were staying at temporary hostels and 'welfare hotels' in Glasgow in early January 1997 found 600 men and 41 women (Crane and Warnes 1997a). This represented 35 per cent of the overall hostel population.

No estimates have been made of the number of older people who are sleeping rough. Between 1992 and 1996, six-monthly counts of rough sleepers in parts of central London, the City and East End found an estimated 80–140 people aged 50 years or more (Homeless Network 1996; 1995; Randall and Brown 1996). These counts covered only a small section of London, they excluded isolated and hidden homeless people, and provide only partial evidence of the problem. In 1989, a count in 17 London boroughs found 226

Table 3.1   Households accepted as homeless and vulnerable due to old age by local authorities

Year	England[1]		Wales[2]		Scotland[3]		Total
	No.	%[4]	No.	%[4]	No.	%[4]	No.
1985[5]	6,579	7	322	6	740	5	7,641
1991[6]	5,860	4	326	3	920	3	7,106
1992[6]	6,230	4	359	3	792	3	7,381
1993[6]	5,920	4	335	3	910	3	7,165
1994[6]	6,050	5	348	3	875	3	7,273
1995[6]	5,890	5	303	3	845	3	7,038
1996[6]	5,510	5	309	3	825	3	6,644
1997	4,230	4	224[7]	5	n.a.[8]	n.a.	n.a.

[1] Tables 1 and 12 (Bramley *et al.* 1988) and Table 3 (DETR 1998)
[2] Table 7.4 (Welsh Office 1997)
[3] Tables 6a, 6b and 6d (Scottish Office 1998)
[4] Percentage of total households accepted as homeless
[5] Represents 1986–87 for Scotland
[6] For Scotland, figures are from April to March of the following year
[7] Verbal report from Welsh Office
[8] Figure not available until early 1999

rough sleepers aged over 50 years (Moore *et al.* 1995). The most substantial evidence of the scale of rough sleeping among older people in London comes from the Lancefield Street Centre Study. Just two out-reach workers at the project found 458 people aged 50 years or more sleeping rough in London at some time between February 1997 and September 1998. Some had been on the streets for years, others for just a few nights. The workers had also been informed about other older rough sleepers but were unable to find them.

Estimating the number of homeless older people in England and Wales

To estimate the number of homeless older people in England and Wales in the mid-1990s requires many assumptions and interpolations. The calculation which follows is a single-point prevalence and does not allow for the flow of people entering and leaving homelessness over a period, but it is the best that can be produced with present knowledge. It would probably be wise to accept that such an estimate must have a wide confidence interval, and the 95 per cent confidence limits could be as much as 50 per cent either side of the best estimate. We have already mentioned that, between 1992 and 1996, an estimated 80–140 people aged 50 years or more slept rough in parts of central London, the City and East End (Homeless Network 1996; 1995; Randall and Brown 1996). In the 12 months ending December 1997, the out-reach workers at the Lancefield Street Centre found 157 rough sleepers aged over 50 years in parts of London not covered by these street counts, and they estimate that around one-third were long-term rough sleepers (Crane and

Warnes 1998). Therefore, approximately 50 older people were long-term rough sleepers in outer London. It is assumed that a further one-fifth to one-third (30–50 older people) were short-term rough sleepers in outer London at any given time. If this situation continues, an estimated 160–240 people over the age of 50 years will sleep rough in central and outer London on any night (Table 3.2).

In the rest of England and Wales, the 1991 census counted 1,428 rough sleepers (Office of Population Censuses and Surveys (OPCS) 1991a). Subsequent counts in some areas, including Bristol, Leeds, Manchester, Nottingham and Oxford, have produced slightly higher or lower numbers (Davies and Leat 1997; Leeds City Council 1997; Shelter 1996). Two areas have reported large differences: a subsequent count in Birmingham found 61 rough sleepers whereas the 1991 Census recorded none, while in Basingstoke the 1991 Census recorded 99 rough sleepers yet a later count found just two (Shelter 1996; Oldman and Hooton 1993). Street counts in London during the late 1980s and 1990s found that between 29–39 per cent of rough sleepers were over the age of 50 years (Homeless Network 1996; Randall and Brown 1996; Moore *et al.* 1995). Assuming that a similar proportion of rough sleepers in the rest of England and Wales are aged 50 years and over, and using the 1991 Census figures of rough sleeping in the rest of England and Wales, it would be estimated that there are 410–560 older rough sleepers in England and Wales outside London.

There are an estimated 22,283 hostel residents in London and 37,759 in the rest of England (Randall 1992). An estimated 14,209 people are 'self-placed' in bed-and-breakfast hotels in London, that is, neither officially registered as homeless nor placed in the accommodation by local authority housing departments; and an estimated 62,471 people are 'self-placed' in bed-and-breakfast hotels in the rest of England and Wales (Carter 1997). Surveys of hostels in London, Glasgow, Birmingham, Bristol and Manchester have found that at least 26–35 per cent of residents are over the age of 50 years (Crane and Warnes 1997a; Moore *et al.* 1995; Garside *et al.* 1990). Assuming that 26–35 per cent of all hostel residents and of people 'self-placed' in bed and breakfast hotels are over the age of 50 years, we can calculate the approximate number of older people in temporary accommodation who are unofficially homeless (Table 3.2).

Using the methodology described, an estimated 36,220–48,780 people aged 50 years and over are unofficially homeless and sleeping rough or staying in hostels and bed-and-breakfast hotels in England and Wales. This is equivalent to 0.2–0.3 per cent of the population in England and Wales of that age (OPCS 1993b: 326, Table II). It has to be stressed that these figures are approximations and only a starting point; more accurate figures would require more detailed surveys and analyses. Because there is no reliable information about the number of 'hidden' homeless people who are staying with relatives and friends, this group is excluded from the estimation. It is known that 5,819 people were accepted by local authority housing departments in England and Wales as homeless and vulnerable due to old age in 1996 (DETR 1998; Welsh Office 1997). This suggests that only 11–14 per cent of older homeless people in England and Wales appear on official statistics.

Table 3.2 An estimate of the number of people aged 50 years and over in England and Wales who are unofficially homeless, mid-1990s

Housing status	All ages No.	Aged 50 + %	Aged 50 + No.[1]
Sleeping rough:			
Central London[2]	273–389	29–39[3]	80–140
Elsewhere in London[4]	n.k.	n.k.	80–100
Rest of England and Wales[5]	1,428	29-39	410–560
In hostels:			
Greater London[6]	22,283	26–35[7]	5,820–7,840
Rest of England[8]	37,759	26–35	9,820–13,200
In bed-and-breakfast hotels (self-placed):			
Greater London[9]	14,209	26–35	3,700–4,980
Rest of England and Wales[9]	62,471	26–35	16,310–21,960
Total unofficially homeless[10]	138,423–138,539[11]		36,220–48,780

[1] Rounded to nearest 10
[2] Parts of central London, the City and East End (Homeless Network 1996; Randall and Brown 1996)
[3] From street counts in London during the late 1980s and 1990s (Homeless Network 1996; Randall and Brown 1996; Moore *et al*. 1995)
[4] Crane and Warnes (1998)
[5] 1991 Census (OPCS 1991a)
[6] Randall (1992). Figure excludes Wales
[7] From surveys in British cities (Crane and Warnes 1997a; Moore *et al*. 1995; Garside *et al*. 1990)
[8] Randall (1992)
[9] Carter (1997: Table 6). Self-referrals to hotels; excludes official homeless people placed in temporary accommodation by local authority housing departments
[10] People sleeping rough, in hostels, and self-referrals to bed-and-breakfast hotels
[11] Excludes rough sleepers in outer London

Demographic details of older homeless people

Sex distribution

The number of older homeless men generally far exceed that of older homeless women, both in hostels and on the streets. There were 159 men (seven-tenths of the sample) and just 66 women in the Four-City Study. Likewise, the out-reach workers at the Lancefield Street Centre found 325 older men sleeping rough in London and just 35 older women. This sex distribution contrasts with that of the general elderly population. According to the 1991 Population Census, 56 per cent of people over the age of 55 years in England and Wales were women (OPCS 1993b: 64, Table 2). In Detroit, New York City, St Louis, Ohio, and Tampa Bay, Florida, between 67 and 92 per cent of older homeless people were also found to be men (DeMallie *et al*. 1997; Rich *et al*. 1995; Ladner 1992; Roth *et al*. 1992; Douglass *et al*. 1988).

In Chicago, two studies of older people in contact with emergency shelter services contradicted these observations, reporting that up to two-thirds of their sample were women (Keigher *et al.* 1989; Kutza 1987). In both studies, the majority of subjects had recently become homeless. The Four-City Study found that the entry to homelessness occurred for men at all ages but for women in later life (see Chapter 7). The preponderance of older women in the Chicago studies may therefore be partly explained by the concentration of recently homeless older people in their sample.

Age distribution

Older homeless people tend to be young elderly. Only 6 per cent of the men and 21 per cent of the women in the Four-City Study were over the age of 75 years. When their age distribution was compared with that of older men and women in England and Wales in the 1991 Population Census, homeless older people tended to be disproportionately younger than the general older population. In the 1991 Census, 21 per cent of men and 31 per cent of women were over the age of 75 years (OPCS 1993b: 64, Table 2). Other reports have also found that older homeless people are relatively young. Only 8 per cent of older homeless people in Detroit and 1 per cent of 103 homeless people over the age of 50 years in Tampa Bay, Florida, were over the age of 75 years (Rich *et al.* 1995; Douglass *et al.* 1988).

Homeless people are a highly vulnerable group and have high rates of mortality (described in Chapter 9). The detrimental effect of homelessness on health over time may mean that people who have been homeless for years die before they reach an advanced age, or they become physically ill and are forced to move into housing or residential homes as they approach old age. Hence, older homeless people are either survivors or those who first become homeless in old age. This would explain why two Chicago studies reported that a much higher proportion of older people referred to emergency shelter services were over the age of 75 years: one sample of 157 subjects included 32 per cent over the age of 75 years, and the other of 475 subjects included 44 per cent over the age of 75 years (Keigher *et al.* 1989; Kutza 1987). The majority of both samples had recently become homeless.

Place of birth

Sixty-three per cent of older people in the Four-City Study were born in England and Wales, 15 per cent in Ireland, and 15 per cent in Scotland. Compared to the general older population in Britain, a disproportionately high number of homeless older people originated from Ireland or Scotland. Nineteen per cent of the Four-City Study subjects interviewed in London originated from Ireland and 15 per cent from Scotland, yet only 8 per cent of the general population over 55 years of age in inner London (as recognized by OPCS) originated from Ireland and 2 per cent from Scotland (OPCS 1993c: 221, Table 2). Similar differences were seen when the birthplace of the Four-City Study subjects interviewed in the North of England (Sheffield, Leeds and Manchester) was compared with the general population in the Yorkshire and

Humberside Region and Greater Manchester Metropolitan County (OPCS 1993c: 173, 275, Table 2). A high proportion of older homeless people contacted by the Lancefield Street out-reach team also originated from Ireland and Scotland: three-tenths were born in Ireland and 15 per cent in Scotland.

Only 4 per cent of the men and 13 per cent of the women in the Four-City Study were born outside the British Isles. Similarly, only 8 per cent of older homeless people contacted by the out-reach workers in London were born outside the British Isles (Crane and Warnes 1998). The reasons why only a few older homeless people in Britain are born abroad can only be speculated upon. It is likely to be partly associated with the relatively small number of older people in Britain who are from a minority ethnic group. By virtue of having immigrated, it is also likely that intercontinental migrants are fairly socialized and competent, or that they are supported by close family networks.

Patterns of homelessness

Entry to homelessness

Collecting information about the age of a person when they first become homeless can be more complicated than is often portrayed. For some people there is a recognizable time when their circumstances change and they become homeless. Instances are when owner-occupiers or tenants abandon or are evicted from their homes, and subsequently stay in hostels or sleep rough. For others, the entry into homelessness is protracted and unclear. It sometimes involves alternating moves between housed and homeless states before continuous homelessness sets in. Some people leave their homes following marital arguments, book into hostels or bed-and-breakfast hotels for a few weeks, and then return home. Eventually they leave their homes permanently and become persistently homeless. One man finally separated from his wife when he was 59 years old. During the previous 14 years, he had left home on several occasions following marital arguments and had slept rough for a few months in the Scottish highlands. He had thus been homeless intermittently several times before he finally left home.

For some people, the entry into homelessness involves a progressive move from conventional, permanent housing as a tenant or owner-occupier to less secure, temporary accommodation with no tenancy rights. Following a crisis, some people volitionally abandon or are forced to leave their homes. They find accommodation in less secure settings, as in holiday camps and hotels, where their stay is limited and a condition of employment. For them, homelessness is in abeyance. One man ceded his council tenancy in the South of England when he was 59 years old. He had been married for 36 years and had become widowed one year earlier. He moved to the North of England and lived and worked in a hotel for one year. He returned to his home town, stayed with friends for a few months, but could not settle. He came to London and slept rough for the first time at the age of 61 years.

At times, people lose tenancies when they are detained in prison or other institutions for long periods. They are only housed temporarily while in the institution and have no legal rights to continuing accommodation. Others 'drift' between insecure housing where they have no written tenancy agreement, such as lodgings and digs, and hostels and **resettlement units** designated for homeless people. These are usually itinerant working men who frequently change jobs and towns (see Chapter 5). They gradually increase their use of hostels and resettlement units as work and income diminish. With such people, it is often impossible to recognize a particular 'moment' when homelessness begins. It is a gradual intensification of an established pattern of hostel use.

Three-fifths of the Four-City Study subjects experienced a sudden and abrupt move from secure housing to homelessness. Others described a less direct transition. Twenty-six men had 'drifted' between lodgings, workcamps, hostels and sleeping rough, 18 people had moved from secure to less secure accommodation usually as the result of marital breakdown, and nine had stayed in hostels or slept rough intermittently for brief episodes and in-between times had lived with marital partners. In New York City, the housing histories of 482 homeless families of all ages were traced and their pathways leading to homelessness were examined (Weitzman *et al.* 1990). Forty-three per cent experienced a rapid decline after having been in a stable housing situation, 13 per cent experienced a slow slide from stable housing to increasingly marginalized housing and eventually homelessness, and 44 per cent had never been securely housed but had lived with family or friends.

Among the Four-City Study sample, 162 people were able to state the age when they *first* became homeless. Others had 'drifted' into homelessness or were unsure when they first used hostels or slept rough. The ages when they first became homeless spanned most of the life course (Table 3.3). Two men became homeless before they were ten years old, yet five men and four women first became homeless when they were aged in their seventies. Whereas the men had become homeless at all ages, women tended to have become homeless for the first time in later life. Twenty-four men and two women were aged under 21 years when they first became homeless. Yet nearly two-thirds of the women and three-tenths of the men experienced homelessness for the first time after the age of 50 years. Few men reported first becoming homeless after the age of 60 years, yet the highest proportion of women were found in this age band. The sex differences were statistically significant. Although few other British or American studies have identified the age at which older homeless people first became homeless, the Four-City Study and Lancefield Street Centre Study report similar findings (Crane and Warnes 1998).

An episode of rehousing

Just as it is sometimes difficult to define an entry into homelessness, so it is equally problematic to define an exit from homelessness. For some people, it is clear whether and when this change has taken place. Such people are rehoused in tenancies and do not use soup kitchens or congregate on the streets with homeless people. For others, an exit from homelessness is less distinct. One difficulty relates to the type of accommodation to which people

Table 3.3 The age when the Four-City Study subjects first became homeless

Age (years)	Men		Women	
	No.	*%*	*No.*	*%*
Up to 29	42	34	4	11
30–39	21	17	2	5
40–49	24	19	8	22
50–59	24	19	10	27
60+	14	11	13	35
Total known	125	100	37	100
Not known	30		24	
Total experienced homelessness	155		61	

move and whether it constitutes being housed. Some move from hostels or sleeping rough into insecure, marginal types of accommodation where they have no tenancy rights, for example those who move in with friends or obtain work with tied accommodation. Although they are accommodated, their housing is not secure and is conditional on other people or on jobs. Another group includes those who are homeless and are admitted to hospital or receive a prison sentence. While in institutional settings, they are no longer on the streets or in hostels, yet they have not been rehoused.

Another issue relates to the duration of time that people remain in accommodation once they are rehoused, and whether brief periods should be regarded as episodes of rehousing and exits from homelessness. Once rehoused, some maintain a tenancy for several years but others leave their accommodation after a few nights and become homeless again. In Chicago, an exit from homelessness is recognized to be a stay in accommodation for at least 14 consecutive days (Sosin *et al.* 1990). Furthermore, some people who have been rehoused do not leave the homeless lifestyle but still maintain homelessness behaviours (described in Chapter 2).

Duration of homelessness

There are considerable variations in the number of times older people have become homeless and the duration of each episode. Some have experienced a single episode of homelessness, others have been homeless and rehoused several times. Of 190 subjects in the Four-City Study, 104 had been consistently homeless while 86 had been rehoused (Figure 3.1). Of this latter group, 49 had become homeless for a second time and, of the 20 who were rehoused again, 16 became homeless for a third time. Some have been homeless for most of their lives with only brief spells of housing. One man had slept rough from the age of 17 until he was rehoused when he was 52 years old. He became homeless again after two years and had been homeless for three years when interviewed. Another man was sent to an approved school for two years at the age of 13 years. From the age of 15 years until his mid-fifties, he slept rough in-between serving numerous prison sentences ranging from nine months to eight years for burglaries and shoplifting. He said that he sometimes committed crimes because 'prison was a home to me; I had a warm bed in prison. I used to sleep in old cars in the winter when I was out, and it was freezing; I spent 21 Christmases on the trot in prison'.

In contrast, some older people have experienced short spells of homelessness but have been mainly housed. One woman became homeless when she was 42 years old and remained so for three years. She then had accommodation for 18 years until she became homeless again at the age of 63 and remained so for one year. She was then rehoused for nine years, became homeless for the third time at the age of 73, and had been so for six months when interviewed. Another woman became homeless in her early thirties after her marriage ended. She slept rough and stayed in hostels for two years and then remarried. She became homeless for a second time at the age of 69 after her marriage of 27 years ended in separation.

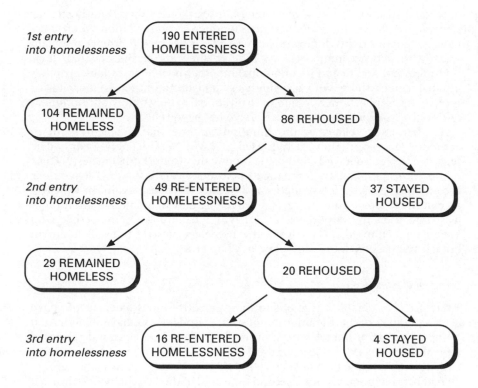

Note: This diagram represents the experiences of the people interviewed for the Four-City Study, most of whom were currently homeless. It is a compilation of their retrospective reports. It is important to note that the pathways, and particularly their relative numbers, do not indicate the distribution of outcomes of resettlement for all homeless people.

Figure 3.1 Movement of the Four-City Study subjects between housing and homelessness

At the time of interview, 173 people in the Four-City Study were homeless. Nearly one-quarter had been homeless for less than 12 months, yet one-third had been continuously homeless for more than 20 years (Table 3.4). Seventeen men and one woman had become homeless before the age of 29 years and had never been rehoused. They had therefore experienced a near-lifetime pattern of homelessness. There is no recognized length of time that constitutes chronic or long-term homelessness. In America, it has been variously described as occurring after a person has been consistently homeless for one or two years (Wright and Devine 1995; Sosin *et al.* 1988; Kutza 1987; Rossi *et al.* 1986). By such definitions, a high proportion of older people in the Four-City Study could be classified as chronically homeless.

Conclusions

The evidence suggests that the extent of homelessness among older people in Britain is more widespread than is documented, and that official figures represent only the 'tip of the iceberg'. It is a much more extensive problem, and a large number of older people are sleeping rough and living in hostels and bed-and-breakfast or welfare hotels. Enumerating or estimating the number of older people who are homeless is complex, and without a detailed enquiry in each town and city over a period, no accurate figure of the scale of the problem can be ascertained. A single-night count is likely to exclude many isolated and hidden homeless people, and does not account for the movement of people over time between housed and homeless states and between towns. Nevertheless, indications are that between 42,000 to 55,000 people aged 50 years or more may be homeless in England and Wales.

Many characteristics differentiate homeless older people from housed older people in Britain, and these findings are generally supported by American studies. In contrast to the general older population, homeless older people tend to be male, young elderly, and only a small proportion are over the age of 75 years. An exception to this is when studies concentrate on recently homeless elderly people. When compared with housed older people in

Table 3.4 Duration of the Four-City Study subjects' current episode of homelessness

Duration of homelessness	Men		Women		Total	
	No.	*%*	*No.*	*%*	*No.*	*%*
Less than 1 year	25	24	6	21	31	23
1–4 years	14	14	4	14	18	14
5–9 years	9	9	5	17	14	11
10–19 years	19	18	8	27	27	20
20 years or more	36	35	6	21	42	32
Total known	103	100	29	100	132	100
Not known	20		21		41	
Total homeless	123		50		173	

Britain, an unusually high proportion of homeless older people have originated from Ireland and Scotland.

Patterns of homelessness among older people are diverse. Some have been homeless since early adulthood and have become elderly while homeless. Others have become homeless for the first time in later life. Some have experienced short spells of homelessness but have been mainly housed. But many are chronically homeless, have been in the state for more than 20 years, and have experienced a near-lifetime pattern of homelessness. Homelessness among older men tends to have occurred at all ages, whereas among older women it tends to be characteristic of old age. This may be related to sex differentials in access to help and support for those who become homeless. Over the years, local authority housing departments have had a duty to rehouse homeless women who are pregnant or who have children and who are therefore likely to be young or middle-aged. No such obligation has existed for single homeless men of those ages. The next three chapters examine older people's pathways into homelessness and highlight their histories and vulnerabilities.

Notes

1 This was launched in 1990 by the government to provide services for people sleeping rough in designated inner London zones (see Chapter 11).
2 This organization acts as a coordinator for voluntary sector organizations working with single homeless people in central London.
3 A technique developed by field biologists and used to estimate the size of populations that are difficult to find and count. It requires obtaining two or more independent observations on the same population. An estimate of the number of people in a population is obtained by multiplying the number of people observed the first time with those observed on the second occasion, and dividing by those observed on both occasions (Fisher *et al.* 1994; Sudman *et al.* 1988).

4

The breakdown of family households

This way of life gets you and you cannot get out of it. I left home as a child and slept rough because my mother didn't want me. It was like being in a family when I came on the road. I would cover myself with blankets at night and think of the warmth of the fires in people's houses.

(Harry, aged 58 years, homeless since childhood)

The breakdown of a family household is cited in many British and American studies as an important factor leading to homelessness at all ages (Rosenthal 1994; Anderson *et al.* 1993; Snow and Anderson 1993; Zozus and Zax 1991). At times, it refers to childhood and parental homes, at other times to marital homes. The disruption is sometimes triggered by strained family relationships and separation, and at other times by the death of a family member. This chapter examines the connection between the breakdown of family homes and homelessness among older people. Following a literature review, the chapter first examines the relationship between the breakdown of childhood homes and homelessness, and second the situation of people who became homeless in middle age after the loss of parental support. The third section describes associations between widowhood and homelessness, followed by the circumstances of those who became homeless after their marriage or intimate relationship ended in separation. Finally, the breakdown of surrogate family homes is discussed.

The breakdown of childhood homes is a critical feature of contemporary youth homelessness. Some young people are raised in dysfunctional and problematic family homes where they experience disruptions, abuse, neglect and rejection. The problems are sometimes caused by parents separating, conflicts with step-parents, and parents abusing alcohol or drugs. The young people either leave home or are evicted by their parents (Hagan and McCarthy 1997; Downing-Orr 1996; Snow and Anderson 1993). Others experience broken childhood homes and become homeless immediately or soon after leaving local authority residential care settings or foster homes (Hutson and Liddiard 1994; Kirby 1994). In one study in London, 161 homeless young people between 16 and 21 years of age experienced 'high levels of domestic turbulence, neglect and abuse' in their childhood (Craig *et al.* 1996:

7). Two-fifths were in care at some time and almost two-thirds had psychiatric problems.

The belief is that young people who are raised in dysfunctional and problematic families become alienated from the family and are not taught the necessary skills to live independently (Downing-Orr 1996). On leaving their family home or care placement, they are prematurely exposed to adult responsibilities of independent living, are not able to cope, and so become homeless. Young people who are placed in foster homes and group homes may also be at risk of homelessness. Being in care might indicate that they have severe emotional and behaviour problems which make them vulnerable, or that they do not have an effective family support network to help at times of crises (Piliavin *et al.* 1993).

The death of a parent or a spouse is an important contributory factor to homelessness. As early as 1911, a study in Chicago noted that some men related homelessness to the death of their spouse (Solenberger 1911). In the 1960s, a British study reported that many middle-aged men 'went to pieces' and became homeless following the death of their mother, and suggested that 'the single man who continues to live with his parents is particularly at risk when the parental home breaks up' (National Assistance Board 1966: 118). More recently, one-twentieth of 390 men at the Alvaston Resettlement Unit in Derby had become homeless in their thirties or forties after the death of a parent, usually their mother (Walker *et al.* 1993). A British survey found that 'the most commonly cited reason [for homelessness] by respondents over 60 was the death of a spouse, relative or other significant person' (Anderson *et al.* 1993: 74). Marital breakdown and separation is another frequently reported reason for homelessness, and was the most frequent reason why elderly men and women presented as homeless to local authority housing departments in Glasgow and Edinburgh (Wilson 1995). Many had been married for more than 20 years, had experienced marital difficulties for some time, but the problems exacerbated on retirement when the couple spent more time together.

Most people whose family or marital relationships end through death or separation do not become homeless, and there is little understanding about the factors that select those people who are vulnerable after such crises. Widowhood is a particularly stressful event which requires significant readjustments (Holmes and Rahe 1967). Some people react atypically and become depressed or develop physical health problems (Parkes 1986). Among those recently widowed, men are more likely than women to experience physical health problems and to have higher mortality and suicide rates. Family and social support networks are important in helping older people to adjust to widowhood (Gallagher *et al.* 1981–82). Widowhood is believed to have a greater impact on men than on women because men are generally more isolated and have fewer close friends (Stroebe and Stroebe 1983).

Heavy drinking, infidelity and long-standing domestic violence have been blamed for relationship breakdown and homelessness (Bahr and Garrett 1976; Bogue 1963). But similar reasons have been given for marriage breakdown among people who never became homeless, suggesting that these behaviours are not sufficient to cause the added consequence of homelessness (Bull 1993; Argyle and Henderson 1985). Divorce is sometimes 'disorderly' in that the severance is incomplete and emotional or role attachments continue, and divorced or separated people, particularly men, have higher rates of mental illness and alcoholism than those married (Duck 1992; Hagestad and Smyer 1982). Social support, time for 'orderly' withdrawal from the relationship, and an ability to adapt to new role demands are factors reported to increase the chance of successful adjustment after relationship breakdown (Argyle and Henderson 1985).

Merton (1968) proposed that widowhood and other events which result in an individual suddenly experiencing a loss of roles and a break in routine behaviours and social relations sometimes produce a state of anomie (Chapter 2). The person has no structure in their lives, no clearly defined norms to follow, and so reacts by 'retreating' from conventional society into homelessness (Merton 1968). But Merton offered no interpretation as to why only a few widowed people behaved in this way. Later theorists have associated the breakdown of family households and homelessness with vulnerability (Rossi 1989; Wright 1989; Sosin *et al.* 1988). Some people are vulnerable, have personal disabilities such as a mental illness, and few resources. They are supported materially and emotionally by their parents, a marital partner or other close relative. When their main carer dies or their family's ability to help is eroded financially or psychologically, their support system is destroyed. Because they cannot cope on their own, they become homeless.

Two main theoretical ideas emerge about family breakdown and homelessness. The first is associated with that of childhood homes and youth homelessness, and identifies the family itself as being dysfunctional and the person who becomes homeless as the 'victim'. The second is associated with the breakdown of family homes in adulthood, and suggests that the root cause of homelessness lies with the disability of the person who becomes homeless. In many instances, it is difficult to separate the disability of the person who becomes homeless from the family pathology. In New England, many homeless people originated from violent or pathological families and then experienced stressful marriages which ended in divorce (Wagner 1993).

Homelessness following the breakdown of childhood homes

A high proportion of homeless people are reported to have experienced disruptive childhood homes. One-fifth of 1,798 women and 13 per cent of 6,253 men in temporary shelters in New York City had grown up mainly in institutions and foster homes (Crystal 1984). Thirty-nine per cent of 338 homeless people in Minneapolis had been placed in care as a child (Sosin *et al.* 1990). Twenty-three per cent of 223 men newly admitted to New York City shelters had been placed in foster care, group homes or other special residences before the age of 17 years (Susser *et al.* 1987). In New York City, 31 per cent of 353 older homeless people grew up in childhood settings where at least one parent was absent (Ladner 1992), and nine of 12 older shelter women lost one parent through death before they were 18 years old (Sullivan 1991).

But few studies have traced the histories of homeless people and examined the connection between disruptive childhood homes and homelessness. In the Four-City Study, 58 per cent of subjects reported broken or disturbed childhood homes. One-fifth had been separated from both their natural parents through death or desertion by the age of 16 years, and had been brought up by relatives, foster parents or in orphanages. One-quarter had been separated from one parent through death or marital breakdown. Thirteen per cent grew up with both parents but recalled disturbed homes in which one or both parents drank heavily, was violent, or was adulterous. A few reported sexual abuse by relatives. More men than women had grown up in homes where their fathers had been heavy drinkers.

For some older people, a broken or disturbed childhood home was the start of homelessness. Twenty-four subjects in the Four-City and the Lancefield Street Centre studies became homeless before they were 18 years old after leaving disturbed family homes, foster homes or orphanages. Two men were just seven and nine years old at the time. One described how he was 'adopted by the men and women on the road; they used to look after me and give me food. It was like a big adventure, and I was away from the arguments at home and from my mother hitting me around the head'. Barry was 14 years old when he returned from school, found his mother in bed with a man (not his father), and left home to sleep rough. Frank stayed with relatives after his mother died when he was eight years old. His father remarried five years later and Frank lived with his father and stepmother. His father died when Frank was 15 years old. He continued to live with his stepmother. They argued and she threw him out of the house when he was 17 years old. He has since lived in hostels and slept rough.

Their histories often indicate the parents' pathology. One man has slept rough since the age of 16 years after his father murdered his mother. He fled from the house and has never returned. Hugh was abandoned as a baby, never knew his real parents, and was adopted when young. His adopted father was in the navy and died at sea when Hugh was six years old. Shortly afterwards Hugh and his adopted mother moved to a seaside resort and lived in a cheap hotel. According to Hugh, his adopted mother was an alcoholic and a prostitute, and she brought different men back to the hotel. From his early teens, Hugh lived with his adopted father's parents and an aunt. He left their home when he was 16 years old, came to London, and has since slept rough.

A further 16 older men became homeless in their early twenties after leaving the army, having served between two and six years. Eleven became homeless immediately after discharge, the others returned to their parents' home but recalled family problems and became homeless within a few weeks. Most had experienced disturbed or broken childhood homes *before* enlisting and eight were drinking heavily by the time they left the forces. Mick, for example, said that his father had been an alcoholic who occasionally slept rough. He died of hypothermia while sleeping out when Mick was three years old. Mick's mother 'had mental problems and she used to wander off after my father died', so Mick lived with foster parents from five years of age until he was 14. He then returned to his real mother, but said 'we were like strangers; we did not know each other'. At the age of 16, Mick was sent to

Borstal for three years for shop-breaking, after which he joined the army for two years. He left the army at the age of 21 and has since slept rough. Although the 16 men described how they became homeless after leaving the army, enlisting may have been a temporary measure used by some to alleviate family problems. Rosenthal (1994) also suggested that military service may be an intervening variable between unstable family backgrounds and homelessness for some people.

The association between disruptive childhoods and homelessness is complex. The 40 subjects who became homeless after leaving childhood settings or after leaving the army in their early twenties, experienced disturbed childhoods which seem to have had a profound and destabilising effect. They were over the age of 55 years when interviewed and had been mostly homeless since their teens or early adulthood. They never sustained work, accommodation or marital relationships. One 63-year-old man has slept rough since he was aged 16. The only time he acquired accommodation was when he married a woman 20 years his senior when he was aged 38. The marriage ended in divorce in less than three years.

But some older people with disturbed childhoods married and worked for years before becoming homeless, suggesting that childhood experiences had little influence on their pathway to homelessness. One woman experienced the death of her mother when she was 14 years old, but did not become homeless until she was aged in her seventies. Many people experience disruptive childhoods and never become homeless. The British National Child Development Study found that three-quarters of children who have been in care do not later have psychological or mental health problems (Buchanan and Brinke 1997). The reason for being in care is believed to be more important than the separation itself. Parental discord and unhappy broken homes are more likely to lead to problems such as delinquency than harmonious homes broken by the death of a parent (Rutter 1971).

Homelessness following the loss of parental support in adulthood

Some people who have always lived with their parents become homeless in middle age following the death of the last surviving parent, usually their mother. This happened to 17 men and eight women in the Four-City and the Lancefield Street Centre studies. Most were aged in their forties at the time, and had experienced the deaths of both parents within ten years (often within five years). Twenty-three had lived with their parents throughout their lives, except for brief episodes in the army, and long periods in a psychiatric hospital (one person for seven years, another for 13 years). The exceptions were one man and one woman who had lived in private rented accommodation for a few years. Only four men had been regularly employed. The others either never worked or had been employed for only a very short period. They never had friends, married, or had intimate relationships. Most never drank alcohol. This group of 25 subjects were poorly socialized, had limited work skills, had lived with and relied on their parents, and two-fifths had mental health problems.

They had all been living in their parents' home at the time of their parents' death. Six continued to live alone in the family home but five were evicted by the council within a few months because they failed to pay the rent. One man said, 'the council just wanted the house; I did no wrong'. They admitted to not paying rent but were vague and could not explain why. Their comments included: 'I bought food with the money.' The sixth was allowed to accumulate rent arrears for a few years and was then evicted by the council. Another man was evicted by the landlord two weeks after his mother died because 'I was frying fish and I did not use enough fat and the house filled with smoke.' Six men said that they abandoned their homes because there were too many painful memories. One man explained: 'Your mother is your best friend; when she goes there's no use staying.'

Three women were turned out of their homes by siblings who took over the property. Four subjects lived with siblings for a short time but became homeless when relationships became problematic and support was withdrawn. Five could not explain clearly how they became homeless, but stated that they had 'drifted' on to the streets after their parents died. The majority had been homeless for more than 15 years when interviewed and had never been resettled. The case study of Alfred (Box 4.1) indicates his vulnerability.

Box 4.1   Case study: Alfred

Alfred was 73 years old and became homeless after his mother died. He believes that he was aged in his forties at the time, and had always lived at home. He left school at the age of 14, and worked for 'a few years' as a labourer on building sites, but never had regular employment. He was not in the armed services and could not explain why, stating 'I just did not go in'. He never married and had no friends. He said: 'I never mixed with people'. He denied ever suffering from mental health problems. He had only one brother who also lived at home and seldom worked. Alfred's father died first, and Alfred continued to live at home with his mother and brother. His brother developed cancer and died at the age of 46 years, and two days later Alfred's mother died. After her death, Alfred lived alone in their council house for 'a couple of months . . . then the council contacted the police and they evicted me. I don't know why.' He had not paid his rent but was vague as to why not, saying 'I did not bother'. He was offered no alternative accommodation, so 'I stayed in a lodging house for three or six months, then I moved about and slept rough'. This happened over 20 years ago, since when he has been homeless and has mainly slept rough.

Alfred's history is similar to that of the others. They had always lived with their parents and it can be assumed that their parents maintained responsibility for cooking, budgeting and paying bills. Once their parents died, they were without their main carer and support for the first time. Most were evicted within six months, generally for non-payment of rent. Another man described an incident whereby he was cooking dangerously, itself suggesting his incompetence when alone. The majority had no support from relatives or lacked family. One man said: 'after my parents died, I was all alone; I had no family'. A few received support from siblings but this ended within a few months because of relationship difficulties and arguments. The siblings were married with families, and it is unlikely that they were prepared or able to offer long-term the intensity of support which the older people needed and to which they had become accustomed.

Besides having no support from relatives, the interviewees were poorly socialized, lacked friends, and many had mental health problems. It is likely that they were unable to articulate their needs and problems and access services. They were left alone to adjust to the loss of one or (in many instances) both parents. Many had also been through additional stresses. Alfred had experienced the death of his brother two days before his mother died. Another man's brother, who had always lived in the family home, died shortly after their mother's death. For most people who are recently bereaved, coping with additional stresses is difficult even when social support is available. Yet these subjects, whose vulnerability is evident, had to cope simultaneously with one or more bereavements and the stress of living alone. They became homeless because of their inability to manage alone and a lack of support once their main carer died.

Among the Lancefield Street Centre Study sample, there is also evidence that some people who have always lived with their parents become homeless in middle-age because a surviving parent is unable to continue to provide the level of support that is required. Four men became homeless in this way; all had mental health problems, inconsistent work patterns, and had never married. Two became homeless when the physical health of their only surviving parent deteriorated, and the parent was admitted to a registered care home. The other two men became homeless because their parent asked them to leave the house. The four men were aged in their 50s at the time, and it can thus be assumed that the parent who was providing care was aged at least middle-70s. The parents had cared for their sons for 50 years or more. It is therefore likely that support broke down because the parents were themselves old, possibly in poor health, and found it too much strain to continue to look after a dependent adult.

Widowhood leading to homelessness

Widowhood is an important contributory factor to homelessness for some older people, particularly men. In the Four-City and the Lancefield Street Centre studies, 17 men and one woman became homeless for the first time after their spouse died. In addition, one man had been successively homeless, rehoused for more than ten years, and then homeless again after his marital partner died. Most (15 people) were over the age of 50 years when they were widowed, and three were in their seventies. Most married in their twenties or early thirties and were married for more than 25 years. Ten were owner-occupiers, the rest had tenancies. The majority worked consistently until they were at least in their late fifties.

Nine wives died unexpectedly, the others were ill for a long time. One man, whose wife died suddenly of a brain haemorrhage, explained: 'it was so sudden; like a blow to my head'. Another man's wife died of cancer. He described it as 'a slow painful death; she suffered; I knew she was dying but she had not been told. I had no one to turn to; I did not want to lean on my children; so I turned to drink.' Three men had cared for their wives for years. One was married for 40 years. In the latter 10 years of the marriage, his wife developed cirrhosis of the liver and severe arthritis, and he used to wash and dress her, and take her out in a wheelchair. Another had cared for his wife who had been intermittently ill for 15 years with breast cancer and Alzheimer's disease. The only woman in this group was widowed in her thirties after her husband was struck by lightning.

Following the death of their spouse, most (15 subjects) volitionally gave up their homes and became homeless. Seven sold their property and five ceded council tenancies shortly after becoming widowed, and three sold their homes within five years. They said that they could not settle and found it too painful and upsetting to remain in the house. In the words of one man: 'the house had too many memories; my wife and I had lived there for 35 years; when I went out I never wanted to go back in the house'. Another man gave up his council home three months after becoming widowed and stayed with his son and daughter-in-law. This arrangement lasted for four years, arguments ensued, his son told him to leave, and he became homeless at the age of 71 years.

The other four widowers lost the right to remain in their accommodation. They said that they had been too distressed to challenge being evicted or to look for alternative accommodation at the time. Tom, for example, was evicted by the council less than three months after his wife died from the three-bedroomed house where he had lived for 25 years, because the premises were considered too large for one person. He had been made redundant the month before his wife died and his rent was in arrears. He said: 'the council started giving me aggravation; everything got on top of me; I was devastated and hit the bottle. I let them have their house. I had uncertain feelings about staying there anyhow; it had too many memories' (see Box 6.4). Another man had been drinking heavily since he was made redundant at the age of 62 years. His wife died a few years later, his drinking became excessive, his home became filthy, and he was evicted by the council.

The subjects reacted to bereavement in various ways. Nine drank heavily. One man sold his house, caravan and lorry, and spent the money on alcohol. Two men were admitted into psychiatric hospitals following suicide attempts. One former carer took an overdose, explaining: 'I was devastated by my wife's death; I was desperate; I tried to commit suicide; I drank poison and ended up unconscious in intensive care'. Another man obtained a job in a mortuary. He explained: 'I was laying out bodies and everyone seemed to be my wife; I didn't realize it at the time; I went to great lengths to make the bodies look nice.' After a few months he had a nervous breakdown and was admitted to hospital. Others sold their homes and possessions and travelled around. One man bought a car and caravan and 'I just drove off. I went all over the States. I came to England and travelled all over Europe. I became a wanderer. I could not settle anywhere.' Another said 'I went on the road after my wife died. I travelled anywhere . . . I just kept going from town to town'. A third said: 'I kept booking holidays to Wales, Cornwall, anywhere. I went on holidays to try and get away. Each time I came back to London it was too painful. I'm still unsettled and want to escape.'

Some men experienced additional stresses and traumas in the months preceding or following widowhood. One man was widowed at the age of 29 years and eight months later his young son died. He sold his house and car. 'I drank the proceeds. It took me a while to drink to freedom and get on the streets'. A second man's daughter drowned two months after his wife died. The case study of Horace (Box 4.2) demonstrates how various factors are likely to have contributed to homelessness.

Box 4.2   Case Study: Horace

Horace became homeless in his early fifties when his wife died of pneumonia. They had been married for more than 20 years. He was born in Ireland and had a disturbed childhood. When he was six years old, his mother had a mental breakdown and was admitted into a psychiatric hospital. She was never discharged and eventually died in hospital. Horace said that her mental breakdown was 'caused by giving birth to me'. He and his four siblings were brought up by their father and an aunt. Horace left school when he was 15 years old, worked as an electrician's mate for one year, and then served in the army for four years. After leaving the army he came to London and lodged with a landlady who 'cooked all my meals'.

Horace married at the age of 27, had five children, and he and his wife lived in council accommodation in London. He always worked; his last job was as a dustman for 15 years. He was a heavy drinker and said that this caused arguments with his wife and children. He hinted that he had suffered from 'nerve problems' while married, explaining: 'I used drink to get over them'. His wife died 15 years ago. By that time, his children had married and left home; one was living abroad, the others in London. After his wife's death, Horace was unable to settle at home because 'there were too many memories'. He gave up his home after a few weeks and became homeless. He first stayed in a bed-and-breakfast hotel, then lived in hostels and occasionally slept rough. He was offered a council flat a few years ago but refused it. He said: 'I do not want to live on my own. I am alright in hostels. I want company. I can't see much future.' He seldom has contact with his children, explaining: 'I don't bother them. I let them live their own lives. They do not approve of my lifestyle.'

Others described a similar history to Horace. Three-quarters came from broken childhood homes and then settled for many years with marital partners. They became owner-occupiers or sustained council tenancies and the majority worked for years. Vulnerability is, however, indicated in their histories. While married, five had been heavy drinkers and five suffered from mental health problems. Wives seem to have been a stabilizing influence. Once widowed, the subjects lost this stability and support. Most had never previously lived independently, having relied on tied accommodation or lodgings until they married. Many also experienced additional stresses. They generally lacked family or relationships were estranged. Horace admitted that his relationship with his children had been poor; his drinking habits had caused family arguments. The subjects became unsettled and restless, some drank heavily, and a few made suicide attempts. Most volitionally left their accommodation.

Homelessness following the breakdown of a marital relationship

Marital breakdown was a commonly reported reason for homelessness among older people. In the Four-City and the Lancefield Street Centre studies, 73 subjects (56 men and 17 women) associated homelessness with the breakdown of a marital or cohabiting relationship. Thirty-five per cent separated after the age of 50 years, including eight people after the age of 60 years. Some relationships had been a brief interlude within an unsettled life history. Others had been long-standing, and had been a central feature of people's lives. Some reported having had stable relationships which had deteriorated just before they separated, while others described long-standing marital problems. Some people blamed themselves for the relationship breakdown, others accused their partners. Several coincident factors were associated with the relationships ending, particularly heavy drinking, violence, infidelity and mental illness.

Relationship breakdown following long-standing problems

Relationship breakdown was sometimes the result of long-standing problems. Twelve men had been heavy drinkers for years, and their marriages ended because their wives could no longer tolerate their drinking. One man explained: 'my wife told me she had had enough and wanted me to leave. She said she would be better off on her own.' Most had been married for more than 20 years, and all except two had children. Although the men knew that heavy drinking was damaging their marriage, they were unable (or unwilling) to explain why they continued to drink. Two said that their fathers had been alcoholics; others associated heavy drinking with stresses they had experienced, such as the death of a child or a close family member, or disturbing events while in the armed forces. After separating, all 12 men slept rough. They already had a drinking problem, and it is likely that they coped with the stresses and changes linked to separation by spending their money on alcohol rather than on securing lodgings and avoiding homelessness. This is illustrated in the case study of George (Box 4.3).

Seven women became homeless after years of physical abuse by marital partners. Although they had been injured on several occasions and had sometimes needed hospital treatment, the women remained with their partners for years (four for more than 25 years). One woman said: 'I was in and out of hospital. He hit me and I got broken jaws, a bruised face and black eyes.' Six associated the violence with their husband's heavy drinking. The

---

Box 4.3   Case study: George

George was in his early sixties and had been sleeping rough for 20 years. He was born and brought up in Ireland, and had five siblings. His family lived in a two-bedroomed house, so George used to share a bed with his father. When George was 17 years old, he found his father dead in bed beside him. He could not settle at home after this and soon after came to England. He stayed for 'a short while and then I took off', and worked in France and Germany as a paint-sprayer for three years. He returned to England, settled in one town, and became a watch repairer with a jewellery firm for 20 years. He lived with a woman for 20 years and had two sons.

He had started drinking at the age of 14 years, his intake increased after his father's death and 'over the years I was drinking more and more'. His heavy drinking affected his ability to work as he needed steady hands for the job; it caused arguments at home, and eventually the breakdown of his relationship. When it ended, his two sons were working abroad, his partner remained in their council home, and George became homeless.

---

seventh believed that her husband was mentally ill: 'he thought I poisoned his food and he heard voices from nowhere; when I said I could not hear the voices, he hit me'. He behaved this way throughout their 27 years of marriage, but 'he has never been to a doctor so nobody knew he was like that'. The police had been called to incidents of violence for four of the women. Three said that their husbands had become increasingly violent in later years. One woman explained: 'he became more violent in the last ten years of our marriage, since he was made redundant from the coal-mines'.

Before their relationships finally ended, four women left home for a few weeks when relationships became intolerable, stayed in hostels or bed-and-breakfast hotels, and then returned to their partners. Three finally separated when they found out that their husbands were committing adultery, two when their husbands tried to strangle them, and another while her husband was in prison for assaulting her. All were over the age of 40 when they separated, and three over 50. For all seven women, the final separation was a sudden, unplanned event, and they booked into hostels or slept rough. Two later acquired jobs at holiday camps for a few years, being accommodated during the summer at camps and staying in hostels during the winter, before they became persistently homeless.

The relationship between these women and their husbands is complex. The women had tolerated physical abuse by their husbands for years and only separated when it became more intense or when they discovered their husband's infidelity. They said that they stayed with their husbands because 'the children were young', or because they had no one to help them. Yet even when their children had grown up they did not separate. In three instances, adult children tried to intervene but help was rejected. The women reported that their husbands behaved intolerably. Yet two women described how they had retaliated on occasions, one explaining: 'I threw hot water over him on many occasions'. The women's role within these pathological, stressful relationships is not clearly understood. Because they tolerated abuse for years and became homeless immediately they separated, one suspects that they were supported in some way by being with their partners. Most had never lived alone, three had experienced broken or disturbed childhood homes, a fourth had been mentally ill as a young adult, and a fifth had experienced an early short-lived marriage in which her first husband had sexual relations with her mother. Their marital relationships, although abusive, may have provided them with some level of security, stability and support.

Three men, aged in their sixties, volitionally left their homes because they could no longer cope with their wives who were mentally ill. They had all been married at least 20 years. Their wives suffered from schizophrenia, had been ill for many years, and had had several hospital admissions. According to the men, although their wives were on medication, the illness was uncontrolled and in recent years their wives had become more disturbed and aggressive. One man, whose wife bit off part of his ear, said: 'I took many beatings from her; she used to think I was the Devil'. Another man's wife accused him of being with other women each time he left the house. On several occasions, she had thrown his belongings out of the window when he returned. In the years preceding separation, two of the men had developed physical health problems and could no longer work. They were thus at home more often, and this seems to have aggravated the situation.

As with the women who tolerated physical abuse for years, the relationship between these men and their wives who were mentally ill was complex. The men had tolerated years of abuse, arguments and difficult behaviour. They had left their wives on several occasions but had returned home. One man divorced his wife and then remarried her a few years later. It is likely that their marital relationships were providing them with some stability and support, and once this was removed, the men became homeless.

Domestic violence was common among marriages in mediaeval times and in the early days of industrialization, and it remains widespread (Giddens 1989). Although men are primarily believed to be the perpetrators of marital violence, the indication is that wives strike husbands nearly as often as the reverse (Straus *et al.* 1980). In 1975 an American study found that 28 per cent of 2,143 couples reported at least one violent incident in their marriage, and in the 12 months preceding the interview, 3.8 per cent of wives and 4.6 per cent of husbands had been severely physically attacked by their spouse (Straus 1978). Domestic violence is often accepted as normative behaviour within families. Violence is sometimes learned through socialization in childhood, whereby it is regarded as appropriate behaviour when one is frustrated or angry. Wives are more likely to tolerate abuse from their husbands if they have been victims of intrafamilial violence or exposed to spousal violence in their family of orientation (Gelles 1979; Straus 1978).

Relationship breakdown following recent stresses

Sixteen men and one woman associated the breakdown of a long-standing marriage and homelessness with recent problems, particularly the infidelity of partners, mental and physical illnesses, redundancy, and heavy drinking. At the time of separation, ten had been married for more than 15 years, and the majority (12 people) were aged in their forties or fifties. For six men, their marriage ended abruptly after their wives committed adultery. They all had long-standing histories of heavy drinking or had worked away from home for long periods, but denied that their behaviour had caused marital difficulties. Six men lost their jobs after becoming mentally or physically ill. Although the illnesses did not result in immediate relationship breakdown, as with the case study of Albert (Box 4.4), marital problems ensued and separation occurred in a few years.

Box 4.4   Case study: Albert

Albert was 60 years old when his marriage ended and he became homeless. He described an unsettled childhood. His parents moved around Britain with his father's work, and Albert sometimes lived with his family and at other times 'I was sent to aunts; I was like a gypsy'. Albert had five siblings but described himself as 'the black sheep of the family; my father used to beat me with a strap. I don't think he wanted me to be born.' Albert left home when he was 17 years old, and joined the army for eight years. He said: 'I didn't like the army. I didn't want to kill people. I was a terror and took all the anger of my childhood out on the officers.' After leaving the army, Albert worked as a bricklayer for almost 30 years. He married when he was 26 years old, lived in a council house, and had eight children.

When Albert was 54 years old, his neighbour's house caught fire and he tried to rescue an elderly woman in the blazing house. He dragged her outside but she was dead. The fire brigade were on strike and it took 30 minutes for help to arrive. His eldest daughter, then aged 22 years, was at the scene and had a succession of epileptic fits. The fire occurred early one morning and an elderly man came to help Albert. This man died six months later of heart problems. For the next five years, Albert suffered from breathing difficulties due to smoke inhalation, developed pneumonia, had several courses of medication, and was unable to work. He said: 'I turned into a miserable, cantankerous old bastard. I was awful to live with. I lost my memory for three years. I felt that people were getting at me and thought I should have got the woman out alive. I was petrified going into the blazing house.'

During the years following the fire, Albert and his wife argued. He said: 'the rows got worse, our relationship fell apart, and she kept telling me, "I want you out of my life"'. They separated six years after the fire and after 34 years of marriage. Albert explained: 'I just upped and went one day. I would never stay somewhere I was not wanted. I only took with me my bricklayer's tools. I left everything else behind.' Since separating 11 years ago, Albert has slept rough and has had no contact with his wife and children. He explained: 'the day my wife turned me out it broke my heart. I feel very angry and bitter towards her.'

According to Albert, homelessness was triggered by a fire which led to physical and mental health problems, strained family relationships, and marital breakdown. He had an unsettled childhood, found difficulties in adjusting to army life, but settled once married. He was married for 34 years, consistently employed, and raised a large family. Similar histories were described by the others in this group. All except two reported unsettled histories in childhood and early adulthood but, once married, the majority worked for years and raised a family. From Albert's history, there was no evidence of especial vulnerability before the fire. But pathological states are indicated in some histories. Seven men had been drinking heavily throughout their marriage, five started to drink heavily when they were experiencing relationship difficulties, six suffered from mental health problems, two had served prison sentences for non-violent offences, three had been charged with assault on their wives, and a fourth had physically assaulted his employer.

At the time of separation, most lacked or were estranged from their families. It was difficult to determine the extent to which estranged family relationships were instigated by the interviewees or by their families. Albert had had no contact with his siblings for years, and felt angry and rejected by his wife when he left home. Another man, whose wife committed adultery, explained: 'I cut myself off from my family when my marriage broke up 30 years ago.' Three men had tried to keep in contact with their children but were denied access rights. All had been mentally ill and admitted into hospital prior to separation, and one man had assaulted his wife. One man said: 'my wife's solicitor got my three sons to sign forms to say they did not want to see me. When I made contact with my nine-year-old son, a contempt of court [order] was issued against me and I had to do a 14-day sentence.' Another said: 'when we separated, my son and daughter were young and I did not see them much. I kept having to go to court to get access. Eventually you give up and just don't bother.'

Once their marriages ended, most made no attempt to find accommodation but instead slept rough. Their reaction may have been caused by a fear of having to cope alone. Or it may have been the result of angry feelings towards their partners who had rejected them (in ten cases, partners were reported to have been adulterous) and towards 'society' which had refused them access to their children. When interviewed, many were still apparently angry with their wives although they had been separated for years. One man who had been refused access rights stated angrily: 'I saw my wife a few years ago in the street; she looked ill and I prayed she had cancer and would die.' He had been separated for 17 years. Another man, divorced for 15 years, referred to his ex-wife as 'a constipated ferret' and said: 'if I ever find out I have a terminal illness, I will get a pistol and shoot her. I wouldn't mind spending my last months in prison.' Besides expressing anger towards their ex-wives, the men described their irritation with people generally and how they wished to be 'apart' from society. One explained: 'for 20 years I have wished I could disappear up a mountain and get away from everybody. People drive me mad and screw me up. It would be nice if the voice boxes were removed from people.' Another commented: 'I was suffering from psychological pain, grief and inner anger [after the divorce]; I have been consumed by that. I want to cut myself completely off from everybody and be totally alone.' Wagner (1993: 56) noted the brutal impact and trauma which separation and divorce have on many homeless men, particularly those over the age of 35, concluding that 'emotional pain, alcohol, and flight [had] led to a sharp and steady downward path'.

The breakdown of surrogate family homes

In some instances, older people have lived in surrogate family homes for years and have become homeless when the arrangement breaks down. Two men and one woman lodged with elderly landladies and became homeless because the property was sold once their landlady died. All had been lodgers for more than ten years, in one case for more than 20 years. They were all over the age of 50 years at the time. One woman had lodged in her aunt's house for 11 years, since she retired. She used to work as a chambermaid in hotels and lived in tied accommodation while employed. After her aunt's death, her nephew sold the house and she became homeless at the age of 76 years. The case study of Fred (Box 4.5) demonstrates how surrogate family households sometimes provide support and stability to vulnerable people.

Conclusions

The breakdown of family homes is an important antecedent to homelessness. It occurs at any stage of the life course. Some people become homeless for the first time in old age following marital breakdown or widowhood. Others have been homeless since middle age following the death of their parents or as a consequence of marital breakdown. Yet others have been homeless since adolescence after leaving broken or disturbed childhood homes. Although homelessness was triggered by different events, several shared characteristics are apparent in the subjects' histories. Many had a dysfunctional relationship with their parents. Some experienced a disturbed childhood and were raised by foster parents, in institutions, or remained at home and witnessed their parents' heavy drinking, violence or adulterous behaviour. Others had always lived with and been dependent on their parents. Disruptive childhood homes are often reported in studies of homeless people, but 'sheltered and protected' family homes may be an equally important antecedent to homelessness once support breaks down.

Many who experienced disruptive childhoods settled with marital partners or landladies, and maintained long-lasting relationships and consistent work patterns. Wives and landladies seem to have acted as a safety net. They provided support and a stable environment in which the subjects could structure their lives and develop a routine. Once this stabilizing influence was removed through death or marital breakdown, the interviewees became unsettled. Some volitionally abandoned their homes, while others had to leave their accommodation but made no attempt to find alternative housing. Although they had settled for years in a supportive environment, vulnerability and pathological states are indicated in some histories, with reports of heavy

---

Box 4.5 Case study: Fred

Fred was 55 years old and had been sleeping rough for two years. His mother died when he was 13 years old, following which he lived with an aunt who had three children. He said: 'my aunt was good to me but it was not the same as my real mother'. Fred had no siblings. His father died when Fred was 18 years old. After his father's death, Fred joined the army for three years and then 'I became homeless, slept rough, and drifted for 12 years'. He eventually rented a room from an elderly woman when he was in his early thirties. She had been recently widowed and had no family. Fred lived with her for 20 years until she died. He worked as a porter in a hospital for a few years, then looked after her for 10 years because she was crippled with arthritis. She did the cooking and housework, and he shopped and grew vegetables in her garden. He said: 'I enjoyed that life; I was like a son to her. When I lodged with her, it helped me to settle down; it was a normal home life.' The elderly woman had herself rented the house privately. When she died he had to leave the house as the landlord wanted to sell the property. He did not seek alternative housing but became homeless for a second time at the age of 53 years.

Fred had long-standing mental health problems, and had received treatment for depression intermittently since the age of 16 years. He said: 'when the old lady died it was a great loss, it reminded me of my mother's death. Losing my mother when I was 13 years old affected me all through life.' He never married, explaining: 'you need to be steady to marry; have a steady job. I never had a firm footing in life.' He had always been a loner and never had friends, 'only mates in passing'. He drank alcohol 'because of loneliness. I'm not an alcoholic. I had nobody in the world until my landlady took me in . . . I was all alone, no one to turn to, no home. When I went into pubs I had company and someone to talk to.'

---

drinking, mental health problems, aggression, and non-violent offences. A third shared characteristic is the lack of social support and estranged family relationships at the time of entry into homelessness. For some, the stressful event which triggered homelessness, such as the death of a last surviving parent, also destroyed their only social network. Some were already estranged from their families and friends, sometimes heavy drinking contributed to strained relationships. Others severed contacts because of conflicts with parents or marital partners.

Differences existed in the histories of those who became homeless after the death of a parent or a spouse, and those who became homeless following a marital breakdown. Only a small proportion of bereaved people reported heavy drinking before the loss, and *none* reported histories of violence or expressed anger towards their family. Yet among the men who became homeless following a relationship breakdown, these behaviours were common and some remained angry and vindictive towards their wives and towards society years after they had separated. To further the understanding of the breakdown of family relationships and homelessness, it would be necessary to collect information from parents, siblings and former partners. Because many older homeless people have been estranged from their families for years through choice or rejection, contacting relatives would be extremely difficult and perhaps unnecessarily traumatic for the subjects and the relatives.

5

Itinerant working lives

In a city like London you can lose yourself in a crowd or sit on a bench all day and no-one will take notice of you. If you are homeless and sit on a bench all day in a village, people will stare at you and talk about you. In London you can be anonymous; in a village you become a marked man.
(Frank, aged 60 years, sleeping rough)

A long-standing association exists in Britain and America between men who have been itinerant workers and have moved about with their jobs, and homelessness. Forty-two men in the Four-City Study and nine in the Lance-field Street Centre Study had been itinerant workers for years before becoming homeless, as merchant seamen, building and construction labourers, seasonal workers on farms and in factories, hotels and holiday camps, and as long-distance lorry drivers. Following an opening literature review, this chapter examines the relationship between itinerant work histories and homelessness. It draws on the experiences of two distinct groups, men who had been merchant seamen and had travelled abroad, and those who had been labourers and seasonal workers and had travelled around Britain. The majority became homeless in the 1970s, and the effects of retirement and redundancy on contemporary older homeless people are discussed.

In early twentieth-century America, migratory and itinerant workers had jobs which were casual and seasonal, and thus required them to move from place to place (Sutherland and Locke 1936; Anderson 1923; Solenberger 1911). Chicago, for example, had become a rapidly growing city with railway connections to many areas and much casual work in construction and the stockyards. During the 1920s, an estimated 300,000–500,000 migratory men passed through each year, seeking shelter in the winter when harvest and seasonal work was finished (Anderson 1923). They were known as 'hoboes' and included lumberjacks, railroad workers, construction labourers, harvest workers, fruit pickers and merchant seamen (Cohen and Sokolovsky 1989). They usually worked outdoors during the summer when they slept in work-camps or bunk-houses, and moved to 'skid rows' of cities during winter where they stayed in flop-houses and were regarded as homeless (Schneider

1984; Sutherland and Locke 1936). By the 1940s, because of mechanization on farms, in factories and the lumber industry, there was a reduction in the number of semi-skilled and unskilled jobs, and the proportion of migrant workers within the homeless population declined (Cohen and Sokolovsky 1989; Schneider 1984).

The association between casual work and **transience** is also long-standing in Britain. In the fourteenth and fifteenth centuries, harvest workers moved around the country looking for seasonal work (Chambliss 1964). In the nineteenth century, during times of high unemployment, labourers, agricultural workers, and railway and canal navvies moved between towns seeking jobs (Burnett 1994). Trade unions operated a 'tramping system', whereby unemployed skilled workmen were encouraged to leave town and look for jobs elsewhere (Mann 1992). They were given an allowance, a planned route, and a list of places (usually public houses) where they could secure a night's lodgings and obtain information about local jobs. The rationale was twofold: to help skilled workers seek jobs in other parts of the country, and to remove surplus labour from the place of origin. By the twentieth century, men who were 'on tramp' in Britain no longer received a travelling allowance nor were they accommodated in 'houses of call', but instead lodged in casual wards of workhouses or stayed in private lodging-houses if they had money.

Hypotheses suggest that economic conditions, unemployment, and the seasonal nature of some jobs force men to become mobile in search of work (Schneider 1984). Partly because of poverty in rural Ireland, unskilled Irish men came to Britain in the nineteenth century and worked as harvesters, building labourers, and navvies constructing canals and railways (Coleman and Salt 1992; Mann 1992). Nearly 23,000 migratory workers came from Ireland to England in 1880 (Jackson 1963: Table XI). Others suggest that the problem is more complex, believing that personality difficulties and irresponsibility dominate (Anderson 1923; Solenberger 1911). Navvies and building labourers sometimes drifted from one job to another without staying until a job was completed, and they became easily piqued or pressurized in work situations (Schneider 1984; Sykes 1969a). The lifestyle is believed to have attracted people with social and psychological problems who were unable to secure alternative work (Bogue 1963). Others left home following the death of a close relative, family conflicts, or to escape from crimes (Allsop 1967; Anderson 1923).

Itinerant working lives are believed to have encouraged homelessness in two ways. First, the majority of men never married or settled in one place, but lived and worked in male-dominated environments where heavy drinking was common. In Britain, railway navvies lived in encampments by railway lines, labourers in work-camps erected at building sites, and other casual workers stayed in resettlement units (Coleman 1965). The work-camps were often in remote areas and the men were alienated from local communities. Such settings fostered social ties among some workers, although many navvies were reported to be isolated in the camps and without friends (Sykes 1969b). Second, using skid row lodgings between jobs habituated the men to homelessness, and they drifted into a lifestyle to which they were already accustomed once unemployed (Bahr and Caplow 1974; Solenberger 1911). Skid row offered them a male-oriented lifestyle with few responsibilities, comparable to the work-camps. Furthermore, when seeking casual workers, American employers often contacted lodging-houses on skid rows and British employers the resettlement units.

Former merchant seamen

Twelve older homeless men had been merchant seamen and had travelled extensively. Ten had been in the merchant navy for more than 20 years, and most had joined by the age of 16. One man who described himself as 'a gypsy of the sea', had been in the navy for nearly 30 years and had made 72 voyages world-wide. The men said that there used to be plenty of work available, they were employed casually, and were always at sea. They would sign up for the next trip after a few days ashore as they were not paid between voyages. This used to be common practice in Britain. At the start of the Second World War, the British Merchant Marine employed over 190,000 seamen, almost all casually, voyage by voyage, with no paid leave and no guarantee of future work.[1] Between voyages, the men stayed in seamen's missions close to docks or slept rough on beaches. In Lowestoft, a night-shelter originated because many merchant seamen were sleeping on the beach (see Chapter 11). A few stayed on ships. One man reported: 'when the ship was in dock, we were allowed to stay on board. We slept there. The ship was my home.'

The majority (nine men) married but most marriages lasted less than five years. Only two men were married for more than 20 years. One man explained: 'my wife got fed up with me being away and said I had to chose between her and the sea. I chose the sea. We were married less than two years.' Heavy drinking was a regular feature of their lives. They used to be given 'a daily tot of rum at 11 a.m. to stop getting seasick'. One man said: 'you wouldn't be in that sort of navy unless you got yourself involved in drinking; we made regular trips to the West Indies where we got strong rum'. Most said that they were forced to leave the merchant navy in the 1970s when jobs became scarce. At the time, most were over the age of 50 years. One explained: 'the navy finished me off because of my age'. On leaving the merchant navy, most had no family support and became homeless immediately. Six had experienced broken childhood homes and the rest had not kept in contact with their parents and siblings.

Although only one man admitted to mental health problems before becoming homeless, ten had apparent memory problems when interviewed. One man answered '12 years' to all questions relating to time. He said that he had been in the merchant navy for 12 years and then admitted: 'although I say 12 years, it could have been 30 years'. It is likely that years of heavy drinking affected their memory. The case study of Henry (Box 5.1) illustrates the former seamen's move to homelessness. Because of poor memory, Henry gave a general account of his circumstances but was unable to remember details.

Box 5.1   Case study: Henry

Henry was 70 years old and had been homeless for nearly 20 years. He said that he had been in the merchant navy for 17 years, but according to his history, he must have been a merchant seaman for approximately 30 years. He left school when he was 17 years old, joined the Royal Navy for four years, and was then a merchant seaman until he was 51 years old. While in the merchant navy, he was married briefly and lived in a council house with his wife. He explained: 'I used to do smaller trips then so that I could spend time with my wife.' They never had children. He said: 'One day I came home on leave and found her in bed with another man.' He left her and 'went back to sea'. He was unable to say how old he was when he married, and could not remember how long he had been married but knew 'it was just a few years'. After he and his wife divorced, he stayed in seamen's missions in East London between trips.

He left the merchant navy almost 20 years ago. He explained: 'I was laid off from the navy when I was 51 years old. I got too old and was told to go. I didn't want to go. When I left I burned my two seaman's books which held the records of all the voyages I'd made.' On leaving the navy, he was homeless. He said: 'the navy gave me my signing off papers in Edinburgh, but did not give me accommodation'. He had no family to help him. His parents had died, his only sister lived in Canada, and he had lost contact with his brother years earlier. He came to London, and at first worked casually on building sites and stayed in hostels. He explained: 'I queued up each morning at the Elephant and Castle and bosses from building sites would come looking for labourers and take us to the jobs. At the beginning it was easy to get work, but later it became difficult.' When he was no longer able to get work, he could not afford to stay in hostels so he slept rough. He was unable to say how old he was when he first slept rough.

Former labourers and seasonal workers

Thirty-two older homeless men had been labourers on building sites, laying cables, building roads, or seasonal workers in factories and at holiday camps, hotels, fairgrounds and farms, or as long-distance lorry drivers (three men). They had travelled around Britain working. Some had stayed in a job until the work was completed before moving to another town. One former labourer said: 'I worked on a building site for two to three years until the job finished, and then moved to another town and the next job.' Others changed jobs and towns through boredom. One man said: 'I could never stick a job because of the monotony.' Several men worked at holiday camps on the coast during the summer and as labourers in towns in winter. One man said: 'I used to go to Kent in the summer and do farmwork or fruit picking, and sleep out.

In the winter I came back to London.' Two men had worked in sugar-beet factories in Cambridgeshire: they were taken on 'for six months if it was a good crop; the job would last until February, and then you would get another job until the sugar-beet was ready again'.

They said that there used to be plenty of unskilled work available and they had been mainly employed. According to one man: 'you could go with a mate to his job and the building firm would take you on straight away. If you did not like that job you could go with another mate to his job and get taken on by his firm.' They changed jobs knowing that they could easily find work and there was no obligation to remain in a job. Another commented: 'if you were out of work you could look in the *Evening News*; they always had long lists of vacancies'. Work-camps were erected next to building sites, sugar-beet factories and power stations to provide accommodation for the men, particularly if the sites were in remote areas. Canteens on site provided meals. The men sometimes chose jobs knowing that they would also get accommodation. One man stated: 'I chose camp jobs because they gave you accommodation and meals.'

Some men lived in digs and lodgings. They said that it had once been easy to get lodgings as rooms to let were advertised by newsagents. The lodgings were often crowded, with several men sharing a room. One man said: 'I shared rooms with my work crew so we then had money left for beer.' The men were often 'looked after' by landladies, who did their cooking, cleaning and washing, and provided them with breakfast, a packed lunch and an evening meal. Some stayed in hostels and resettlement units and slept rough intermittently. One man used to work at holiday camps during the summer and book into resettlement units during the winter because 'employees would contact the unit and offer you jobs'.

From the 1970s, they had found it difficult to get regular work and digs. They shifted from being regularly employed to working intermittently and casually as kitchen porters, before eventually stopping work. Those who had been labourers reported that their health had also started to deteriorate at the time and the building work had become too heavy. They blamed their poor health on years of working outdoors and being exposed to bad weather and digging in wet trenches. They increasingly slept rough and relied on hostels and resettlement units, stayed less in lodgings and work-camps, and 'drifted' into homelessness. The majority were in their forties or early fifties at the time, although 16 had first used accommodation for homeless people or slept rough before the age of 30. Many had therefore experienced many years of moving between marginal housing and homelessness before becoming persistently homeless.

Fifteen of the 32 men originated from Ireland, most of whom had come to England by the age of 19 years, and eight were born in Scotland. Hence, 72 per cent were Irish or Scottish. One-third had experienced broken or disturbed childhood homes, and only six had remained in contact with their family. Others had lost contact while moving around. Seven-tenths had never married or cohabited. Fifteen men admitted that they drank heavily while working. Those who had been building labourers described a typical drinking cycle. They worked from Monday to Friday until they were paid, drank heavily all weekend and spent their earnings, returned to work on Monday and were given a 'sub' by the boss to last until Friday. Employers often arranged transport to take labourers from their lodgings to building sites, and the men used to drink in the vans in the morning while going to work. The case study of Bill (Box 5.2) demonstrates how he came to England at an early age, spent nearly 30 years travelling around, and drifted into homelessness.

Box 5.2 Case study: Bill

Bill was 59 years old and had been sleeping in a shed for more than ten years. He was born on a farm in Ireland and had nine siblings. His father died of meningitis when Bill was four years old. As Bill's siblings got older, they left home or went out to work. Bill said: 'I was the youngest son and was expected to do the farmwork. I was running the farm when I was 16 years old. I had to do all the ploughing by hand and look after the pigs. My brothers and sisters would come home from work nicely dressed and I would be filthy dirty.' He left home at the age of 18 and came to England. He explained: 'I had to leave and get away or else I would never have left. I had to escape and see life. Because I would not stay and run the farm, I became the black sheep of the family.'

After coming to England, he travelled around the country, working as a labourer on building sites. He said: 'I would stay in a job until it finished, and then move to the next town and the next job.' He stayed at work-camps attached to building sites and in lodgings. When he stayed in lodgings, 'my landlady would cook my breakfast and evening meal. Even if I came in at 10 p.m., I would find my dinner in the oven. She made sandwiches for me to take to work for lunch.' He occasionally worked on farms in the summer, during which time he slept rough. By the 1970s, he found it hard to get jobs and digs and so remained in London. He occasionally booked into hostels and resettlement units, but mainly slept in derelict buildings. He once 'lived' in a derelict house for ten years. He said: 'I would get wood, make a fire in the house, and cook on the fire. I lived there and nobody knew.'

He used to go back to Ireland and visit his family every year, but 'this dwindled off when I was out of work and had no money. I've had no contact with them for over 12 years.' He said: 'I hate going back there. People have changed and you don't know your family anymore. If you cannot afford to go back every year they think you're not achieving, and they look on you as a bum and a no-gooder.' He never married nor had a girlfriend: 'I've been let down so many times in life that I don't bother with people.' He said that he used to get depressed about his situation and, as a result, he drank heavily and moved around to try and improve his circumstances. He was given a council flat 12 years ago but said: 'I kept the tenancy for seven years but hardly lived in the flat; I slept in the shed where I'm now living. When I had the flat it was a lot of aggravation and worry with the bills and rent.'

Distinctive features of the itinerant workers

Long-standing transience

The men who had been itinerant workers had travelled around for years, in many cases for more than 20 years. For some, the lifestyle started in adolescence after they left disturbed or broken childhood homes; for others it began in early adulthood after leaving the army or after failed marriages. The men who had been merchant seamen had jobs which by their very nature required them to be mobile. Others had moved between jobs and towns of their own volition. Once homeless, the merchant seamen tended to have remained in one town but many who had been labourers and seasonal workers still moved around. This suggests that work may have largely contributed to itinerant behaviours among the merchant seamen, but for those who were labourers and seasonal workers, and who continued to be transient even when it was no longer required, the implication is that personality difficulties (or other non-work factors) contributed to unsettled behaviours. Several, including Bill, said that they had moved around because they had felt depressed. Because the information collected in the interviews was retrospective, the depth of depression which the men experienced at the time when they were moving between jobs and towns is unknown.

Poor family and social relationships

The majority of men described poor family and social relationships. Many came from broken and disturbed childhood homes, and left home in adolescence to join the merchant navy or become labourers. Most others lost contact with their families once they left home. Bill referred to himself as 'the black sheep of the family'; others used similar phrases, 'the gypsy' and 'the bad apple', to indicate estranged family relationships. One man reported that his brother had said to him: 'You'll be a great guy when you're dead; now you're a drunken bastard.' In America, many homeless people also described themselves as the 'black sheep of the family' (Wagner 1993: 47). Most remained single and never cohabited, or their relationships had been short-lived. Only a minority experienced lasting relationships with women. Whereas labourers and seasonal workers tended never to have cohabited or married, merchant seamen had more often been involved in short-lived intimate relationships.

The effect of being away from home for long periods is likely to have had an influence on relationships. One man said: 'I was working away from home six days a week; I came back and my wife was with another guy.' Another explained: 'all the travelling affected my marriage; I was never at home. My children were growing up and I was away. You are a complete and utter stranger when you come back to your kids and they ask who you are.' Yet another reported: 'I was never close to my children. I was away working for days and weeks. I would promise to take them out and then my boss would ring me with a job. I was the wage earner so I had to do the work. But the children never understood and they hold that against me still.'

The men had spent much time in male company, their social relationships had focused around their working lives, and they had rarely formed other social links. Merchant seamen had been on voyages which had lasted up to 15 months, they had lived on ships, and affiliated only with fellow crewmen. One said: 'I sailed from Birkenhead and sailed back into the same dock nine months later. It was like returning to a strange world.' They had stayed in missions and mixed with seamen while ashore. The majority of former labourers described themselves as 'loners' who lived in work-camps, and who used to work, eat and drink together. One said: 'I've never bothered to make friends; I keep myself to myself.' Another explained: 'I put drink before women; my work-mates were my drinking partners.' Hotel workers also stayed in their rooms when off-duty and occasionally socialized with each other.

Heavy drinking

Alcohol featured prominently, and many men admitted that they had been heavy drinkers while working. The former merchant seamen talked about the availability of alcohol and their daily ration of rum to prevent seasickness. The former building labourers described how they used to drink on the way to work and heavily at weekends; for them, the pub was a focal point. One man said: 'the pub was a labour exchange and a place to get lodgings when you arrived in a town. You slept on the floor in the pub until you could fix yourself up with digs.' Others described how employers used pubs to seek workers and wages were paid in pubs at the end of the week. This practice is long-standing. In nineteenth-century Britain, pubs 'served important social, cultural and economic functions . . . it was a common practice for contractors to pay Irish labourers their wages in public houses' (Swift 1989: 168).

Many started drinking before the age of 17 years. One man, whose father had been a heavy drinker and a sailor, was expelled from school when he was 13 years old for being drunk. Another, whose father also was a heavy drinker, was drinking by the age of 14 years. Others related the onset of heavy drinking to horrific events while in the armed forces, and said that they used alcohol to obliterate bad memories (Chapter 6). Alcohol then became an integral part of the men's work and living circumstances, and a focus of their social activities. Their earnings were spent on alcohol with little regard for future investments. One man described, 'I was like most Irishmen; I would work all week and then have a good drink at the weekend. By Monday morning I would be skint. I've worked for 35 years but have nothing to show for it.'

No home base or experience of independent living

Only a few married itinerant workers sustained tenancies and a 'home base' while working. The majority stayed in lodgings, work-camps and missions, with no security of tenure. Two-thirds used hostels or slept rough periodically. Many relied on employers for accommodation. Those who were seeking work were encouraged to stay in reception centres as these were used as labour exchanges by employers. When the men changed jobs, they also changed accommodation. Hence, they did not establish 'roots' or connections in any one town. Most never lived independently but stayed in settings where they had few responsibilities, and where meals were provided by landladies or in works canteens. At the time that the men became homeless, three-fifths had *never* lived in secure accommodation since leaving their childhood home. This included three men who had been raised in orphanages and had *never* lived in conventional housing.

Their inability to manage independently in accommodation is evident from their histories once they became homeless. The majority had either never been resettled or had become homeless again soon after being rehoused. Twenty-seven had been rehoused but 22 had become homeless again, all except three within one year. When Bill acquired a tenancy for a few years, he was unable to cope and slept rough. Of the five who had secure accommodation when interviewed, three said that they felt lonely, were unable to settle and manage a home, and preferred to live with others. One man explained: 'I was disappointed when I got my flat. I was living in bed-and-breakfast and I used to sit and chat to the landlady in the kitchen. When I went into my flat I was lost. I don't like living alone.' One former merchant seaman who had lived in missions when not at sea said: 'in the mission everything was done for you. Now it may be two or three months before I change my bedclothes.'

Conclusions

The men became itinerant as merchant seamen, labourers or seasonal workers after leaving broken childhood homes, on discharge from the armed forces, or following marital breakdown. Having been itinerant workers for many years, most 'drifted' from regular work to casual work, and from insecure housing into homelessness in the 1970s. During this period, unemployment increased in Great Britain, particularly within the manufacturing and construction industries, and the demand for unskilled manual workers fell sharply (Burnett 1994; Coleman and Salt 1992). Only 15–17 per cent of male unskilled manual workers were unemployed, however, and most did not become homeless (Bennett *et al*. 1996: Table 7.5). This suggests that unemployment alone was insufficient to account for the transition to homelessness.

Their progression into homelessness resulted from aggregated economic, social, health and psychological factors. While working, the men had relied on employers for accommodation or had stayed in digs and lodgings. The availability of privately rented accommodation had been declining in Britain since 1918 and, by the 1970s, when the men could no longer obtain regular work and tied accommodation, it was also difficult to secure cheap lodgings (Greve 1991). They were heavy drinkers, generally lacked savings, their health was deteriorating, and they only worked casually (if at all). Their income was thus irregular and low-paid, and this would have affected their ability to afford privately rented accommodation. They were estranged from families who might have been able to offer support. They had never settled in one location, were unknown to local housing authorities, and would not have been considered a priority group for council housing.

The undersocialization theory of homelessness proposes that young adults who are poorly socialized and dependent leave their childhood homes and move into semi-protective institutional environments, such as military barracks, railroad and labouring work-camps, and hostels, which relieve them 'of responsibility for coping with problems of food, housing and related needs' (Pittman and Gordon 1958: 128–9; see Chapter 2 above). The 51 itinerant workers had few social relationships outside the work setting, and some had frequently changed jobs because of difficulties at work. They had become accustomed to living in male-oriented communal settings and in lodgings where they had few responsibilities and were 'looked after' by landladies. Most had never lived independently and managed a home. After becoming homeless, many who were resettled soon re-entered homelessness, while a few sustained tenancies but preferred living in hostels where they had companionship and few responsibilities. Although economic and housing circumstances may have contributed to homelessness, poor socialization and a dependency on institutional-type settings also seem to have been influential.

This chapter has examined ways in which itinerant workers became homeless in the 1970s. There is a reduction in this type of workforce nowadays and few older people in the Four-City and Lancefield Street Centre studies became homeless in recent years having been merchant seamen or itinerant building labourers. But there remains an association between redundancy or retirement and homelessness in later life. Some older men become homeless aged in their late fifties and early sixties after having worked abroad or in another part of Britain for years, and having returned to their native area on retirement without family, friends or accommodation (Wilson 1995). Five men and one woman in the Four-City and the Lancefield Street Centre studies became homeless at or near the official retirement age on return to this country after having worked abroad for years. One such man became homeless at the age of 62 years after having worked and lived in lodgings in Australia for more than 20 years. He had no family and had assumed he would be able to find accommodation once he arrived in London. He said, 'I felt I needed to come home once I stopped work. I wanted to eventually die in my own country.' Another man, an architect, went to Spain to work at the age of 53 years after his long-standing marriage ended in divorce. He stayed in Spain for five years but his business failed and he returned to London in early 1998 with no money and no home. A woman returned to this country aged 63 years, having lived and worked in Los Angeles for more than 30 years. She had no family, stayed in a hotel for a few weeks, used up her savings, and became homeless in August 1998.

Homelessness also occurs when some people retire having lived in tied accommodation (Wilson 1997b; 1995). In the Four-City and Lancefield Street Centre studies, this happened to six men and seven women who had never married, and who had no family contact or support when they left their job. The men had been in the army for more than 15 years, had lived in barracks, were heavy drinkers, and said that they had found it hard to adapt to civilian life. One who had been in the army for 24 years said: 'I did not want to leave the army but my time was up. In the army the men were my comrades.' Other studies have also found that many ex-servicemen experience difficulties in settling after leaving the forces (Randall and Brown 1994a; Cohen and Sokolovsky 1989). The women mainly originated from Ireland or European countries, and had been domestics and had lived in hospitals and hotels for years. One woman had been at one hospital for 30 years.

A further eight men in the Lancefield Street Centre Study lost tenancies and became homeless because they could not cope once they stopped work. All were single and had no contact with relatives. Four were born outside Britain and had no family in this country. They had all worked for years until they retired or were made redundant. From their histories, two common patterns were apparent. After retiring, four men started to drink heavily and were evicted from council tenancies for non-payment of rent. One man came to England from the West Indies in 1956 and worked continuously for 40 years as a factory worker and a hospital porter until he retired at the age of 65. He said that he became lonely and bored after retiring, and allowed homeless people to stay in his council flat. He cooked for them but only one man helped with bills. He acquired rent arrears and the local authority arranged an appointment with him to discuss the problem. He did not respond to their letter as he was scared. He was evicted at the age of 68, and subsequently slept rough each night in the corridor outside his flat.

The other four men experienced financial problems once they stopped work because they did not claim relevant welfare benefits or a pension. They were thus unable to afford rent and utility bills, and were evicted because of rent arrears. One such man became homeless for the first time at the age of 66 years, having lived alone in a housing association flat in south London for 25 years. After serving eight years in the army, he worked continuously until he retired when he was 65 years old. His last job was as a hospital porter for 15 years. When he retired, he received a state pension but did not receive housing benefit towards his rent because, 'I filled out the forms wrong . . . I did not understand them'. He acquired rent arrears, was evicted from his home in July 1998 just 18 months after stopping work, and had to abandon his two pet cats which he had looked after for years. Another became homeless at the age of 68 years, having worked as a laboratory assistant in a university for years. He retired at the age of 65 years, did not claim a state pension, but instead used his savings. When his savings were exhausted, he could not pay rent and was evicted from his lodgings. He was vague about why he had not claimed a pension, saying that he did not understand how to make a claim and fill in the forms.

The number of itinerant workers in Britain nowadays is greatly reduced, and it is less common for men to become homeless in middle or old age having been merchant seamen or casual labourers. But retirement and redundancy still lead to homelessness for some older people, particularly for those who have no family support. Some become homeless when they return to their homeland after having worked abroad. Some become lonely and bored when they retire, drink heavily, and this leads to financial problems. Others do not claim appropriate benefits and soon acquire rent arrears. A job provided them with stability, structure and support, and sometimes accommodation. Once this was removed, they were isolated, unable to manage, and became homeless.

Note

1 Information from the Merseyside Maritime Museum, Liverpool.

6

Mental illness and stressful events[1]

I had to leave my flat in a hurry as monsters were attacking me. They were like tigers and alligators. They had machinery in them and laser rays which were 12 feet long. The doctors and dentists nearby were experimenting on people. They cut up people. The court found out, and the doctors and dentists were put in chains and manacles, and were given the death penalty.

(Rose, aged 62 years, sleeping rough)

A high prevalence of mental illness is reported among homeless people in Britain and America (see Chapter 9). Between 40 and 68 per cent of *older* homeless men in London, New York and Detroit were found to be depressed (Cohen and Sokolovsky 1989; Douglass *et al.* 1988), and a similar proportion of older homeless women in London, New York and Chicago were severely affected by persecutory ideas or memory problems (Cohen *et al.* 1997; Cranc 1994; Kutza 1987). But only a few studies have examined the histories of homeless people and demonstrated the ways in which a mental illness progresses to homelessness. This chapter examines the role of mental illness in contributing to the entry to homelessness among older people, and how stressful and traumatic events can sometimes lead to depression and heavy drinking which progress to homelessness.

Until recently, it was believed that the increase in the number of mentally ill homeless people in Britain and America was due to the closure of large psychiatric hospitals over the past four decades and inadequate support for former long-stay patients. It is now recognized that many mentally ill homeless people have never been hospitalized. The problem is related to the declining number of psychiatric beds, poor service integration, the failures of community mental health services, and the pattern of hospital psychiatric admissions which are often short and which exclude many people with chronic mental illness (Rosenthal 1994; Snow and Anderson 1993; Bachrach 1992; Craig and Timms 1992). Once homeless, mental health problems are exacerbated by the inability or unwillingness of people to use services and take medication, and by the reluctance of general practitioners and hospital staff to treat them (Pleace and Quilgars 1996; Lamb and Lamb 1990).

The belief is that mental illness affects a person's ability to develop or deploy coping skills. It diminishes the available social supports over time and leads to the breakdown of family relationships (Craig 1995; Rosenthal 1994; Snow and Anderson 1993; Wright 1989). As a result, those who are unable to cope on their own and lack support from statutory services become homeless. Two studies, in Los Angeles (Lamb and Lamb 1990) and Scotland (Crockett and Spicker 1994), examined the role of mental illness in contributing to homelessness. Some subjects had lived with their family and became homeless when the main carer (usually the mother) died or moved elsewhere; some became mentally ill and homeless following a marital breakdown, and for some women this was interlinked with domestic violence; some had a paranoid illness, refused help, and abandoned their accommodation; and others with a long-standing mental illness had been unable to cope when discharged from hospital to accommodation.

Mental illness and diminished mental functioning due to loss of cognitive capacity are reported to be important contributory factors to homelesness in old age: 'psychiatric and cognitive impairment . . . play a major role in situations that lead to homelessness among the elderly' (Keigher *et al.* 1989: 63). They have resulted in some older people being evicted for not paying rent, while others have abandoned their homes because of paranoid ideas about neighbours (Crane 1994; Kutza 1987). Although not empirically tested, a New York City report suggested that the faulted and delusional thinking patterns of some older 'bag ladies' were instigated by real, complex, stressful experiences (Schwam 1979). Some forms of mental illness are known to present in later life. Dementia, characterized by impaired memory, comprehension and judgement, is either a progressive organic disease of somatic origin (Alzheimer type) or is induced by factors such as alcohol, head injury, metabolic disturbances and cardiovascular problems. Its estimated prevalence increases from 1 per cent at the age of 60 years to 32 per cent by the age of 85 years (Jarvik *et al.* 1992: 332). Ten per cent of schizophrenic conditions manifest for the first time after the age of 50 years. Referred to as paraphrenia, late-onset schizophrenia is characterized by paranoid symptoms such as delusions, hallucinations and abnormal behaviours (Gurland and Fogel 1992; Kay and Roth 1961). It most often occurs in people who have lived alone for years and have few intimate friends. The annual incidence of paraphrenia is estimated to be 17–26 per 100,000 of the population (Holden 1987).

Stress and psychological trauma have been associated with homelessness for several years. Psychological disturbances following military experiences have been reported since the 1970s among ex-servicemen who are homeless (Randall and Brown 1994a; Robertson 1987). Homeless Vietnam veterans on the Bowery, New York, were recognized to be suffering from a 'delayed post-traumatic psychotic state', characterized by constant war nightmares, extreme irritability to noise, paranoid ideas, flashbacks, self-destructive behaviours, and disaffiliation (Reich and Siegel 1978: 198). Before becoming homeless, some people have experienced physical abuse, rape, assault or other traumas. It is hypothesized that psychological trauma directly contributes to unsettledness and homelessness, or it results in mental health, alcohol and drug problems which progress to homelessness (Rosenheck and Koegel 1993; North and Smith 1992; D'Ercole and Struening 1990; Goodman *et al.* 1991). Some trauma victims are believed to lose support networks because they become depressed and withdraw from or are rejected by families and friends (Elder and Clipp 1988; Sosin *et al.* 1988).

In 1987 the American Psychiatric Association defined post-traumatic stress disorder as a syndrome resulting from exposure to a recognizable stress or trauma. Its features include the re-experiencing of mental trauma through nightmares, flashbacks or intrusive memories, and emotional numbing, memory impairment, irritability, self-mutilation and substance abuse (Goodman *et al.* 1991; Elder and Clipp 1988). Active service is recognized to be particularly stressful. It is repetitive and lasts for long periods, and servicemen face fear and apprehension before a battle, fear of being wounded or killed, distress at seeing comrades killed or severely injured, and guilt at having killed the enemy or civilians (Crocq 1997; Holmes 1985). Active service can cause fatigue and stress, lead to emotional and behavioural problems, survivor guilt, disaffiliation and feelings of alienation, and can have a long-lasting influence on people's lives (McManners 1993; Hunter 1988; Laufer 1988). War-related stress symptoms are sometimes in remission while men are aged in their thirties and forties, and intensify in later life when other stresses and personal losses are faced (Schreuder 1997).

The role of mental illness in contributing to the entry to homelessness

Mental health problems sometimes precede homelessness. In the Four-City Study, 41 per cent (of 175 subjects) experienced such problems before becoming homeless (Table 6.1). Nearly a quarter had been in a psychiatric hospital, including three for more than 10 years. The women were more likely than the men to admit to having had such problems and to having been hospitalized. Other studies have also found that 14–17 per cent of older homeless men (Elam 1992; Cohen and Sokolovsky 1989) and 27–53 per cent of older homeless women (Cohen *et al.* 1997; Sullivan 1991; Douglass *et al.* 1988) have histories of past psychiatric hospitalization, although it is not always stated whether the hospital admission preceded homelessness.

Seventy-two Four-City Study subjects reported mental health problems at some time before becoming homeless. For nine, there was no apparent association between previous mental health problems and the entry to homelessness. They had been treated for a mental illness in early adulthood, denied having had subsequent mental health problems, and had become homeless many years later due to events such as widowhood which had no apparent relationship to a mental illness. Careful examination of the life histories suggests that mental illness had an influence on the entry to homelessness for 38 subjects. For others, the association was less clear or they were unable to give detailed histories. The designation 'probable association' relied partly on self-reports, and partly on the chronology of events and the synchronicity of a mental illness, a disruptive event and entering homelessness. Their pathways into homelessness are now examined.

Table 6.1   The Four-City Study subjects' self-reports of mental health problems before becoming homeless

Mental health problem	Males		Females		Total	
	No.	%	No.	%	No.	%
In hospital	28	20	13	35	41	23
Treated by doctor: not hospitalized	9	7	5	13	14	8
Self-reported problem: no treatment	16	12	1	3	17	10
No self-reported problem	85	61	18	49	103	59
Total known	138	100	37	100	175	100
Not known	17		24		41	
Total experienced homelessness	155		61		216	

Discharge from a psychiatric hospital

As found by other studies, no direct connection was established between discharge from a mental hospital and homelessness. Although 41 subjects had been in a psychiatric hospital before becoming homeless, most had returned to their childhood or marital home or to other accommodation, and only two men had been homeless immediately on discharge.

Loss of family support for those with long-standing mental health problems

Four men and four women in the Four-City Study, with long-standing histories of mental illness, became homeless aged in their forties closely following the breakdown of previously effective social support. In most cases, this was related to the death of their mother, although all eight subjects had been bereaved of both parents within five years. The subjects had always lived at home, none had married or cohabited, and they had had few friends. Most had never worked or had been employed for only a short period. All had been admitted to psychiatric hospitals while their parents were still alive. Two had been diagnosed schizophrenic, one man had spent seven years in a psychiatric hospital during which time he had a leucotomy, and one woman had spent more than ten years in a hospital for the mentally subnormal. They were all living in their parents' home when bereaved. They continued to live in the family home but were evicted within six months. They were vague about why they had been evicted but it often seemed to be through failure to pay rent. For them, a mental illness was not the precipitating cause of homelessness. Their illness had been adequately contained for years by the support they received from their parents. Homelessness was instigated by the death of their carer and the subsequent lack of support. Their situation is described fully in Chapter 4.

Long-standing mental health problems exacerbated at a time of stress

In the Four-City Study, five men and four women with long-standing histories of mental illness became homeless closely following stressful incidents, namely retirement, redundancy and burglary. Two could not settle after their homes had been vandalized, and four ceded their tenancies or were evicted because they found difficulty with paying the rent or mortgage after being made redundant. All were over 40 years of age when they became homeless (four in their fifties, and three in their sixties). Eight had been in-patients in psychiatric hospitals, while the ninth man had been treated for depression for more than ten years by his general practitioner. Most had maintained employment and had lived alone for years without family support. They had competently managed everyday problems and minor challenges until a major stress required considerable adjustments to their lives. From their histories, it seems that long-standing mental health problems were exacerbated at that time. This is illustrated by the case study of Clive (Box 6.1), for whom it seems that an underlying paranoid illness was exacerbated by the stress of redundancy and the loss of finances. He was unable to cope, his support networks had seemingly become targets of his delusions, and he ended up homeless.

Box 6.1   Case study: Clive

Clive had been homeless for seven years when interviewed. He was paranoid and believed that he was a member of the Anti-Terrorist Squad and was working for an intelligence agency. He was born in Ireland and his parents separated when he was young. He was brought up by foster parents and came to England when he was aged 18. Clive married in his early twenties, had ten children, and owned his house. He worked in the building trade. He and his wife divorced after 18 years of marriage. After separation, Clive bought a house and lived alone for 15 years. He was employed for ten years until he was made redundant, after which he was unable to find work. He could not pay his mortgage so sold his house and became homeless at the age of 58. He stayed in hotels until his money was spent, and then slept rough.

Clive had suffered from mental health problems while married and had been admitted to a psychiatric hospital three times. He explained: 'My wife was the reason I was admitted to the loony bin. She put toxic substances in my food; she was trying to do away with me.' He had had no contact with his family since he and his wife separated because 'two-thirds of the children were not mine'. He did not claim social security benefits after being made redundant because 'the authorities started to mess about with me and were trying to destroy me'. He refused to contact his three sisters as 'they were in the enemy camp; they'd got £500,000 of my money and were paying social workers to keep quiet'.

The interaction of mental illness with marital breakdown

In Scotland, some people became mentally ill and homeless following a marital breakdown, and for some women this was interlinked with domestic violence (Crockett and Spicker 1994). The combination of factors was also present in the histories of some older homeless people. In the Four-City Study, four women became homeless following the breakdown of a long-standing marriage. They had tolerated physical abuse for many years and at the same time had had treatment for depression. They finally separated from their husbands when the violence became more intense or when they discovered their husband's infidelity. For these women, homelessness was triggered by a marital breakdown, and it is difficult to determine whether mental health problems increased their vulnerability and contributed to homelessness.

Seven men and two women, however, with a short history of a mental illness became homeless following marital breakdown. Most were aged in their forties or fifties at the time. Several coincident factors were reported during the preceding years, particularly heavy drinking, infidelity and redundancy. From their histories, it was impossible to determine the sequence of problems, to identify how they had interacted, or to assess the extent to which each had contributed to marital breakdown and homelessness. This is illustrated by the case study of Malcolm (Box 6.2). For Malcolm, it is extremely difficult to determine the extent to which mental illness contributed to strained relationships, marital breakdown and homelessness, or whether relationship difficulties instigated stress and mental health problems. In the nine years preceding separation, he had experienced the death of his mother, lost his job through an accident, was admitted to a psychiatric hospital, started drinking heavily, and his wife committed adultery. He reported that he had a settled marriage until this time. He denied ever suffering from mental health problems before his accident. For him, it appears that several adverse events, including a mental illness, interacted and contributed to homelessness.

The increased severity of a recent mental illness

In the Four-City Study, five men and five women became homeless for the first time soon after developing paranoid ideas or confusion. According to their reports, they had no previous psychiatric history. Nine were over 50 years of age when they became homeless, three were in their sixties and three in their seventies. All were living alone at the time and had no family contact. Two became homeless in their seventies after being evicted from their council flats because their homes had become squalid and their behaviour disruptive, yet they refused to accept help. Both had become confused in the years preceding the eviction, and had been unable to cope at home. Their histories were confirmed by reports from service providers.

According to self-reports, four men and four women became homeless after developing paranoid ideas. Many had been homeless for years and, although they said that at the time they became homeless neighbours were trying to harm them or government officials had bugged their homes, their mental

---

Box 6.2   Case study: Malcolm

Malcolm became homeless in his late forties after he and his wife separated. He was born and brought up in the North of England, and spent two years in the army. After leaving the army, he trained as a carpenter. He married at the age of 24, had four children, and he and his family lived in their own house. Malcolm worked until he was 42 years old, when he injured his hand at work, and could no longer continue his trade. He remained unemployed for the next six years. He said that arguments increased between him and his wife during this time, his wife committed adultery, he became depressed and took an overdose and was admitted into a psychiatric hospital for a few weeks, and he started to drink heavily. Three years before his accident, his mother had died and this had also upset him.

Six years after his accident and after 24 years of marriage, Malcolm and his wife separated and later divorced. Their children were in their early teens at that time. He signed the house over to his wife and he was homeless. He denied that there had been marital problems before his accident. He said that he had felt depressed since the accident because he was no longer able to work, and this was why he started to drink heavily. He explained: 'I used to go out drinking once a week; but after the accident I went out most nights. I thought drinking would take my depression away.'

---

states at that time are unknown. They may have been extremely paranoid or their delusional ideas may have intensified with time. Five owned their property, the others had council tenancies. Three abandoned their homes, while the rest were evicted. One man sold his property and left his home town at the age of 70 years because 'an atomic bomb was planted nearby'. Another sold his house because 'the government bugged my home. They put a transmitter in the attic and were broadcasting my affairs to the world.'

Examination of their histories shows that they had all coped with responsibilities for many years. Some had maintained full-time jobs, three had single-handedly raised dependent children after experiencing broken marriages, they had sustained tenancies or had owned property, and one woman had been a foster parent. They had fulfilled these responsibilities until shortly before becoming homeless, so it is likely that they were mentally healthy until the latter years. They had all been through major stressful events shortly before becoming homeless, and these seem to have contributed to paranoid beliefs. Some reported multiple stresses and pressures in close succession. One woman abandoned her council flat at the age of 66 years because 'my neighbours were plotting to harm me'. She had never married and had worked in a hospital until she retired at the age of 60 years. She lived in the hospital until she acquired a council flat when she was in her late fifties. In the years preceding homelessness, she had therefore experienced two major life changes: a first move to independent living, and then retirement. Within six years of retiring, she had become paranoid and home-less.

The subjects reported that they had no support from their family or friends when they were experiencing difficulties. One woman believed that her only brother was plotting against her, and so refused to have contact with him. Another believed that her life-long friend, and her main source of support, had been stealing from her. Their reports suggest that their support networks became targets of their delusions, and were destroyed either by wrongful accusations which caused their family and friends to withdraw, or by false beliefs which caused the respondents to initiate withdrawal. Schwam (1979) suggested that the paranoia of some older homeless women may have been instigated by complex stressful experiences. The case study of Trudy (Box 6.3) also indicates that there may be an association between stresses, a late-onset paranoid illness, and homelessness.

For Trudy, it was impossible to determine when her paranoid ideas started although, if she was given power of attorney over her father's property at the time he moved into her house, she was then likely to have been mentally healthy. Before she became homeless she seems to have been under con-siderable pressure: she was caring for her father who had become confused, and her teenage son, maintaining two jobs, in financial difficulties, and without electricity. It is likely that these pressures proved too stressful, and triggered paranoid ideas which exacerbated the situation. She stopped work, believing that her colleagues were against her, and so her financial difficulties intensified. At the same time her son had just left home, a separation which was also likely to have been distressing. From her account, she received no help from statutory services. She went into arrears with her mortgage, and eventually her home was repossessed.

A 'drift' into homelessness for those who are confused or mentally disturbed

From the Lancefield Street Centre study, there is evidence that some older people who are confused or mentally disturbed may 'drift' into homelessness because they wander away from their accommodation and stay on the streets. The centre has two out-reach workers who work on the streets most nights. Their role is to locate and build trust with older people who are sleeping rough, and to persuade them to accept help and move into accommodation. Nine older men with no history of homelessness were found by the out-reach workers sleeping rough in London. All had severe memory problems or dis-turbed mental states and had wandered away from registered care homes and psychiatric hospitals. One man aged 75 years was found in central London. He was very confused, unable to provide details of his circumstances, and had left a care home in Streatham (approximately 8 miles away). It took six days to trace his address. An older confused person who wanders away from home can easily drift into homelessness unless their situation is recognized and acted upon. It is likely that the subjects described in this section would have continued to sleep rough without the interventions by the out-reach workers. In Chicago and London, some older homeless people were extremely con-fused when contacted and were unable to provide information about their

---

Box 6.3   Case study: Trudy

Trudy became homeless in 1981 at the age of 53 years after being evicted from her own house because of mortgage arrears. She was brought up in the West of England, and had one brother. Trudy's grandmother died when she was eight years old. She said: 'I was left money by my grandmother but I couldn't touch it; it was put in a trust fund and managed by two trustees.' Trudy married when she was in her late twenties, had one son, and she and her husband owned their house. She described her husband as a gambler, and they divorced when their son was six years old. She continued to live in the house and raised her son single-handedly. She received no maintenance from her ex-husband and said: 'I did not pursue it; I didn't want anything to do with him.' Instead, Trudy worked as an upholstress and 'neighbours used to look after my son whilst I was working'.

In 1972 Trudy's mother died and her father had a road accident and was hospitalized for several months. Following discharge, Trudy's father lived with her for six years. She said: 'I was under a lot of pressure at that time. I was holding down two jobs, and looking after my son and my father. I was also having to deal with the legal matters associated with my father's property, because he owned his house and I had been given power of attorney.' In 1978, she stopped paying her electricity bills because 'I had no money and the government were plotting against me'. Her electricity was disconnected, so while she was at work 'I used to leave my father a flask of tea. My father's mind was going . . . he used to wander around the streets whilst I was working. One day he was picked up by Social Services and taken into care. I had been without electricity for eight months when this happened.' Her father died shortly afterwards.

In the same year Trudy stopped work because 'the firm was plotting against me; everybody was involved in the plots, even my brother and niece. Everyone was trying to siphon off the money I had been left by my grandmother.' In 1981 her home was repossessed because 'I had no money to pay my mortgage and rates. I was taken to court and my house was taken from me. I had had no electricity for three years.' Four months earlier, her son had left home and joined the armed forces. She had been divorced for 15 years when she became homeless.

---

preceding circumstances (Crane 1993; Kutza 1987). Some may have first become homeless because they had wandered away from home, had not been traced, and their circumstances had not been recognized.

Mental trauma

Many older people in the Four-City Study experienced stressful and traumatic events before becoming homeless, namely widowhood, the death of a child or parent, a serious physical illness, an accident, war traumas associated with active service, and incidental events such as a fire. Some reported multiple stresses in a short time. Although these events did not directly result in homelessness, they contributed to depression, heavy drinking, unsettledness and eventual homelessness. Nine men with no previous psychiatric history became depressed after experiencing traumatic events. Four were admitted to psychiatric hospitals following overdoses, while the remainder were treated with medication. One man experienced the death of his grandson, two months later his wife died, 15 months later his son was experiencing marital problems and committed suicide, and four years later his mother died. Soon after his mother's death, he took an overdose and was in hospital. After being discharged from hospital, he abandoned his home at the age of 60 years. Likewise, Albert (Box 4.4) suffered from depression and amnesia following a fire, and these problems contributed to marital breakdown and homelessness.

Two-fifths of the heavy drinkers in the Four-City Study had been drinking heavily *before* they became homeless. Some associated the onset of heavy drinking with traumas and stresses in adolescence and early adulthood. Beth grew up with her father and her stepmother after her parents separated when she was a toddler. She did not get on with her stepmother so left home at the age of 15 years and stayed with friends. Her natural mother died when Beth was 18 years old and her father died two months later. Beth was traced by the police and asked to identify her mother in the mortuary. She said: 'I've never been the same since . . . that is when my troubles started . . . when I saw my mum in the mortuary I had my first drink, and I've been drinking ever since.' Beth married when she was in her early twenties but continued to drink heavily. Her marriage ended after a few years and she became homeless. Similarly, George (Box 4.3) had been drinking heavily since the age of 17 years when he found his father dead in bed beside him.

Ten men associated the onset of heavy drinking with widowhood and marital breakdown in middle or old age. Two who experienced the deaths of both their wives and daughters within a few years, used drink as 'a way to get through the bereavements'. Tom experienced several stresses in close succession, started to drink heavily, and became homeless at the age of 60 (Box 6.4). In New York City, one-fifth of older Bowery men who were heavy drinkers, started to drink heavily after the age of 50 years, associating it with widowhood, isolation, depression and boredom (Cohen and Sokolovsky 1989).

Seven-tenths of the men in the Four-City Study had been in the armed forces, mainly the army, or in the merchant navy. One-third had left within three years, but 23 per cent had served for at least 10 years. Three-tenths (28 of 94 who provided details) reported horrific experiences during active service which seemed to have had a profound and enduring destabilizing effect. They described the fear of being under attack, the horror of seeing their comrades badly injured, and the revulsion of killing the enemy. Many still experienced nightmares, panic attacks, and night sweats, triggered by incidents such as a car backfiring in the street, or fireworks. The majority (16) had started to drink heavily to obliterate bad memories. One man said: 'I was a paratrooper and an SAS man. I was in Korea on the front line, and I was trained to shoot

---

Box 6.4   Case study: Tom

Tom became homeless when he was 60 years old. He had been fostered as a child after his mother died giving birth to him. He joined the army at the age of 18 and served for three years. After leaving the army, he returned to his foster parents' home until he married when he was 25 years old. He and his wife lived in a council house, they had two children, and were married for 35 years until his wife died suddenly. She had not previously been ill. Tom had always been employed until one month before his wife's death when he was made redundant. After his wife's death, Tom was 'devastated and I hit the bottle . . . I drank beer, brandy, anything'. He drank heavily, did not pay his rent regularly, and acquired arrears. Before this he only drank occasionally. He explained: 'after my wife died I would go into a pub at 11 a.m. and stay there until 11 p.m. I could not stand to be alone . . . I wanted to be with people . . . I had no job and had nothing to do with my life'.

Tom was evicted from the three-bedroomed council house where he and his wife had lived for 25 years less than three months after becoming widowed. He said: 'they wanted the house as the premises were considered too large for one person . . . the council started giving me aggravation . . . I had uncertain feelings about staying there anyhow; it had too many memories'. He sold most of his furniture and possessions, including a caravan, and spent the proceeds on alcohol. After being evicted, he stayed in a bed-and-breakfast hotel for a few months and then slept rough when his money ran out. He maintained contact with his children but they were unaware of his circumstances. He said: 'if they knew that I'm homeless they'd want me to stay with them . . . I pretend that I have a flat . . . they have their own lives to lead; I do not want to impose'. He added: 'I'll never forget this year. They say that things come in threes . . . I have lost my job, my wife, my home; there is nothing more to lose.'

---

and kill. Since coming out of the army, I have hated myself for what I did. I wake up at 3.30 a.m. screaming.' Other works have noted the guilt that some ex-servicemen feel at having killed civilians (Crocq 1997).

Three men had been tortured in Japanese prisoner-of-war camps for up to four years, had since been heavy drinkers, and were extremely distressed when recounting the experience. One man had both his eardrums damaged when the Japanese butted him in the ears with their rifles, and has since been deaf. A second man was held prisoner for nearly three years, during which time the Japanese severed the nerves in his toes and fingers, slashed his stomach, and damaged his kneecaps by hitting them with rifles. On release, he weighed only five stone and was admitted to a naval hospital for 11 years where he received surgery and psychiatric treatment. He said: 'I didn't care whether I lived or died . . . I was nearly dead anyhow'. The third man was held prisoner for nearly four years and still has ulcers on his body. He explained: 'these are tropical ulcers through lack of vitamins . . . we lived on rice. I survived the camp but many didn't.' Approximately 11 per cent of British and American prisoners-of-war during the Second World War died in captivity, mostly from malnutrition or deliberate neglect (Hunter 1988). Since leaving the armed forces, some men who had been through traumatic war experiences had married but heavy drinking contributed to marital break-down and homelessness. Others, such as Charlie (Box 6.5), had been home-less and had never settled.

Box 6.5 Case study: Charlie

Charlie left school when he was 14 years old and worked in the coal-mines for four years until he joined the Royal Navy. He was in the Royal Navy for four years. He became tearful when talking about his experi-ences. He described how he was on a ship in the Atlantic Ocean, it was stormy and 'there were 20-foot high waves . . . they came over the ship and some men got washed into the ocean and drowned . . . it was awful . . . we were rescued'. He volunteered on D-Day to be a stretcher-bearer. He said: 'I helped remove the dead and wounded from the battleground at Normandy . . . it was 5.30 a.m. and there was a young soldier who had been killed, lying on his back. I turned him over and his face had been blown away . . . in his pocket was a wedding photo . . . I felt devastated . . . it's a fucking awful world we live in'.

By the time he left the Royal Navy, Charlie was drinking heavily. He returned to his parents' home but could not settle and left after a few months. He lived and worked on a farm for three months and then 'I travelled all over England, working casually, drinking heavily, sleeping rough, and staying in hostels . . . I left the navy when I was 22 years old and have never been able to settle since.' He was 71 years old when interviewed, had never married or had friends, and had lost contact with his family years ago.

Conclusion

The associations between mental illness, stress and homelessness are intricate. For some older people with histories of mental health problems, their illness was only a background factor and had no obvious influence on their becom-ing homeless. But for others, it interacted with poor daily living skills and vul-nerability to produce various pathways into homelessness. Those with a long-standing mental illness became homeless following the collapse or ter-mination of a previously effective structure of social support, or following a major adverse event which required them to make considerable changes to their lives. Although the illness is likely to have increased vulnerability, family support or a job had been a stabilizing influence. It was only when this was disturbed, through the death of a carer or redundancy, that the respondents became unsettled, could not cope, and homelessness followed.

In the Four-City Study and two Chicago studies, there are indications that a mental illness can be an important contributory factor to homelessness in old age, particularly among those who lack cohesive support networks (Keigher *et al.* 1989; Kutza 1987). Some people with no known history of psychiatric problems became homeless for the first time in later life after developing a paranoid illness or confusion. The illness affected their ability to cope, distorted their perceptions of reality, and influenced their capacity to seek and accept help. Many people experience major changes in later life, such as retirement and widowhood, which require considerable readjustment. Some may have to contend with multiple changes in a short time. A minority are unable to cope, become mentally ill or start to drink heavily, and their mental, social and housing situation deteriorates until they eventually abandon or are evicted from their homes. Craig (1995: 60) suggested that the association between mental illness and homelessness is 'the result of an initial failure to develop adequate coping skills'. Although this applied to some Four-City Study subjects, it was not always the situation. Some had lived alone, maintained tenancies, worked, and coped with stresses and changes for many years before becoming mentally ill and eventually homeless.

Many Four-City Study subjects with mental health problems became homeless because their needs had been neglected or undetected by social services, health services and housing departments. Some had untreated mental health problems which increased in severity, while others were mentally ill and vulnerable and received inadequate community support at home when their circumstances changed. They had no family or social network to initiate help. For some, mental health problems affected family and social relationships and support networks were destroyed by wrongful accusations or false beliefs.

As people age, there is an increased likelihood that they will experience one or more major stresses, such as the death of family members or friends, retirement and serious physical illnesses. Yet there is limited understanding of the relationship between such stresses and homelessness. Many older men have served in the armed forces. War-related stress symptoms are known sometimes to be in remission while men are middle-aged, and intensify in later life when other stresses occur (Crocq 1997; Schreuder 1997). But little research has examined the relationship between military experiences, subsequent losses and homelessness.

Note

1 Parts of this chapter are published in *Aging and Mental Health*, 1998, 2(3), 171–80.

7

The aetiology of homelessness among older people: a synthesis

This life is the alternative to suicide. If someone is in a house and feels suicidal because of relationship problems, the answer is make yourself homeless. You will then live because you will start behaving like us homeless people and develop our mentality. Our main aim is to survive each day; we spend our time working on survival. By learning this, the man who was thinking of suicide will no longer have time to think of killing himself; he will have been saved from that at least.

(*Harold, aged 63 years, sleeping rough for more than 20 years*)

The previous three chapters have examined states and events which preceded homelessness for older people. This chapter draws on the empirical findings to advance knowledge of the aetiology of homelessness and to make contributions to present theory. It establishes that homelessness is a complex process, disputes theories that it is due to structural and economic conditions, and demonstrates how personal and social factors were more critical for most respondents in the Four-City and Lancefield Street Centre studies. Two hypotheses are presented to explain the reasons for and processes leading to homelessness. They have been informed by American sociological theories and hypotheses, and developed from findings in the empirical field studies. Because of the heterogeneity of homelessness, no single theory can encompass or explain the problem. The discussion which follows pertains to older people in the field studies and does not claim to reflect the situation of all homeless people.

Histories preceding homelessness

Prior to becoming homeless, older people have diverse histories. Some have limited experiences of work and marriage, have rarely sustained tenancies or lived independently, and have been homeless since early adulthood. But others have become homeless for the first time in old age, having previously married, raised children, worked, and managed tenancies or owned their homes. In the Four-City Study, 42 per cent of men and one-third of the women worked consistently until at least 50 years of age. Three-quarters of the men had been unskilled workers but others had had more responsible jobs. One man had his own building firm and employed up to 20 men until his wife's death.

The men were more likely than the women to have become homeless in early adulthood, to have been living in marginal accommodation such as lodgings, and to have entered homelessness having never, as adults, had a tenancy. Prior to becoming homeless, almost one-half of the men were insecurely housed, and had been living in lodgings, tied accommodation, work-camps, barracks, ships or cohabitee's tenancies (Table 7.1). Five had been in prison. In contrast, the women tended to have become homeless in old age and to have been living alone in conventional accommodation as sole or joint owner-occupiers, or as tenants of local authorities, housing associations or private landlords. Less than one-fifth had been living in tied housing or lodgings.

States and events triggering and contributing to homelessness

The histories of the older people in the Four-City and the Lancefield Street Centre studies were often complicated and characterized by problems and difficulties stemming back to childhood. It was possible to distinguish between events and states which triggered homelessness and those which contributed to the problem. A single incident such as a relationship breakdown sometimes acted as a 'trigger' and directly resulted in a subject leaving or being evicted from their home. Such proximate incidents were usually reported by the subjects as being the 'causes' of homelessness. But other states and events were usually involved which were less evident. They did not directly cause homelessness but contributed to the process.

Table 7.1 The accommodation of the Four-City Study subjects before first becoming homeless

Type of tenure	Males		Females		Total	
	No.	%	No.	%	No.	%
Owner-occupation	19	14	7	18	26	15
Tenancy[1]	27	20	17	44	44	25
With parent(s) who had tenancy	24	18	9	23	33	19
With partner or relative who had tenancy	10	7	2	5	12	7
Lodgings and digs: no written tenancy	15	11	1	3	16	9
Tied accommodation with job, e.g. hotel	3	2	3	8	6	4
With armed forces or merchant navy	28	21	0	0	28	16
Institution: prison, hospital, orphanage	8	6	0	0	8	5
Total known	134		39		173	
Not known	21		22		43	
Total experienced homelessness	155		61		216	

[1] Local authority, housing association or private landlord

Different events and states triggered and contributed to homelessness at different stages of the life course, and sex differences existed (Table 7.2). For the men, triggers to homelessness included itinerant work histories, and discharge from the armed forces and merchant navy, none of which applied to the women. A minority of women did, however, become homeless after retiring from hotel and hospital work and losing tied accommodation. Although only one woman expressly linked homelessness to widowhood, the association was made by some men. This may partly be explained by the sex-role differentiation which was strong during the early adult lives of the cohorts. Men usually worked full-time, while women stayed at home and looked after the children and house. Women would be more accustomed than men, therefore, to managing mundane household responsibilities such as shopping, settling bills and paying rent. Both men and women had become homeless after the death of their last surviving parent. Similarly, both men and women associated homelessness with a marital breakdown, although they often reported different reasons why their marriage ended. Other less commonly reported triggers were release from prison, arguments with family household members, and eviction from private rented accommodation due to the sale of the property.

The case histories of the subjects demonstrate the multi-faceted and complex nature of homelesness. In some instances, the pathways to homelessness overlapped. A few men adopted itinerant working lives or moved

Table 7.2 States and events in the life course that antecede homelessness in old age

Approximate age	*Antecedent states (S) and preceding events (E)*
Childhood and adolescence	• Broken and disturbed childhood homes (S & E) • Discharge from orphanage (E)
Early adulthood	• Discharge from the armed forces (E) • Mental illness (S) • Heavy drinking (S) • Itinerant working life (S)
Mid-life	• Death (E) or deteriorating health (S) of last surviving parent • Marital or relationship breakdown (S&E) • Drift by itinerant workers to less secure work and accommodation (S) • Mental illness (S) • Heavy drinking (S)
Later life	• Marital or relationship breakdown (S&E) • Death of spouse (E) • Discharge from the merchant navy or armed forces (E) • Retirement (S) and loss of tied accommodation (E) • Retirement followed by loneliness or an inability to manage finances (S) • Return to homeland after having worked abroad (E) • Mental illness (S)

back to their parents' home after marriages failed. The former drifted into homelessness, the latter became homeless when their parents died. Homelessness was often the result of the interactions between several events and states, and it is difficult to determine the ways in which factors interacted and generated vulnerability. Vulnerability stemmed from several causes. These were broken and disturbed childhood homes, mental illness, heavy drinking, a marginal coping ability, limited social skills, and unsettled lifestyles. They affected the respondents to various degrees and increased their vulnerability at times of stress.

Some subjects became homeless soon after developing a mental illness, yet others with mental health problems remained housed for years until other factors incited homelessness. Two-thirds of the Four-City Study subjects were raised either in broken or disturbed childhood homes, or in protected settings within which they continued to live with their parents in adulthood. The extent to which these situations affected socialization is unknown. Disturbed childhood homes triggered homelessness for some people in adolescence, while many recalled traumatic childhoods but did not become homeless until old age. Some were poorly socialized, had seldom worked, and had always been supported by their parents. Their family homes may have created dependency and poor socialization; or problems such as a mental illness and an inability to work and be self-supporting may have made it necessary for them to live in such circumstances.

The relevance of structural and economic theories of homelessness

Homelessness is commonly associated with a lack of low-cost rented housing, poverty and unemployment (Greve 1991). Yet these factors had little influence on the entry to homelessness for many subjects in the Four-City and Lancefield Street Centre studies. The aetiology of homelessness was more complex and was related to personal inadequacies, stresses accumulated over years, and mental illness. At the time that they became homeless, many had homes which they ceded or from which they were evicted because of difficulties associated with coping abilities, mental illness and emotional distress. Others had been without secure housing for years, had not sought a tenancy, but preferred to live in lodgings, tied accommodation, and occasionally hostels and resettlement units.

The belief is that unemployment and poverty contribute to homelessness because people are unable to afford low-cost rented housing (Avramov 1995; Greve 1991; Wright 1989; Ropers 1988). For most respondents, unemployment had not been a factor in the progression to homelessness. In the instances where it had a contributory role, it was instigated by the interactions of social and psychological states and events, and economic conditions had little impact. Some respondents gave up their jobs and homes at the time of a bereavement or relationship breakdown. Others were unable to function effectively at work due to heavy drinking and mental illness. Although the men who had been itinerant workers reported that in the 1970s jobs were scarce and it had become more difficult to get work, some had frequently

changed jobs because they were unsettled. This suggests that personal difficulties contributed to inconsistent work histories and eventual homelessness.

Poverty was a feature of many respondents once they became homeless,
but few were poverty-stricken before they became homeless. Many men had
worked and earned a regular wage until or near the normal age of retirement,
and 15 per cent of the subjects had owned property (as sole or joint owners).
A minority had owned cars and caravans and had holidayed abroad. Former
building labourers reported that they had earned 'good money', but this had
been spent on heavy drinking, with little attention to savings or investment.
Mental illness, distress and poor coping skills sometimes led to financial difficulties and homelessness. A few sold their homes and assets after their wives
died and spent the proceeds on alcohol, or gave the money to their children.
Yet others did not know how to budget and claim relevant benefits after their
main source of support was removed. Although they had experienced financial difficulties, the reasons for homelessness were intricate and related to
complex personal difficulties and not simply economic constraints and destitution. Two hypotheses about the reasons for and processes leading to homelessness are now described.

Vulnerability and stress leading to social disconnection and homelessness

For many older people in the Four-City and the Lancefield Street Centre
studies, homelessness was the outcome of vulnerability interacting with
stressful events. They had been supported by a parent, a spouse, a landlady,
a job, or in tied accommodation and institutional settings. They became
homeless when this structure, stability and support broke down because of
events such as the death of the last surviving parent, widowhood, retirement
and the loss of tied accommodation. While they were in a structured and
stable environment, their behaviour was regulated and controlled, and they
functioned well to varying degrees. Once the stable influence was removed,
their lives became chaotic and uncontrolled.

Merton (1968) proposed that when people suddenly experience social
change, as in widowhood or retirement, they lose established social relations
and routines. This can produce a state of anomie and a retreat from society
(Chapter 2). For the Four-City and the Lancefield Street Centre subjects, a
critical factor in the progression to homelessness seems to have been the
extent to which they were loosely bonded to society *before* they experienced
the stress which disrupted their lives and led to homelessness. Theories of
social control have rarely been applied to studies of homelessness, yet have
been used to explain delinquent behaviour (Reckless [1973] in Pfohl 1994;
Hirschi 1969). Hirschi (1969) proposed that a person is bonded to society
through inner beliefs and values, and through attachment, commitment and
involvement. 'Attachment' refers to the strength of a person's ties to others,
'commitment' to the degree to which a person is tied to conventional ways
of behaving because of social rewards, such as prestige and prospects, and
'involvement' to the proportion of a person's time which is spent pursuing
conventional activities. The components collectively encourage conformity,

act as a buffer during periods of social change and upheaval, and prevent a person from deviating. Social change may disrupt one or more of the components of bonding, and weaken or suspend its other features.

Hirschi's theory of social control is a useful model in understanding a person's relationship to society and how that person might become socially 'disconnected'. Social networks are important in providing emotional and practical support, impeding a distressing event, and acting as a buffer once stress has occurred (Thoits 1982). It can be hypothesized that those who have weak social bonds are more at risk of becoming homeless following a stressful event than those who have strong social ties. Retirement or widowhood, for example, is likely to have a major impact on a person's social connections if that person is poorly socialized and their job or spouse has been their principal tie to society.

From the subjects' histories, different dimensions of social bonding were affected by stressful events and contributed to social disconnection. One woman had worked and lived in hospitals for 40 years, and became homeless shortly after she retired. She had no family or friends. She had been committed to work but not to society's norms of having her own home and raising a family. She had been highly involved with her job, it had occupied most of her time, and this had been her main social link. Retirement destroyed her involvement in society and her only social attachment and commitment. Likewise, one man became homeless on discharge from the army after 24 years' service. He had no family and the army had provided him with occupational and social ties.

For those who had always lived with their parents, a different pattern is seen. They had poor social relationships, were not involved in work and community activities, and were not committed to society's norms of achieving and goal-striving. They were attached to society through the strong ties they had with their parents. The death of the last surviving parent destroyed their only attachment to society and they became socially disconnected. Some itinerant workers frequently changed jobs and accommodation, and moved from town to town. They had no social or family ties. They were not highly involved or committed to their work: they would, for example, take days off if they had been drinking heavily. They were not committed to norms such as marriage and securing stable accommodation. They were weakly bonded to society and, once they could not find work and lost their accommodation, they had no social connections.

But social detachment does not necessarily progress to homelessness. Many people are isolated yet not homeless. Homelessness occurred because the 'disconnected' person was vulnerable and unable to function alone. Some remained at home, attempted to cope alone, it was beyond their capabilities, and they were evicted for reasons such as non-payment of rent. Others avoided and distanced themselves from their problems by abandoning their homes and not finding alternative housing when they lost accommodation.

The hypothesis that vulnerability and stress interact and lead to social disconnection and homelessness suggests that the person is already vulnerable and weakly bonded socially. At the time of a stressful event, the structure and stability in their lives is destroyed, they become socially disconnected, are unable to function independently, and become homeless. This was a common pattern among itinerant workers, those who became homeless after being bereaved, and some who became homeless following a marital breakdown or a mental illness. The undersocialization theory was first related to homelessness fifty years ago when it was proposed that men who were poorly socialized and dependent left their childhood homes and moved into protected, institutional environments, before finally drifting into homelessness (Pittman and Gordon 1958; Straus 1946). The findings from the Four-City and Lancefield Street Centre studies support this pathway into homelessness, but also propose that some people with limited social skills live in conventional households with parents, partners or landladies, and become homeless with the removal of this structure and stability.

Traumatic and stressful events leading to alienation and homelessness

The histories of some respondents who became homeless following a mental illness or a relationship breakdown did not, however, suggest that they were highly vulnerable, poorly socialized and unable to cope alone. Some had lived alone and worked for years, single-handedly raised children, sustained tenancies, and accepted additional responsibilities such as caring for a confused parent (Box 6.3). Others married and raised families and, although they lived with spouses, were employed for years and did not report histories of heavy drinking or mental illness until the later years of their marriage (Box 4.4).

From their histories, homelessness was the outcome of trauma and stress, which led to states and behaviours such as mental illness, heavy drinking and unsettledness, and progressively to the breakdown of family and social relationships and the loss of coping skills. Stressful events included the death of family members, family problems, the onset of a physical illness, war traumas associated with active service, and incidental events such as a fire or a burglary. Some experienced a single stressful event, others reported multiple stresses in close proximity. The events did not directly result in homelessness but led to heavy drinking or mental illness. These are likely to have been escape mechanisms to cope with trauma and distress. But such behaviours can be alienating, and it seems that they led to estranged family and social relationships.

In some instances, the family rejected the respondent, and in other cases the subject withdrew from relatives and friends. Albert (Box 4.4) developed mental and physical health problems after trying to rescue a neighbour from a fire, lost his job, his marriage deteriorated, and he became homeless. According to him, his family asked him to leave the house and he has subsequently refused to have contact with them. His family therefore withdrew from him, he resented this, and has since alienated himself. Some respondents, whose homelessness was triggered by a mental illness, described estranged social relationships which seemed to have been the outcome of delusional ideas. In such instances, they could have withdrawn from their family and friends because of false beliefs, or the family could have rejected them because of false accusations.

Alienation in itself was not responsible for homelessness. Deteriorating coping skills also seem to have been a critical factor. A mental illness or heavy drinking had impaired their ability to cope effectively and independently. Some were no longer able to work. A few abandoned their homes to 'escape' from paranoid fears. Some were evicted by local authority housing departments for rent arrears. They retreated into homelessness rather than try to secure accommodation. When interviewed, many expressed anger and resentment towards relatives even though they had been homeless for years, and such vindictive feelings are likely to have been contributory factors to retreatism and homelessness.

The two pathways into homelessness describe different preceding states and events but suggest that the outcome is the same at the point of entry into homelessness: people are disconnected or alienated from society, and are unable to function independently. But the histories differ. Those who were vulnerable and became homeless following a stressful event had limited social skills and were always weakly bound to society, whereas those with no reported history of vulnerability who became homeless following stress seem to have had strong social links but were either rejected by or withdrew from society. Although both groups were unable to cope and function alone at the time of entry into homelessness, this was also for different reasons. Those with histories of vulnerability had always relied on others without acquiring the skills to survive independently. But those with no long-standing history of vulnerability had such skills and these were destroyed in the process leading to homelessness.

Preventing homelessness

Two pathways have been described which identify situations contributing to vulnerability, events which trigger changes in the circumstances, and the progression to homelessness for a minority of people. The histories of some subjects strongly suggest that homelessness may have been prevented if appropriate action had been taken and support had been provided. Thirty subjects (24 men and 6 women) first became homeless after being evicted by statutory housing providers. Four had been owner-occupiers whose homes were repossessed, 21 had been housed in local authority accommodation, and five had housing association tenancies. Seventeen were living in London at the time and 13 elsewhere in England and Wales. Many were evicted because they had rent or mortgage arrears, and others because they neglected their home, or disturbed neighbours. Yet many had mental health problems or poor coping skills and were experiencing problems with claiming benefits, budgeting and paying bills, and managing household tasks. As recently as mid-1998, a woman aged in her fifties was evicted from a council tenancy for rent arrears. She had mental health problems, had not claimed benefits nor paid rent since 1982, and had acquired arrears of more than £15,000.

Many other subjects became homeless because they could not cope at a time of stress or emotional distress and so abandoned their homes. Some ceded tenancies on becoming widowed or after the death of their parents. Others had always lived in lodgings or tied housing and never had the responsibilities of a tenancy. Yet they received no help to find accommodation on discharge from the armed forces and the merchant navy, or when they retired having worked and lived in hotels and hospitals for years. Some British prisoners prior to discharge receive housing advice through specially trained prison officers, attend pre-release courses and workshops, as provided by the National Association for the Care and Resettlement of Offenders (Carlisle 1996). Nonetheless, at least two-fifths of prisoners are homeless on discharge (Carlisle 1997; Paylor 1992). The armed forces provide similar resettlement help for dischargees but it is often targeted at married men. Many single men leave the forces without help to adjust to settled living (Gunner and Knott 1997; Randall and Brown 1994a).

There needs to be a greater emphasis on preventing homelessness. A policy statement adopted by the Governing Council of the American Public Health Association in November 1997 noted: 'there have been considerable achievments in terms of providing services to homeless people, but little or no progress in preventing homelessness . . . there needs to be greater emphasis on prevention . . . methods must be developed to identify individuals at special risk' (Anon. 1998: 519–20). In Britain, the Social Exclusion Unit's Report on *Rough Sleeping* (1998, p. 17) noted the importance of preventing homelessness, highlighting the need 'to improve preparations for independent living amongst care leavers, and people leaving the services and prisons, [and] better coordination of housing authorities' approach to people at risk'. Situations which indicate vulnerability and to which agencies should pay heed include people who are housed but:

- experience the death of a parent or a marital partner and are left alone, particularly if there is a history of mental illness, heavy drinking, poor work history, or no prior experience of independent living;
- are unable to manage alone, and live with a parent who is elderly and whose health is deteriorating;
- experience a major stressful event, such as widowhood or retirement, and have no close relatives or friends;
- repeatedly have rent arrears or default with paying bills, particularly if they have recently acquired a tenancy or there has been a change in their circumstances (for example, they have taken over a tenancy after the death of their parents);
- suddenly stop paying rent or mortgage, having previously maintained regular payment;
- are mentally ill or have alcohol-related problems and live alone;
- leave tied accommodation, the armed forces, or an institution, have never lived alone, and have no family contact or connections with a local community;
- frequently present at casualty departments, psychiatric units, general practitioner surgeries, social services departments or housing departments with mental health and social problems, e.g. repeated physical abuse by a marital partner;
- have previously experienced homelessness, particularly if there is a history of mental illness, heavy drinking, or repeated episodes of homelessness.

Building on the knowledge gained of the aetiology of homelessness, it is possible to identify measures which are likely to prevent homelessness for some people. It is unacceptable for statutory housing providers to allow vulnerable people to accumulate rent arrears or neglect their property and then evict them. Such people require help and support at home with claiming benefits, budgeting and paying bills, and managing household chores. In recent years, floating and tenancy support schemes have been introduced into some areas to help people with mental health or alcohol problems maintain tenancies (Audit Commission 1998; Douglas *et al.* 1998; Quilgars 1998; Morrish 1996). Support workers assist people at home with claiming housing benefit and other entitlements, paying rent and utility bills, teaching domestic skills, and with confidence-building. Floating support is funded through the Special Needs Management Allowance by the Housing Corporation and is restricted to housing association tenants. Tenancy support is more flexible, can be provided for as long as a person requires support, and can operate in any tenure. Statutory housing providers should introduce support workers to people who are vulnerable and at risk of losing tenancies because of rent default or other problems.

Many people become homeless on discharge from the armed forces or when they leave tied housing or institutions. The suggestion is that there is a role for pre-release courses, resettlement programmes and housing advice to help people adjust to the transition. Some people may have the skills to manage a home and only require assistance with finding accommodation. But others may have been 'looked after' for years in institutions and never had the responsibilities of a tenancy. They may require skills-training in claiming benefits, paying bills, budgeting, shopping and cooking. Although many large organizations have pre-retirement courses for workers, there are indications that a minority of employees are vulnerable and need help to claim welfare benefits or a pension at the time they cease work. This may be a role that could be fulfilled by personnel staff.

Advancing the understanding of homelessness

By analysing partial life histories of older homeless people, it has been possible to identify events and states which trigger and contribute to homelessness, and the processes and pathways through which people become homeless. The origins of homelessness are complex and deep-seated, are intricately related to psychological and sociological factors, and extend far beyond a lack of housing. By ordering preceding events and states, and examining stages and processes, it has been possible to make interpretations of the ways in which events and states interact, the effects of these interactions on the respondents, and the reasons for the progression to homelessness. Two common pathways were identified: vulnerability interacting with stress and leading to social disconnection and homelessness; and traumatic and stressful events leading to alienation and homelessness. These have been developed into hypotheses about the aetiology of homelessness.

It is specious to seek a single cause or to formulate a single theory which encompasses homelessness. It has multiple causes for most individuals, it results from the interactions of several states and events, and is usually the end result of the failure of numerous coping tactics and support systems. For any event to occur, it is necessary for a series of causal chains to converge at a given moment in time (Hirschi 1969). Events are difficult to predict, and specification of some of the conditions necessary for them to occur often leaves a large residue of indeterminacy. Certain conditions may be necessary for homelessness to ensue, yet others might be sufficient to cause the problem directly. Unemployment, for example, might be a necessary condition for homelessness but, in itself, is unlikely to cause the problem. Hypotheses can only propose that an unemployed person is more likely than an employed person to become homeless when other sets of circumstances are present. At present, studies report a coexistence of factors, for example mental illness and homelessness, yet we are nowhere near developing theoretical propositions setting out the processes.

Individuals react differently in similar situations, and factors which produce vulnerability in some people may lead to homelessness for others. People have different thresholds, determined by factors such as resources, social support, coping skills and psychological well-being. There needs to be more penetrating information on each person's cause of homelessness, in order to understand the ways in which states and events interact and make people vulnerable, and to identify the situations or changes which are most responsible for the entry to homelessness. Such information could then be translated into measures to prevent and alleviate the problem. This type of understanding requires in-depth biographical information from homeless people about their histories and experiences of events and states, followed by sequencing and detailed analyses of factors through different stages of the life course.

There is also a need for controlled trials to determine ways in which homelessness can be prevented or minimized. Such trials may involve providing extra support at home to people with mental health or alcohol problems; assisting vulnerable people to claim a pension before they retire; arranging pre-release courses for people who are leaving prison or the armed forces; employing specialist housing workers to ensure that people have accommodation on discharge from the armed forces; and providing counselling or support to those who are alone at a time of a stress or loss. Comparisons should be made with matched clients who do not receive the additional help.

PART II

Meeting the needs of older homeless people

Part I of the book has concentrated on pathways into homelessness for older people. This second part focuses on the circumstances, attitudes, problems and needs of older people who are homeless, and the types of interventions and services which are required to help the group resettle in conventional society. Some have been homeless continuously for years, while others have been rehoused but are unsettled and still display homelessness behaviours. It is thus apparent that present services in Britain are not effectively meeting the needs of some homeless older people. Raising awareness of the distinct problems and needs of those who have not been helped will increase understanding of the circumstances of the group and assist policy-makers and statutory and voluntary organizations with planning and developing services.

Part II draws on five types of material. It presents profiles of the subjects in the Four-City and the Lancefield Street Centre studies, and their circumstances, behaviour and problems. These are integrated with field reports from the subjects about their activities and lifestyle, the reasons why they behave in certain ways, their hopes and expectations, and their experiences of using services. Third, reports from other British and US studies, and from service providers working with older homeless people in Britain, America and Australia, are described. Historical information is presented of how policies and services for homeless people have evolved through the years. Last, this part draws on evidence from the author's experience while working at soup kitchens, from visiting services for older homeless people in Britain and America, and from innumerable discussions with staff working with the client group.

There are five chapters. Chapter 8 describes the circumstances of older homeless people, the ways in which they acquire basic necessities such as shelter, food and clothing, and their social and occupational activities each day. Homelessness is a stressful and demoralizing state, and living on the streets or moving around hostels for years leads to multiple health problems. Psychological and physical health problems among the group are examined in Chapter 9. Older homeless people have different histories, their circumstances, problems and needs differ, and various services are required to help them. Yet the few existing studies of older homeless people in Britain and America have rarely addressed this issue. Chapter 10 presents a synthesis of the characteristics, behaviours and problems of older homeless people in the form of a typology. It identifies sub-groups of older homeless people with different problems and needs who require particular services.

The way forward is developed in Chapter 11 by reviewing how British policies and services for homeless people have advanced and the ways in which these have been conditioned by different conceptualizations of homelessness. The suggestion is that the problem is likely to have been reinforced by some of the interventions intended to help homeless people. Since the late 1970s, however, extensive efforts have been made by some organizations to understand and tackle the problem, and there have been marked changes in policies and services for homeless people. The ways in which these have elaborated are examined, with particular attention to innovative services established in the 1990s to work specifically with older homeless people. Finally, Chapter 12 highlights how older homeless people, even if they have long histories of unsettledness and homelessness, can be helped and their quality of life improved. It draws on the experiences of several projects around Britain.

8

The circumstances of older homeless people

The tide I'm swimming against is too strong for me, and life's going the wrong way. I was in the merchant navy and travelled to the Canary Islands, Russia, Spain and South Africa. I've worked as a docker in Ireland, London and New-castle upon Tyne. I never thought I'd end my days in a doorway.
(Martin, sleeping rough at the age of 70 years)

This chapter describes the circumstances of older homeless people and high-lights how their lifestyle is very different to that of most housed older people in Britain. Most older people take for granted necessities such as shelter, food, warmth and clothing, but for some homeless older people these have to be searched for and acquired each day. Early sections describe the behaviour of older homeless people and how their basic needs are met, from personal appearance and hygiene to sleeping arrangements, sources of income and food, and daily activities and routines. There follows a discussion of excep-tional behaviour displayed by some people, focusing on scavenging and hoarding garbage, and on transience. Finally, family and social contacts are examined.

Personal appearance and hygiene

Some older homeless people are well groomed, carry few possessions, and their homeless circumstances are not immediately apparent. They regularly wash and change their clothes. Those who are not in temporary accommo-dation use showers at day centres or wash in public toilets. One man who sleeps in a derelict building collects water each day from a tap inside the gate of a nearby cemetery to wash and shave. Some launder their clothes at day centres; others obtain clean clothing from day centres or street hand-outs and discard their dirty clothes. One man, interviewed in Manchester, carried with him a large hold-all containing toiletries, razors, plasters, blan-kets, food and clothes. He explained: 'I'm a survivor. I have everything I need; I keep clean clothes and food in case I reach a town and there are no handouts.'

Others, particularly some sleeping rough, neglect their cleanliness and appearance and their homeless situation is readily apparent. They are filthy, have matted hair and beards, dress in several layers of tattered and ill-fitting clothing, are without shoes, and have head and body lice. Lack of self-care is sometimes due to poor access to washing facilities, but often to mental health problems, or low self-esteem and morale. One elderly mentally ill woman had been living in a hostel for six years, during which time she constantly wore an old raincoat. It was filthy, in shreds, but she refused to change it even when the staff purchased her a new raincoat. In Chicago, homeless people over the age of 40 years, particularly men, were found to be dirtier and dressed more shabbily than younger homeless people (Table 8.1). Similarly, one-quarter of older men sleeping rough around the Bowery, New York City, were filthy and had a strong body odour (Cohen and Sokolovsky 1989).

Sleeping arrangements

Hostels and temporary accommodation

Over the last three decades, there has been a marked change in the temporary accommodation which is available for homeless people in both Britain and America. In Britain, some older men used to stay in large hostels, reception centres (the former casual wards), and lodging-houses such as the privately owned Rowton Houses in London. Some facilities housed up to 1,000 men in cubicles or large dormitories. Other men slept in church crypts and night-shelters, in wooden boxes known as 'coffins' or sitting on benches and leaning on a rope for support (Rose 1988; Orwell 1949, writing in 1933). Since the 1980s, such spartan accommodation has gradually been replaced by smaller hostels with improved conditions and amenities, although traditional hostels and poor standard accommodation still exist (see Chapter 11). In America, older homeless people used to stay in missions, flop-houses, and **single-room occupancy** (SRO) hotels in skid rows. Nowadays, many flop-houses and SRO hotels in America are closed and homeless people are accommodated in widely dispersed public and private shelters (Hoch and Slayton 1989).

Table 8.1   Interviewers' ratings of the appearance of homeless people, Chicago (percentages)

Appearance	Aged under 40 years		Aged 40 years and over	
	Men	*Women*	*Men*	*Women*
Not neat and clean	39	31	56	46
Shabbily dressed	24	19	42	36
Dirty	18	5	31	20
Carrying belongings in packages	8	3	10	27
Total number in sample	271	89	272	88

Source: Adapted from Rossi *et al.* (1986: 81, Table 4.21)

Contemporary older homeless people in Britain use diverse temporary accommodation, including direct-access hostels, night-shelters, **cold-weather shelters**, and 'welfare' or bed-and-breakfast hotels (Chapter 10). Some accommodation provides 24-hour shelter and services, others have restricted services. Some impose limits on the number of nights people can stay. Cold-weather shelters open only from December to March each year to encourage people off the streets during severe weather. Night-shelters require residents to leave the premises in the early morning and not to return until the evening. Older people using night-shelters have to linger on the streets and circulate soup kitchens and day centres during the day. This is tiring and demoralizing, provokes physical ill health, and increases vulnerability and feelings of unsettledness. An elderly woman staying at a night-shelter in London described how she had to leave the shelter by 7 a.m. She went to a day centre until it closed at 2 p.m., following which 'I am on the streets until the shelter reopens at 9 p.m. I feel that people are watching me standing about. I don't look any different to anyone else carrying shopping bags, but I feel that people know I'm homeless.'

Although direct-access hostels, night-shelters, and bed-and-breakfast hotels are intended as temporary accommodation, some people become long-term residents. In Glasgow, some older people have lived in hostels and 'welfare' hotels for more than 30 years (Crane and Warnes 1997a). Five hostel residents in the Four-City Study had created a 'home' in the hostel instead of being resettled in suitable permanent housing. One man had bought an electric radiator, a fridge, an electric cooking-pot, a bookcase, and a television for his bedroom. He had pictures and photographs on the walls, and window-boxes in which he was growing flowers. A 70-year-old woman, who had been resident in one hostel for more than 20 years, had decorated her room with wallpaper and bought rugs and cushions for her room.

Sleeping rough

Some older homeless people refuse to use hostels and shelters because they fear violence and intimidation from younger residents. They instead sleep rough or **skipper** in open or public places at night. A few skipper in sites with several others and form encampments, as in 'Cardboard City' under Waterloo Bridge, London, in Lincoln's Inn Fields, London, and in the secluded tunnels underneath New York City. But many older rough sleepers avoid communal sites for safety reasons, preferring to stay alone in isolated and hidden places away from city and town centres. In London, Manchester, Liverpool and Glasgow, they have been found sleeping in obscure places such as in rubbish skips, graveyards and bushes. Some go to great lengths to conceal their existence. One elderly man sleeps in an abandoned warehouse. He gains access by climbing up a rope to the first floor. An 80-year-old woman slept for several months in the coal-cellar of an uninhabited mansion in a central London square. She had no bedding, and slept on the floor among used tins of paint, strips of wood and building materials. Another elderly man once worked as a toilet attendant in London and, after locking the toilets at night, slept in the building.

An elderly man slept under these steps behind a church hall in West London

For safety reasons, some older rough sleepers do not 'bed down' at night but walk around the streets. According to Jack London (1903), they are 'carrying the banner'. Nowadays some ride on night-buses, or linger in cafés and airports which remain open 24 hours. One 72-year-old man journeys by bus each night from London to the suburbs in the late evening, and returns on the same bus. He arrives back in London about 4 a.m. and walks around the streets until a day centre opens at 7 a.m. A second man has purchased an annual pass for National Express coaches, and travels around Britain at night sleeping in coaches. Another elderly man lingers at night in hospitals where he feels safe and warm, and has access to toilets. He sits in the corner of a casualty department for a few hours before being moved on by security staff. In Los Angeles, one-quarter of homeless people (of all ages) reported that they slept during the day and stayed up at night (Farr *et al.* 1986).

On occasions, members of the public assist older homeless people to conceal themselves. One man has slept for seven years in a shed used by market stallholders to store barrows and goods. He has a bed in the shed, the stall-holders allow him to sleep there, and in return, he pushes their barrows into the market in the early morning. Another has slept in a storeroom for two years. He returns to the storeroom early each evening and the owner locks him in for the night before going home. Others sleep in underground car-parks with the knowledge of the car-park attendants. In New York City, older homeless men were sometimes befriended by a doorman and allowed to sleep in a storage room (Cohen and Sokolovsky 1989). In *Writing Home*, Alan Bennett (1997), one of England's leading playwrights, described how an elderly woman lived in a van across the street from him in Camden Town, north London, for a few years. She then lived in a shed and a van in his garden for 15 years until she died in 1989 at the age of 78.

Some younger homeless people erect makeshift shelters, known as 'bashes', using cardboard and other materials. Older homeless rough sleepers tend not to build elaborate shelters, but some create beds from cardboard and sleeping bags placed on bread-crates. Others have no bedding and sleep exposed in doorways or under bridges. A few modify an area into a makeshift home on the streets. One woman in her seventies slept in the same doorway in London for a few years. She swept the doorway with an old broom each evening, arranged numerous bags and boxes around her, and hung her clothes which she washed in the public toilets over the boxes. An elderly man interviewed in London also created a 'home' in doorways, although he changed doorways every few weeks. One evening when contacted, he was lying on blankets, reading, and drinking wine from a paper cup. In the doorway entrance, he had laid out several books about war, a handwritten notice stating his name and army number, some flowers in an old paper cup, and a candle burning in a saucer.

Movement between accommodation

Some older people stay in the same hostel or sleep rough for years, but others alternate between hostels and sleeping rough. One man in his seventies changed accommodation six times in London within 13 months. He moved successively from a hostel to sleeping rough, a bed-and-breakfast hotel, sleeping rough, and to two bed-and-breakfast hotels. Some sleep rough for long periods, and intermittently book into hostels as respite from the streets when they are physically ill or drinking heavily. One elderly man in Sheffield had been homeless for more than ten years. He slept rough most of the time but stayed in a hostel for two or three months each winter. Some older people who move into hostels find it difficult to adjust after having slept rough for years. Two men slept on the hostel floor because they could not get used to a bed. A third man frequently fell out of bed.

Sources of income and management of personal finances

The majority of older men who have slept rough or stayed in hostels for years have worked while homeless. Casual jobs were plentiful in London until the

An elderly woman preparing to sleep in a doorway for the night in Camden Town, London

early 1980s, and men used to work as pearl divers (dishwashers in hotel and restaurant kitchens), as labourers on building sites, as market barrow-boys, as cleaners at cricket grounds, and on farms picking vegetables and fruit. They were employed on a daily basis and queued each morning outside employment agencies in central London for jobs. Some slept on the streets near private employment agencies to ensure that they were first in the queue. Sometimes they waited for more than four hours only to be told that there were no jobs that day. Employees from building sites used to visit hostels and reception centres looking for workers, and vans would transport willing men to building sites. Today, however, most older homeless people do not work because of age, health problems, and the lack of casual jobs. A minority make money by busking, collecting coins left in telephone-boxes, returning luggage trolleys to train stations, collecting aluminium cans for recycling or phone-cards which they sell, and by selling *The Big Issue* on the streets. Begging is common among some younger homeless people in Britain, but rare among older street people.

Most older homeless people are entitled to social security benefits. Those who have worked regularly for years and have paid National Insurance contributions are entitled to a state pension when they reach the statutory retirement age (65 years for men and 60 for women). Those under pensionable age who are unable to work due to illness or disability, are eligible to claim incapacity benefit if they have paid adequate National Insurance contributions. In 1998, the weekly rate for a state pension and incapacity benefit for those with long-term illnesses was £64.70. But many older people have been homeless since early adulthood or middle age, did not work regularly, and have not paid (sufficient) National Insurance contributions. They are not entitled to a state pension and incapacity benefit. They can claim income support if they are too old or unable to work, or a jobseeker's allowance if they are considered fit for work. Only a minority of older homeless people fit the latter category. In 1998, the average weekly rate for income support or a jobseeker's allowance was £50.35.

Additional premiums averaging £20 a week are available to help with extra expenses. These include the pensioner premium for people over the age of 60 years, and the disability premium for those under the age of 60 who have a disability or long-term illness. The Benefits Agency,[1] however, differentiates between homeless people in hostels and bed-and-breakfast hotels with no fixed address, and people without accommodation (Pugh, no date). The latter are not entitled to claim additional premiums, for these are intended to help meet the costs of living in accommodation. By living nowhere, it is assumed that they do not have these extra living costs.

Most older people in hostels receive a state pension or welfare benefits and, because they are generally on low income and unable to afford hostel charges, means-tested housing benefit as well. Housing benefit is an essential source of finance for hostels without which many would be unable to operate, and it is generally paid directly to a hostel's finance department instead of to claimants. Some hostels and shelters will not accept homeless people who have no proof of identity and are not receiving benefits. In London, just over one-half of direct-access hostels in 1996 did not accept homeless people without proof of identity (Harrison 1996). Yet a British survey found that one-fifth of homeless people of all ages who used day centres and soup runs received no income (Anderson *et al.* 1993).

Ignorance of the benefits system is more common among older homeless people than fraudulent scrounging. Many older rough sleepers claim no entitlements and have no income because they do not understand how to make a claim, are unaware of their entitlements, and are unable to complete the complex forms and manage the bureaucracy of benefit offices. Some are illiterate or have learning difficulties or mental health problems, and in the past have relied on partners or families to deal with finances. Homelessness has often resulted because their support network has broken down, they have not claimed benefits and have accumulated rent arrears and been evicted. One elderly man had slept rough for more than 15 years without claiming money until he accepted hostel residency and the staff helped him claim benefits.

Even experienced hostel staff have difficulties when preparing residents' claims. At the Lancefield Street Centre, several residents had no proof of identity on admission. They came from travelling families in Ireland and their birth had never been registered. Proof of identity has to be obtained before a claim can be processed. It can take months for a claim to be sorted out if a person has slept rough for years, has not received benefits, and is unknown to services. Housing benefit can be backdated for 12 months, but other benefits for only three months and only where the claimant can demonstrate a good reason for not claiming earlier. Problems also arise because some older people move between hostels and the streets. Hostel staff have to notify the local benefit office of a person's change of address, and sometimes new claims have to be processed when a person moves.

In 1994, the habitual residence test was introduced into income support regulations. To qualify for income support, a jobseeker's allowance or housing benefit, a person must have a 'settled intention' to reside in Britain and have been 'habitually resident' for 'an appreciable period of time' (George *et al.* 1997). The terms are not clearly defined and some older people have been affected by the legislation. After having lived abroad for years, some have returned to the UK following a divorce, the death of their spouse, the loss of a home, or a business collapse, and have failed the habitual residence test. They have been homeless yet have been unable to book into a hostel because they were not entitled to housing benefit. One 58-year-old man returned to Britain in 1997 because he was no longer able to work through ill health. He was born in England and emigrated with his parents to South Africa when 13 years of age. He was in the merchant navy for more than 30 years. On return to Britain, he was homeless and destitute but failed the habitual residence test. He appealed, but hearings take up to six months. Because he was destitute and not entitled to benefits, the local authority social services department had a duty to provide him with food and shelter under the National Assistance Act 1948. They paid for him to stay in a bed-and-breakfast hotel, arranged meals-on-wheels as he was not well enough to travel around London to food hand-outs, and gave him a single payment of £20 for necessities such as toothpaste.

Once in receipt of benefits, older homeless people spend their money in various ways. Some spend their money on alcohol and cigarettes, with little regard to necessities such as food and clothing which they obtain free or cheaply at day centres and street handouts. Others prefer to buy food, toiletries and clothes. Some hostel residents purchase belongings for their bedroom such as a television, a radio, a clock and ornaments. A few have savings accounts. Some older homeless people have difficulty in managing personal finances due to illiteracy, mental health problems, heavy drinking and poor budgeting skills. Among the hostel residents at the Lancefield Street Centre in December 1997, over half (54 per cent) needed help with budgeting. Some would spend their money on alcohol if they were not reminded frequently to buy meal tickets and to pay a small weekly contribution towards rent. Others were unable to budget and the staff managed their money, distributed it daily, helped them buy clothes and belongings, and opened savings accounts for them. The proportion who needed help with budgeting was high because many were mentally ill or heavy drinkers.

Although most older homeless people have little income and no savings, this is not the case for all, contradicting the widespread belief that homelessness is synonymous with poverty. One elderly man slept rough in London although he had substantial savings and could easily afford to rent or even purchase accommodation. Another man who had slept rough in London for at least 20 years suffered a heart attack and died on the streets. He was found to have £1,500 in his socks (Meikle 1992). He had mental health problems.

A few older men have stayed in hostels although they have been in receipt of a state pension and an occupational pension and could have afforded to rent accommodation. This indicates that homelessness is a complex behaviour which is not always the consequence of poverty.

Sources of food

The way older homeless people obtain food depends on their willingness and ability to access services. Hostel residents are generally provided with subsidized meals, but many in night-shelters and bed-and-breakfast hotels only receive breakfast. In some towns and cities, there are soup kitchens and day centres for homeless people where food is provided, from soup and sandwiches to free or subsidized hot meals. At some missions in London, Liverpool, New York City and Milwaukee, free food is distributed to homeless people but after they attend a religious service. Soup, hot drinks and sandwiches are also distributed on the streets by religious and voluntary organizations, and occasionally by shopkeepers. There are several food distribution points in cities such as London and Manchester, but in many towns and rural areas they do not exist. One man explained: 'in the country you may go for days without eating'. In the past, some men sought jobs as kitchen porters because they were given meals while working and food to take away.

Many older rough sleepers, particularly women, avoid soup kitchens and day centres, stay away from food runs, and instead eat discarded food from litter bins. An elderly street man described that one Christmas he was hungry, but cafés and stations were closed and there was no food in the litter-bins. He stole some bread from a shop. He said: 'I looked through the windows of houses; I could see people with plenty of food; all I had was a loaf of bread.' Among those sleeping rough in the Four-City Study sample, 64 per cent of the women and 31 per cent of the men never used day centres or soup kitchens (Table 8.2). Some were confused and were unable to appreciate the help available, while some were paranoid and believed that they would be harmed by staff if they used the centres. Others found the centres noisy and overcrowded, and feared intimidation and violence from younger homeless users. A few men said that when they were hungry they visited convents because, 'the nuns always give you something to eat if you knock at their door'.

Little is known about the diets of older homeless people. Some never have hot meals, and some who drink heavily do not eat for days. A large-scale survey in American cities of more than 1,700 homeless people of all ages found that the diet of the majority was inadequate 'to maintain good health' (Burt and Cohen 1989: 520). In Britain, sandwiches donated by supermarkets are the mainstay of the food which is distributed on the streets and at some soup kitchens, and even the meals offered in many hostels and day centres are reported to be 'nutritionally unbalanced' (Balazs 1993: 82). In Detroit, 43 per cent of older homeless people reported that there were times when they had little to eat for two or more days (Douglass *et al.* 1988). The Bowery men in New York reported similar problems; two-thirds of those on the streets sometimes went without meals (Cohen and Sokolovsky 1989).

Table 8.2   The Four-City Study subjects' use of soup kitchens and day centres by type of accommodation

Frequency of use	Permanent housing		Temporary accommodation		Sleeping rough	
	No.	*%*	*No.*	*%*	*No.*	*%*
None used	10	21	71	74	28	42
Occasional use[1]	14	29	12	13	31	46
Regular use[2]	24	50	13	14	8	12
Total known	48	100	96	101	67	100
Not known	4		6		4	
Total subjects	52		102		71	

[1] One to three times per week
[2] Four or more times per week

Daily activities

Most housed older people are occupied each day with shopping, cooking, household chores, gardening, visiting or being visited by family and relatives, watching television, and attending pensioners' clubs or bingo. Homeless older people do not have a home to look after, they have no need to shop as most have no opportunity to cook, and many are estranged from relatives and mainstream social groups. Most housed older people sleep at night. Many older rough sleepers have disturbed sleep as they are fearful to bed down until late, they get up early before people start leaving home for work, and they have to be alert during the night for intruders. Some therefore sleep during the day in parks, libraries, and at day centres. One man who described himself as a tramp said that he sat in a pub until it closed, bedded down in a hidden place around midnight, and got up at 4.30 a.m. 'when the birds started to sing'.

The daily routines of homeless older people are therefore very different from those of most housed older people. Those who are sleeping rough, or staying in hostels and shelters which they have to vacate during the day, have many hours to fill each day, and because they are inevitably in public places their activities are overt. A few are employed full-time, work casually in markets, or engage in marginal occupations such as selling *The Big Issue*. For them, a job provides a role and some structure and purpose to their day. But most are not working and have no goals to pursue. Some develop routines. One woman, who sleeps rough in the North of England, collects free loaves of bread from bakeries each morning and walks around the city, feeding pigeons. Some circulate from morning until evening around day centres and street handouts. Because the centres open for a limited number of hours at different times, they walk for miles from one to the next.

For another group of older homeless people, mainly men, their day is focused around drinking alcohol (see Chapter 9). This involves going to the shops and purchasing drink, consuming it, and then sleeping for a few hours. Some drink in small groups, and some housed older people join homeless drinkers on the streets. Most older rough sleepers leave their sleeping site each morning and return at night. A few, however, are passive, stay in one place, and spend most of the day and night asleep. One woman aged in her seventies spent most of her time in a doorway on a busy street, she was given food and beverages by passers-by, and she only left her site to urinate or defecate in the gutter nearby. Another woman had slept rough for years around Waterloo Station in London. She spent each day in the waiting room of the ladies' toilets mostly asleep on the chairs, she had a shopping-trolley laden with old clothing and food, and commuters regularly brought her food and hot drinks. One evening, she was observed to receive in one hour sandwiches, chips, a burger, three cups of tea, one cup of coffee, and one cup of hot chocolate from commuters. Although she rarely conversed, her presence attracted the attention of the general public.

Exceptional behaviour

Among the Four-City Study sample, a few people displayed idiosyncratic behaviour which had come to the attention of official establishments. According to one man, he was known to the police in central London as 'the teddy-bear' and had been arrested many times for shoplifting. While sleeping rough, he used to steal teddy-bears from a stall, give them to children, and generally their parents would remunerate him. Another man, who was smartly dressed and well spoken, has travelled around Britain for years staying in hotels and leaving without paying bills. He has been in prison many times for swindling and making false claims for welfare benefits. He said: 'I'm a con-man. I'm different to most dossers, I've come from a posh family. I fiddled anybody that had money.'

Scavenging and hoarding garbage

Some older homeless people spend each day rummaging through litter bins. They hoard clothing, old food, newspapers and garbage in carrier bags and shopping-trolleys, known in America as 'ships of the ghetto' (Hill and Stamey 1990). Women so presenting are referred to as 'shopping-bag ladies' and men as 'grate men' (Coston 1989; Damrosch and Strasser 1988; Fischer and Breakey 1986; Schwam 1979). Little is known or written about the circumstances of older **bag people**, particularly grate men. They tend to be seen in doorways or in corners of railway and bus stations. Although they linger in crowded places, they are generally alone, seldom engage in conversation, and are 'off to one side in a private niche clearly separate from the crowd' (Hand 1983: 156). In Chicago, older homeless people were more likely than younger homeless people to hoard garbage in bags (Table 8.1). Twenty-six per cent of the older women and 10 per cent of the older men were bag people (Rossi *et al.* 1986). Among the Four-City Study sample, 54 per cent of the 22 women and 18 per cent of the 49 men sleeping rough were bag people. One woman had 14 carrier bags tied to a shopping-trolley laden with 'goods', and one man collected garbage on a bread-crate which he pulled along the street with a piece of rope.

Possessions have practical use and personal significance, and they convey a person's identity and status (Dittmar 1992; Goffman 1959). Observers have claimed that those who cart things around in bags or boxes are trying to express their identity and social position (Russell 1991; Hand 1983), and preserve some sense of home (Baxter and Hopper 1981). A shopping-bag lady 'may start out with nothing more than what she is wearing. She then acquires first a bag, then another, puts them on a wheeled cart, attaches more bags to the cart . . . until she eventually has an unmovable mound' (Hand 1983: 164–5). One elderly woman who had been sleeping rough for nearly 20 years in the North of England, had a shopping-trolley piled with bags and garbage and numerous carrier bags tied to the handles. She explained: 'When I started sleeping out I only had two carrier bags and a blanket; I could easily move around the town . . . now it takes me ages to get about because my trolley is heavy to push. I unloaded it once, but it soon got full up again.'

The behaviour of scavenging and collecting garbage in shopping-trolleys and bags is not fully understood. Although it has been associated with a homeless person's attempt to preserve a sense of home, not all bag people sleep rough. A few older hostel residents and people in conventional

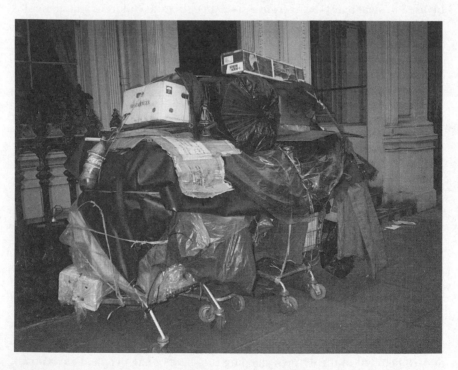

Hoarded garbage in several shopping-trolleys strapped together

accommodation also typify bag people. They leave their hostel or tenancy daily with their possessions in numerous bags, and stay on the streets until evening. In Manchester, one 70-year-old woman who had been homeless for at least eight years was rehoused in a **shared house**. She hoarded in black bags old clothing which she obtained from day centres, street handouts and rubbish skips. She had more than 30 bags of old clothing at home, she left some with car-park attendants in the city, and carried some around with her. An 80-year-old woman who slept rough spent more than six hours each day rummaging through litter bins in London and retrieving food, drink, newspapers and clothing. Yet she declined offers of money, food and drink from the general public.

'Diogenes syndrome' has been noted among some older people, and is characterized by self-neglect, living in squalor, reclusiveness and hoarding of rubbish (syllogomania) (Lishman 1998; McLoughlin and Farrell 1997). As we learn from the *Shorter Oxford English Dictionary* and the *Encyclopaedia Britannica*, Diogenes was a Greek philosopher who showed his contempt for the amenities of life by living in poverty, sleeping in public buildings and a barrel, and begging for food. Approximately 50 per cent of elderly people with Diogenes syndrome are suffering from dementia or, less commonly, schizophrenia or alcohol dependency (McLoughlin and Farrell 1997; Macmillan 1966). The remainder, however, show no evidence of psychiatric disorder or cognitive decline. The suggestion is that the behaviour of some may be a reaction to stress, bereavement or loneliness (Lishman 1998; Clark *et al.* 1975). Many older homeless bag people have apparent mental health problems but, because they are often isolated and hostile when approached, it is difficult to collect histories or to determine the reasons for their behaviour.

Mobility between towns

Transience is a behaviour traditionally associated with itinerant workers and vagrants. Many homeless people nowadays remain in one town, and only a few wander from place to place (Snow and Anderson 1993; Weiner 1984). In Los Angeles, those who are transient tend to be young, newly homeless and physically healthy, and move from town to town in the hope of finding employment (Wolch *et al.* 1993; Rahimian *et al.* 1992). Some homeless mentally ill people also move from place to place. The opinion is that they 'drift' around cities in an attempt to escape from social relationships, commitments, problems and distress (Belcher 1988a; Bachrach 1987; Lamb 1984).

Most older people have remained in one town since becoming homeless. However, a small group of older men are mobile and addictively travel from town to town. Eleven per cent of the men in the Four-City Study had stayed in at least four towns in the six months before being interviewed. One said: 'I never remain in one place longer than five or six weeks.' Between November 1997 and March 1998, one 66-year-old man moved from Birmingham to London, to Derby, to Leeds, and back to London. Those who were transient tended to be young elderly (55–64 years). The mobility of older men who move from place to place *while* homeless can be differentiated from that of building labourers and other itinerant workers who moved around the country in search of work *before* becoming homeless (see Chapter 5). For the former, mobility often followed homelessness. For the latter, it preceded and subsequently led to homelessness.

According to the men's reports, there are two main reasons why they move from town to town while homeless. For some, it is related to their biographies and is a continuation of a long-standing behaviour. Some had been itinerant workers or had been homeless for years. They had become accustomed to the lifestyle since the time, during the 1950s and 1960s, when they used reception centres and were only allowed to stay in any one centre for one or two nights and then had to move on (see Chapter 10). Orwell (1949: 178–9) writing in 1933 noted, 'a tramp tramps . . . because there is a law compelling him to do so . . . each casual ward [later known as reception centres] will only admit him for one night, he is automatically kept moving'. Transience had become a way of life, and they said that now they could not settle in one place. One man explained: 'all us old tramps on the road had a reason for opting out of society and choosing this life-style. We had all suffered some pain. But we then got into the habit of moving about.' Some referred to themselves as 'original tramps' or 'men of the road'. Many admitted that they were now too old to continue travel-ling and that they ought to settle. One man explained: 'this travelling is a way of life; but there comes a time when it has to stop; I'm getting too old for it.' Another said: 'I know this unsettledness comes to an end one day, because of age, illness or death.'

For a second group of men, mobility is related to mental states, depression and disaffiliation, and is their attempt to escape from uncomfortable circum-stances. Its onset occurred at the time a person became homeless and was often instigated by a traumatic event. Several left their home town following widowhood or a marital breakdown. One man lived in Cornwall with his wife for more than 35 years until she died. He abandoned his home and has since travelled around Britain. He said that it was too distressing to remain in Corn-wall. Another has been unsettled for 11 years since his marriage of 28 years ended in divorce. He has a tent, travels from place to place, and camps in fields. He occasionally stays for a week with Benedictine monks at their abbeys when 'I want to meditate and think over what has happened in my life'. Some said that they move around because people irritate them. One said: 'I move about all the time. I stay in a place two or three days, or two or three weeks. People drive me mad and screw me up, and when that happens I just take off.' Another said: 'I keep on the move; a moving target rarely gets hit.' Several associated transience with depression:

> I don't want to travel but my head keeps telling me to go; depression makes me travel; I just need to go anywhere. I go to a bus station and look at the destination of the buses and then go. If I have no money at the end of the journey, I steal and end up in prison. I travel because I have to get out of the situation; I don't think of the consequences.
>
> (Man aged 67 who has been homeless for 30 years)

> Depression is at the root of all this travelling. You are in a place and seem to be getting nowhere in life, so you move to another town as you imagine that the grass is greener on the other side of the fence. After a

couple of weeks, nothing has changed and you realize that it is not changes in places that you are looking for but changes in yourself. As you get older, you realize that your life is over, you cannot change anything, and that you're a failure. Only then do you stay in one place and accept the situation.

(Man aged 60 who has been homeless for more than 20 years)

Homelessness behaviours by housed people

Some older people display homelessness behaviours although they are housed. They regularly congregate with homeless people at soup kitchens and day centres, sit in doorways drinking, and scavenge through litter bins. Some return to their accommodation for just a few hours at night, while some stay on the streets all night (see Chapter 2). There has been little acknowledgement of this group in studies of homeless people. Among the Four-City Study sample, 52 subjects were housed but displayed homelessness behaviours. All except nine had been homeless and had continued the lifestyle even though they had been rehoused. Interestingly, they used day centres and soup kitchens more frequently than those who slept rough (Table 8.2). One elderly woman impersonated a homeless person. She sat on the pavement each day and begged for long periods. She had a dishevelled appearance, a plastic bag which contained her 'possessions', a cardboard sign stating that she was homeless, and she gave a convincing account of the circumstances which contributed to her 'homeless' state. By following her one evening, it was confirmed that she had and used a council flat.

Fifty-seven per cent of the group had been housed for less than two years, including a quarter for less than six months. They said that they stayed on the streets and used day centres because they were lonely and needed company; they had nothing to do during the day; and they were finding it difficult to manage at home, and were unable or unmotivated to cook. A few said that the centres deterred them from drinking alcohol. Many had therefore not only been resettled for a relatively short while but were experiencing difficulties at home. One man explained: 'I've been in the flat for one year and I hate it. The loneliness is the thing that destroys you. I've travelled the world and always been out and about. How can they expect me to stay in four fucking walls? It's not a home, I just spend a few hours there at night.' An elderly woman allowed young homeless alcoholics to stay in her flat because, as she said, 'I want company'. She always left her front door open, her flat was filthy and carpetless, the bedclothes were dirty and smothered in flies, and beer cans, wine bottles, cigarette butts and dirty clothes were strewn around.

A comparison of the daily activities of two subjects in the Four-City Study, Bert and Freda, demonstrates the diverse yet deviant behaviours of some older homeless people (Figure 8.1 and Figure 8.2). Both have been in London for years and have daily routines. Bert is a 67-year-old man who spent years homeless and now has a tenancy in London. Although he has been rehoused for three years, he still displays homelessness behaviour. He spends a few hours each night in his flat and the rest of the time he circulates around day centres and soup kitchens, and stays on the streets until late with homeless

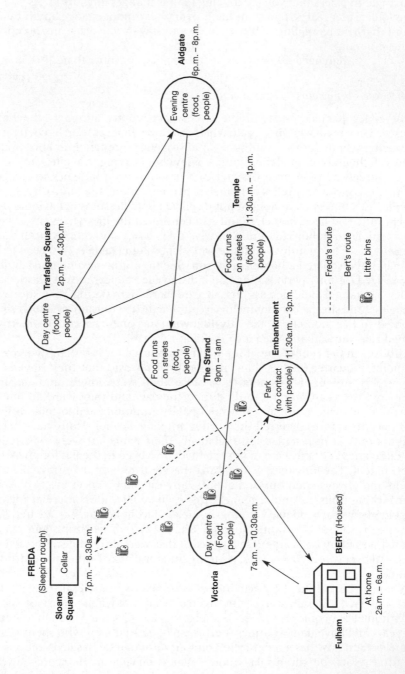

Figure 8.1 The daily routine of a homeless person and a housed person

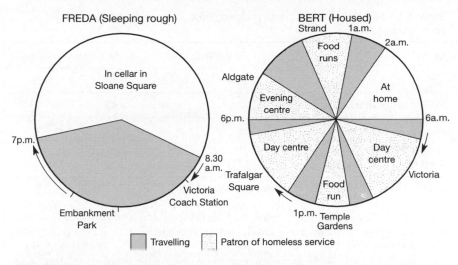

Figure 8.2 The contact with services over 24 hours by a homeless person and a housed person

people. He walks from one place to the next. Freda is 80 years old and has been sleeping rough for at least 10 years. At the time of interview, she stayed alone at night in a cellar. She never used day centres, soup kitchens or street handouts, had no contact with homeless people or services, and scavenged in litter bins for food and drink.

Although Bert is housed, he only spends an average of four hours each day at home. He is on the streets for 12 hours daily and at day centres for eight hours. He accesses services for homeless people and, besides using day centres and soup kitchens for eight hours each day, he remains at sites where street handouts are distributed for $5\frac{1}{2}$ hours daily. On the other hand, Freda spends $10\frac{1}{2}$ hours on the streets daily and the rest of the time is 'hidden' in a cellar. Although she sleeps rough, she never uses services for homeless people. During the day she walks from Sloane Square to the Embankment and rummages through each litter bin that she passes.

Family contacts

Homeless people have often been described as 'family-less' or 'kin-less' (Liebow 1993; Rossi *et al.* 1986; Bahr and Garrett 1976; Wallace 1965). Many lack family, while many others are estranged from relatives. Older homeless people are less likely than younger homeless people to have family contact (Gelberg *et al.* 1990). In Chicago, 42 per cent of homeless men and 48 per cent of homeless women aged 40 years and over had no family involvement (Table 8.3). Yet only 28 per cent of homeless men and 9 per cent of homeless women below that age had no family contact (Rossi *et al.* 1986). Two further studies, in Chicago and in Tampa Bay, Florida, found that only 9–14

Table 8.3   Family and social contacts among homeless people, Chicago (percentages)

Contacts	Aged under 40 years		Aged 40 years and over	
	Men	Women	Men	Women
No contact with relatives, spouse or children	28	9	42	48
No contact with family and no friends	21	7	27	41
Total number in sample	271	89	272	88

Source: Adapted from Rossi *et al.* (1986: 152, Table 9.8)

per cent of older homeless people had family contact, and 9 per cent of the men and 17 per cent of the women in Chicago had no living relatives (Rich *et al.* 1995; Kutza 1987). In contrast, more than half of older Bowery men in New York City were in contact with at least one relative (Cohen and Sokolovsky 1989).

The marital status of homeless older people contrasts greatly with that of housed older people in England and Wales. The majority of subjects in the Four-City Study were single, separated or divorced. The men tended to have remained single, whereas the women were more likely to have been married. Three-fifths of the men were single and one-third divorced or separated, whereas two-fifths of the women were single and nearly one-half divorced or separated. Yet in the 1991 Census, less than 10 per cent of housed people aged over 55 years were single and only 5 per cent were divorced (Table 8.4).

Table 8.4   Housed and homeless older people's marital status (percentages)

Marital status	Men			Women		
	Housed	Homeless		Housed	Homeless	
	England[1]	England[2]	New York[3]	England[4]	England[5]	New York[6]
Single/never married	7	59	42	8	39	27
Married[7]	76	0	10	51	2	1
Widowed	12	9	17	37	11	19
Divorced/separated[8]	5	32	31	5	48	53

[1] Calculated from 1991 Census enumeration of 5,748,161 men in England and Wales aged 55+ years (OPCS, 1993b: 64, Table 2)
[2] 151 men aged 55+ years in Four-City Study (Crane 1997)
[3] 281 men aged 50+ years in New York City (Cohen and Sokolovsky 1989)
[4] Calculated from 1991 Census enumeration of 7,421,496 women in England and Wales aged 55+ years (OPCS, 1993b: 64, Table 2)
[5] 52 women aged 55+ years in Four-City Study (Crane 1997)
[6] 237 women aged 50+ years in New York City (Cohen *et al.* 1997)
[7] For the housed people, includes those who are separated: the Census data do not distinguish this group from those who are married and living together
[8] For the housed people, does not include those who are separated: see note 7

Table 8.5 The Four-City Study subjects' contact with relatives

Most recent contact with a relative[1]	Males		Females		Total	
	No.	%	No.	%	No.	%
Within past year	22	16	13	28	35	19
1–5 years ago	12	9	2	4	14	8
Over 5 years ago	79	58	23	50	102	56
Has no living relatives	23	17	8	17	31	17
Total known	136		46		182	
Not known	23		20		43	
Total respondents	159		66		225	

[1] Parents, children, brothers and sisters

High rates of never marrying or separation and divorce were also reported among older homeless people in New York City, Detroit, and in Tampa Bay, Florida (Rich *et al.* 1995; Douglass *et al.* 1988). In the Four-City Study sample, 59 men and 29 women had children. However, only 12 men and nine women had brought up their children to 16 years of age, for most had left them as minors usually through marital breakdown. Most had little or no subsequent contact with their children.

Most older people in the Four-City Study either lacked family or had had no contact with relatives for years (Table 8.5). Estranged family relationships often dated back more than 20 years, and several were unaware if their family were still alive. Only 27 per cent had seen a family member (parent, child or sibling) during the five years before being interviewed. The women were more likely than the men to have maintained family contact and this was mainly with a child. The findings have to be assessed cautiously. Some people who have experienced relationship difficulties or traumas may deny the existence of relatives and children. Or they may falsely indicate that they have been in contact, refusing to admit estranged relationships. One elderly man maintained that he saw his sister and that she regularly wrote to him. He produced a Christmas card which he had found on the streets, and alleged that it had come from her (even though it did not bear his name).

When comparisons are made with housed older people in Great Britain, homeless older people are clearly differentiated as estranged (Table 8.6). At least seven-tenths of housed older people see one or more relatives each month, yet only one in five of the Four-City Study subjects had seen a relative within the previous *year*. Only a small minority of housed older people are estranged from families and relatives (Bennett *et al.* 1996; Wenger 1994). Yet over half of the homeless subjects had had no family contact for more than five years. Compared to older people in the general population, the Four-City Study subjects were more likely to have no relatives and, for those who had relatives, they were more likely not to see them.

The reasons for older homeless people's estranged family relationships are complex. Some have never married and have no siblings. As they age, they

Table 8.6   Housed and homeless older people's frequency of contact with relatives (percentages)

Frequency of contact	Housed samples			Homeless sample
	North Wales[1]	England[2]	Great Britain[3]	Four-City Study[4]
Within last month	69	70	94	19[5]
No contact	2	5	3	56[6]
No relatives	6	5	n.a.	17
Sample size	289	2,622	3,475	182

[1] People aged 50+ (Wenger 1994: 111–12)
[2] People aged 65+ (Hunt, 1978: 95, Table 12.8.1)
[3] People aged 65+, General Household Survey 1994 (Bennett *et al.* 1996: Table 6.39). Includes contact with friends
[4] People aged 55+ (Crane 1997)
[5] Within the last year
[6] For five years or more

lose their parents. Among the Four-City Study sample, 17 per cent had no living relatives, including some who were raised in orphanages or foster homes and had never had a close family. At a shelter for homeless women near Washington, DC, Liebow (1993: 83) described a 72-year-old resident who had never married, her only living brother was killed in the war, and she had been without a family since her mother died in 1965. Among the Four-City and Lancefield Street Centre studies samples, some older people experienced dysfunctional childhood homes which they abandoned when young and have never renewed family contact. Others became estranged from their family following widowhood or a marital breakdown. Four men who abandoned their homes when their wives died said that they did not keep in touch with their adult children because they did not want the children to know about their circumstances and they did not want to be a burden on their children. Some men who became homeless after a marital breakdown described feeling angry and rejected at the time of separation. They deliberately severed family contacts and some were refused access to their children.

Alcohol problems and mental illness also contributed to estranged family relationships (described in Chapter 7). Some older people led chaotic lifestyles while raising their children and drank heavily or tolerated physical abuse. This is likely to have contributed to poor parenting and had an impact on family relationships. Ruth, for example, has two sons and a daughter whom she has not seen for years because they refuse to visit. According to Ruth, her marriage ended after ten years through her husband's physical abuse. She moved with her children back to her parents' home, but drank heavily and this caused arguments. Ruth left her parents' home, came to London, and slept rough. Her children, then aged between 11 and 15 years, remained with her parents and Ruth never saw them while they were growing up.

Peer-group contacts

The extent to which homeless people socialize with each other is variously reported. Some reports suggest that they affiliate in groups as 'communities' and 'subcultures' (Toth 1993; Underwood 1993; Wagner 1993). In contrast, other reports suggest that homeless people have few social contacts and their relationships are transitory, tenuous, fragile and loose-knit (Rosenthal 1994; Koegel 1992; Hill and Stamey 1990; Glasser 1988). Snow and Anderson (1993: 172) noted that 'peer relationships among street people are infused with a paradoxical combination of isolation and sociability'. Although the relationships provide a source of reference and a nexus for the sharing of meager resources, they are without strong ties or commitments. Some other marginalized groups, such as Liebow's (1967) Negro street-corner men in downtown Washington, DC, and Anderson's (1978) street-corner men in Chicago, are similarly described as having loose-knit social relationships without strong ties. Although there is little longitudinal information about the ways in which social patterns change, the opinion is that some homeless people become increasingly isolated while others gradually integrate with homeless people on the streets and at service points (Rosenthal 1994; Grigsby et al. 1990).

Older homeless people are generally reported to be more isolated than younger homeless people (Sheridan et al. 1993; Gelberg et al. 1990). However, they associate with each other in various degrees. Some older rough sleepers are exceptionally isolated. Bag people are often found in crowded places but many are isolated, refuse to converse, and are hostile and shout 'sod off . . . fuck off . . . get away' if approached. One man aggressively said: 'I'm anonymous; I have no name and no age.' The opinion is that they stay in populated areas because they want to be with people even though they do not want to talk, and because they feel safer and more protected in busy areas (Hand 1983; Baxter and Hopper 1981). A second, particularly isolated group are transient men who frequently move from town to town. Most travel alone and shun social contacts, although some meet in different towns and keep each other informed of the whereabouts of other men. One man explained: 'I'm a loner; I always travel on my own so that I have no incumbencies; I don't want to listen to other men's problems.'

Although some older homeless people use hostels, this does not mean that they are sociable. At the end of 1997, 14 of 33 Lancefield Street hostel residents spent most of the time alone in their bedrooms (Crane and Warnes 1998). One woman refused to converse with residents or staff, and was hostile when approached by staff. Among the Four-City Study sample, one woman had been living in a hostel for six years after out-reach workers found her sleeping rough. She refused to converse or answer questions except in a hostile and sarcastic manner, and the staff were unaware of her circumstances before entering the hostel. Several ethnographic studies in the 1970s of American SRO hotels found that many elderly residents were loners and socially isolated (Eckert 1980; Lally et al. 1979; Stephens 1976; Hertz and Hutheesing 1975).

Some older homeless people develop social networks on the streets and at service points. They socialize in hostels, at day centres and street handouts, and congregate on the streets with homeless people. Older homeless men who are heavy drinkers are particularly likely to socialize. Several in London have known each other for years, having worked together on building sites or in hotel kitchens. Likewise, most older Bowery men in New York City were heavy drinkers who affiliated in small groups (Cohen and Sokolovsky 1989). But the relationships of older homeless people who do socialize are often not deep-rooted. They refer to each other as 'companions' rather than 'friends', and contact is often severed as soon as a person changes accommodation or stops using a day centre. One 69-year-old man who has slept rough for 12 years explained:

> intimate friendships do not form on the streets, but you know about people's habits and how they tick. You know when to speak to a person and when to leave him alone. You need each other to a certain degree to share information, food and money, but you never ask anyone about their problems or past life. The friendships on the streets are different to those of people in houses. On the streets, people do not want you for what you've got because you've got nothing . . . they want you for yourself.

By integrating with each other, people learn how to manage on the streets and where to obtain food and clothing, and it may thus help to sustain the problem. When first homeless, several older men found out about soup kitchens, hostels and handouts in London from other homeless people. For many, the 'homeless community' provides their only social and support links and some are reluctant to break these ties. Furthermore, some display disturbed behaviour or neglect their hygiene and appearance and, although welcomed at day centres for homeless people, they would often be regarded as deviant at mainstream older people's day centres. One man at a soup kitchen in London explained: 'everyone in this place has some sort of problem; we come here because we're all in the same situation'. In the Four-City Study sample, 52 people were rehoused but still spent most of their time at day centres, soup kitchens, and on the streets with homeless people.

The majority of older homeless people are poorly affiliated and do not have strong social ties. Over three-fifths (62 per cent) of older homeless people in Tampa Bay, Florida, were described as isolates (Rich *et al.* 1995). Similarly, two-fifths of older homeless women and 27 per cent of older homeless men in Chicago had neither friends nor family contact (Table 8.3). Their isolation is highlighted when they need emotional support or when they die. Many have no relatives or friends, and sometimes a hostel or out-reach worker performs a role usually fulfilled by family, such as accompanying an older homeless person to the cemetery to visit the grave of their spouse. A worker is sometimes the only person who attends the funeral when an older homeless person dies. Quotes from older homeless people about family and social relationships are displayed in Box 8.3.

Box 8.3   Quotes from older homeless people about family and social relationships

'I have no friends, only acquaintances.'

'You have no family and friends in this life . . . you are on your own.'

'I'm a lone wolf . . . it's the best way.'

'I've detached myself from people and have become anonymous. I don't participate in life, I'm just an observer.'

'I don't mix or talk to people . . . hardly anybody knows that I exist.'

'I came into this homeless life to escape . . . I have now successfully cut myself off from all people that mattered.'

'Homeless men are always alone . . . that is because they don't trust anybody. You are let down too many times in life and in the end you don't bother with people any more.'

'I am a reject . . . my children and family do not want to know me.'

Conclusions

The behaviour of older homeless people differs considerably from that of most older people in Britain. They sleep in places which would be inconceivable as night-time residences for most people, and some exist by eating food from litter bins and washing in public toilets, behaviour which is abhorrent to most elderly people. Compared to the housed older population, homeless older people are disaffiliated. Many are socially isolated, for they have no friends and they either have no relatives or they have not been in contact with their families for years. Those who have been in marital relationships are estranged from their partners, and often from their children. Unlike housed older people, the majority of older homeless people have no responsibilities or roles to fulfil except those of survival.

Compared to their younger counterparts, older homeless people are less visible. They tend to be more isolated, sleep alone in hidden sites, rarely beg in public places, and many refuse to use hostels, soup kitchens and day centres designated for homeless people. Some are well groomed and it is not evident from their appearance that they are homeless. Others neglect their hygiene and self-care and their situation is obvious. Although many older people sleep rough and others are forced out of night-shelters in the day and thus spend long periods in public places, they hide in secluded spots or congregate in large cities where they are less noticeable, and only a minority with exceptional behaviour come to the attention of service providers or the media.

Some older homeless people have acquired skills to survive on the streets or in hostels. Some have little or no money but have learned how to obtain

The isolation of an older homeless man in Piccadilly Circus, London

food, clothing and other necessities. Others work casually or engage in marginal occupations to make money such as collecting phone-cards. Some have developed daily routines, such as scavenging, drinking in groups, or circulating around day centres. Although the majority are estranged from their family and lack or have severed links with housed friends, some have formed social networks with homeless people on the streets and at service points. Some are reluctant to break their social ties and the routines which they have developed while homeless, and thus continue to display homelessness behaviours when rehoused.

Many older rough sleepers are not coping, claim no benefits, do not use day centres, hostels or street handouts, forage for food in litter bins, have poor diets, inadequate sleep, poor hygiene, and lack warm clothing. As a result they are at risk of physical and mental health problems (described in Chapter 9). Some display passive behaviour and spend most of the day and night asleep or dozing, without engaging in activities. Some are depressed and demoralized, unable to settle in accommodation or even in one town, and move between hostels and sleeping rough, and a few men move around the country. They are generally isolated and have no peer-group contacts. Some are hostile when approached, which deters people from making contact and exacerbates estranged social relationships. This is particularly seen among older men who are transient, and among older women sleeping rough and some in hostels.

Homelessness is a complex issue which is difficult to understand. Since becoming homeless, many older people have not sought a conventional home but have stayed on the streets or relied on hostels, even in a few instances when they could afford accommodation. A few have tried to create a makeshift home in a hostel or in a doorway instead of exploring ways to establish a permanent home. This suggests strongly that psychological factors are important contributory states to homelessness, and these are examined in the next chapter. Services may also contribute to the problem by, for example, allowing people to become long-term residents in temporary hostels, and by forcing people to vacate accommodation during the day, thus increasing unsettledness and vulnerability. This is discussed in Chapter 11.

Note

1 An Executive Agency of the Department of Social Security.

9

Psychological and physical health problems

Being homeless is a life of mental and physical torture. At least in prison you have warmth, food and a bed, and your sentence comes to an end. Homelessness is a living hell that never ends. Homeless people drink to numb their minds and escape from this torture.

(David, aged 65, sleeping rough for the past 20 years)

Being homeless is stressful and exacerbates health problems. Since the late 1970s, many British and American studies have reported on the health problems of homeless people and on the difficulties of delivering health-care services to the group. Only a few have focused on *older* homeless people. Using information from their reports and from the empirical field studies, this chapter describes the psychological and physical health states of older homeless people. First, psychological problems are discussed, starting with generalized feelings of demoralization, depression and hopelessness, and moving on to heavy drinking, mental illness, and complex syndromes of mental illness and alcoholism. A second section focuses on common physical illnesses, mortality rates, and the problems of accessing health-care services and treating older homeless people.

Psychological problems

A minority of elderly people in the general British population suffer from a diagnosed mental illness. Depression affects 12–16 per cent of elderly people, with up to 2 per cent suffering from a major depressive illness (Gurland and Fogel 1992). Paraphrenia and dementia are mental illnesses which are present in later life. Between 1 and 2 per cent of elderly people suffer from persistent paranoid states, sometimes a late-onset primary paranoid disorder; and 3–9 per cent of those aged 65 years and over suffer from moderate or severe dementia (Gurland and Fogel 1992; Jarvik *et al*. 1992). It is difficult to diagnose mental illness among homeless people, particularly those sleeping rough. Homelessness is a downhill, degrading and stressful situation, and 'depression might be interpreted as a fairly normal response to a strikingly abnormal situation' (Snow and Anderson 1993: 348). The homeless lifestyle, with its associated stresses, poor diet and inadequate sleep, may produce symptoms of depression or memory impairment which are conducive to physiological and not psychological problems (Koegel and Burnam 1992; Snow *et al.* 1988; Baxter and Hopper 1982).

Since the late 1970s, there has been great interest among British and American psychiatrists in the mental health states of homeless people. The reported prevalence of such problems varies, depending on definitions of mental illness, the instruments used (which vary from self-reports to standard diagnostic tools and psychiatric scales) and whether the sample includes rough sleepers (Koegel and Burnam 1992; Susser *et al.* 1989). To assess depression among this population, measures such as the Center for Epidemiologic Studies' Depression Scale have been used (La Gory *et al.* 1990; Douglass *et al.* 1988; Rossi *et al.* 1986). But the design of the questions is likely to produce responses which suggest high rates of depression. Subjects are asked, for example, if they feel unhappy about the way their life is going, and if they feel discouraged and worried about the future. Some homeless people may be clinically depressed, while many others report and would generally be described as depressed.

It is particularly difficult to assess the mental health states of older homeless people. Some are hostile when approached, shout and swear, and refuse to converse. It is impossible to know whether their behaviour is the result of mental health problems or is their way of avoiding contact. A dirty, dishevelled appearance may be symptomatic of functional impairment, poor access to washing facilities, or low self-esteem and poor motivation. Elderly people living at home have newspapers, television and other orientation cues to stimulate their memory. Older homeless people often do not have access to these cues, they spend every day wandering the streets, and are therefore more likely to become disorientated. One elderly woman, interviewed in London in September, believed that it was Christmas as the shops were displaying Christmas decorations. Another woman, who slept near a train station, said that she knew when it was a weekend because no commuters passed by.

Demoralization, depression and hopelessness

Homelessness has been associated with a downward spiral characterized by demoralization, depression, loss of self-esteem, self-neglect, and feelings of helplessness and hopelessness (Rosenthal 1994; Baum and Burnes 1993; Snow and Anderson 1993; Underwood 1993). The opinion is that people become increasingly despondent, apathetic, and resigned to their circumstances with the prolongation of homelessness, and they concentrate on short-term needs, such as acquiring food and shelter, rather than on planning ahead and developing strategies to change their situation (Liebow 1993; Morse 1992; Rowe and Wolch 1990). In the 1930s, Sutherland and Locke (1936) observed that homeless men in Chicago shelters became apathetic over time, neglected their appearance, and gave up the struggle to find work and accommodation.

Demoralization, depression and hopelessness not only prolong homelessness, but these negative states often preceded and contributed to the *entry* to homelessness for many subjects in the Four-City and Lancefield Street Centre studies. Many had felt desperate and hopeless when their wives died or their marriages broke down and they drank heavily, made suicidal gestures, became unsettled, and abandoned their homes or did not seek alternative housing when they had to leave their accommodation. One widower explained: 'I was married for 35 years; when my wife died I sold my house and slept rough; I was unsettled, desperate and never thought about not having anywhere to live; I just wanted to get away from everything.' One woman left her home at the age of 69 years after a succession of arguments with her son and her daughter-in-law who had been living with her for six years. Just before becoming homeless, she was depressed and had taken an overdose.

From the subjects' reports, feelings of desperation and hopelessness continued once they were homeless, and many never tried to secure accommodation and leave homelessness. One man explained: 'once homeless, you do not think about getting a place; your life just goes along one track and you think this is your lot and you have to survive it. You become so numb and used to it that you do not think about getting out of it.' Negative feelings were related both to the dire circumstances of being homeless and to stresses and losses preceding homelessness. Many became distressed and tearful when talking about the death of their spouse or a child, and from their behaviour it was apparent that some had never come to terms with the traumas which had contributed to homelessness. Some men who had become homeless after a marital breakdown years earlier, said that they still felt upset and angry towards their wives, and preferred to be alone and have no contact with people (Chapter 4). Comments included, 'I cry about living' and 'I'm laughing but I'm crying at the same time'. Several associated heavy drinking and transience with depression and hopelessness, and two men were writing a book 'to try and get rid of the past'.

Hopelessness has been defined as 'an expectation that highly desired outcomes are unlikely to occur or that highly aversive outcomes are likely to occur, and that no response in one's repertoire will change the likelihood of occurrence of these outcomes' (Alloy *et al.* 1988: 7). People who experience negative life events are more likely to have low self-esteem and feel helpless, hopeless and depressed if their situation appears to be enduring rather than short-lived, if it affects a range of circumstances rather than a specific situation, if they blame themselves for the situation rather than external factors, and if they perceive the events as important (Abramson *et al.* 1978). Homelessness among some older people has lasted for more than 15 years and has affected their entire lifestyle. Most have given up tenancies, severed family ties, and abandoned all links with mainstream society.

Depression is reported to be the 'silent problem of homelessness' which immobilizes people and deters them from seeking and accepting help (La Gory *et al.* 1990; Lamb and Lamb 1990). Some reports suggest that one-half to three-quarters of homeless people are depressed and demoralized (Belcher and DiBlasio 1990). In Chicago, the highest rates of depression were found among homeless people aged under 25 years and over 45 years (Rossi *et al.* 1986). In New York City, two-fifths of older street men were described as being 'pervasively depressed' and nearly one-third wished that they were

Homelessness is a state of demoralization and depression

dead (Cohen and Sokolovsky 1989: 166). Self-reports of depression were common among the residents at the Lancefield Street Centre, who had few aspirations or hopes for the future. In the month before being interviewed, three-fifths (of 70 subjects) had felt depressed some or most of the time. Less than half (43 per cent) felt hopeful about the future, and 29 per cent described it as bleak. When asked what they hoped to be doing in six months' time, 27 per cent said that they hoped to be rehoused while a similar proportion said that they were likely to be dead. Those who denied feeling depressed described the future as hopeful, whereas those who reported feeling depressed viewed it negatively.

The majority of those who talked positively about the future had recently become homeless and were motivated to re-establish roles and ties in mainstream society. One man had first become homeless at the age of 58 years and had been homeless for three months when interviewed. He had worked until the time he became homeless, and said that his goal was 'to get my pride back again. I want a job, accommodation, and sufficient money to look after myself. I want to be self-reliant, happy and content again.' Many of those who talked negatively about the future were heavy drinkers.

Heavy drinking

Alcoholism has been strongly associated with homelessness in Britain and America, with terms such as 'bums', 'winos' and 'alcoholic derelicts' being applied to heavy drinkers (Edwards *et al.* 1966; Peterson and Maxwell 1958; Jackson and Connor 1953). Some homeless people drink together in 'schools' or 'bottle gangs', while others are solitary drinkers. Many older Bowery men changed from drinking in groups to solitary drinking as they aged and half said that they mostly drank alone (Cohen and Sokolovsky 1989). Although many still drank heavily, their consumption level had diminished with age due to poor health, loss of interest and limited finances. At the Lancefield Street Centre, some older heavy drinkers form a drinking school, some are solitary drinkers and drink alone in their bedroom or with just one or two companions, while a few drink with friends on the streets. Some older homeless men have been drinking heavily for more than 25 years. They tend to drink cheap but strong beers, lagers, cider, wine, and occasionally spirits. Several admitted to once drinking 'jake' (methylated spirits) and 'white lady' (surgical spirits and water).

Heavy drinking sometimes precedes homelessness, but in other cases is a consequence or at least a sequela of homelessness (Rosenthal 1994; Cohen and Sokolovsky 1989; Koegel and Burnam 1988). One elderly man who became homeless after serving 22 years in the army, said that he had always been a regular drinker while in the armed forces as 'it was part of the culture and lifestyle'. His consumption increased once he left the forces and was homeless. He said, 'alcoholism is an insidious illness; it creeps up on you'. The belief is that homeless people use alcohol as a means to escape from the problems which contributed to homelessness, a device for coping with the physical conditions and stresses of homelessness, and as a way of alleviating loneliness and boredom by socializing within a 'drinking group'. Spradley (1970: 177–8) noted that drinking provides homeless men 'with a group of friends . . . if a man stops drinking and sharing drinks, he cuts himself off from the most valuable of all resources, human companionship and acceptance'.

Among the Four-City Study sample, older homeless men associated heavy drinking with several factors. Some related it to stresses they had been through before becoming homeless. One man said: 'I drink to blot out memories. You have a drink to escape, but you cannot really escape.' According to another: 'I still get nightmares at night. I remember the torture I suffered as a prisoner of war. If I've been drinking, I'm less likely to wake up screaming.' Several men associated heavy drinking with depression and feelings of despair and hopelessness. Comments included: 'you drink to numb your mind; to escape from this torture; being homeless is a life of mental and physical torture'; 'alcohol is a substitute for depression . . . when I drink it blots out unhappy memories'; and 'you drink when you realize that there is nothing ahead for you; when you look at your life, you realize that any future you had is now in the past'.

Among the residents at the Lancefield Street Centre, heavy drinking is associated with higher levels of self-reported depression and pessimism

(Crane and Warnes 1998). Some drink heavily, neglect their self-care, repeatedly fall, are doubly incontinent when drunk and have to be assisted with bathing. Some continue to drink even though they have serious physical health problems including renal failure, cirrhosis of the liver, and peripheral neuropathy, and know that alcohol is damaging their health. One man said: 'the doctors have told me that if I don't stop drinking I shall be dead in six months'. To decline to such degrading behaviour whereby one entirely loses self-respect and responsibility for one's life indicates the severity of desperation and hopelessness among people who have once held responsible jobs, married and raised families, and owned their homes. Similar problems of alcohol dependence, self-neglect, loss of self-respect and self-esteem, and 'giving up' were noted among older homeless men at a shelter in Seattle (Elias and Inui 1993).

Some Lancefield Street Centre residents were admitted to hospital or a **detoxification unit** for a few weeks, during which time they did not drink alcohol and their appetite improved. When they were discharged, however, they soon started drinking again. Abstaining from alcohol is likely to be difficult. Many have lost their family, home, job and friends, they have severe and incurable physical health problems caused by years of heavy drinking, they are depressed and perceive their situation as hopeless, and thus may have little motivation to stop drinking. Furthermore, the decision not to drink means avoiding drinking companions who are generally their only social contacts, and finding ways to fill the hours that have formerly been spent drinking.

Heavy drinking is generally associated with homelessness because such people tend to drink in groups in city centres and parks and are easily visible. But many older homeless people are non-drinkers. In Los Angeles, New York, the Tampa Bay cities (Florida), and in the British Four-City Study, 36–47 per cent of older homeless people were found to be non-drinkers, and only 13–40 per cent regular or heavy drinkers (Rich *et al.* 1995; Ladner 1992; Welte and Barnes 1992; Gelberg *et al.* 1990). Older homeless women are less likely than older homeless men to drink heavily. In New York City, 63 per cent of 281 older homeless men but only 8 per cent of 201 older homeless women were moderate, binge or heavy drinkers (Cohen *et al.* 1997; Cohen and Sokolovsky 1989). The men sleeping rough were more likely than those in shelters to drink heavily. At a shelter for homeless people in New York City, it was also found that elderly men were three times more likely than elderly women to be heavy drinkers (Ladner 1992). In the Four-City Study sample, only 12 per cent of the women but 42 per cent of the men drank regularly (Table 9.1). The sex differences were statistically significant.

Compared to elderly housed people, older homeless people are more likely to be either non-drinkers or heavy drinkers. The British General Household Survey of 1994 found that among those over the age of 65 years, 12 per cent of men and 24 per cent of women never drank alcohol, and one-third of the men and 17 per cent of the women were moderate or heavy drinkers (Bennett *et al.* 1996: Table 5.7). Older homeless people in the Four-City Study were therefore more likely than elderly housed people in Great Britain to be non-drinkers, older homeless women had especially low consumption, but a

Table 9.1   Drinking patterns of the Four-City Study subjects

Drinking pattern	Men		Women	
	No.	*%*	*No.*	*%*
Does not drink	36	25	47	80
Drinks occasionally[1]	50	34	5	8
Drinks regularly[2]	61	42	7	12
Total known	147	101	59	100
Not known	12		7	
Total subjects	159		66	

[1] Twice a week or less
[2] At least three times a week or excessively for one or two days

higher proportion of older homeless men were heavy drinkers. Similarly, in New York State, homeless people over the age of 50 years were more likely than housed people of that age to be both non-drinkers and heavy drinkers (Welte and Barnes 1992).

Mental illness

British studies indicate that 30–50 per cent of single homeless people have mental health problems, including 12–26 per cent who have schizophrenia or other serious mental illness which severely impairs social functioning (Pleace and Quilgars 1996; Connelly and Crown 1994; George *et al.* 1991). The prevalence of mental health problems is reported to be considerably higher among single homeless people in Britain and America, particularly rough sleepers, than among the general population (Bines 1994; Fischer and Breakey 1991). Mental illness sometimes occurs after the onset of homelessness, but in other cases precedes it (North *et al.* 1998; Winkleby and White 1992). High rates of mental illness have been reported among older homeless people in Britain and America. Between 40 and 68 per cent of older homeless men in London, New York and Detroit were estimated to be depressed (Crane 1994; Cohen and Sokolovsky 1989; Douglass *et al.* 1988), and 40–65 per cent of older homeless women and 28–31 per cent of older homeless men in London, New York and Chicago displayed psychotic symptoms or were found to have memory problems (Cohen *et al.* 1997; Crane 1994; Cohen and Sokolovsky 1989; Kutza 1987). In New York City, some 'bag ladies' were found by physicians to be suffering from 'paranoia, organic brain syndrome, senility and psychosis' (Schwam 1979: 22). In Chicago, homeless women over the age of 40 years were found to be more 'confused and incoherent' than other age–gender groups (Rossi *et al.* 1986: 81).

Two-thirds of older homeless people in the Four-City Study reported or were observed to have mental health problems (Table 9.2). One-third denied having any problem (and there was no sign to the contrary). One-half denied

Table 9.2 Mental health of the Four-City Study subjects at the time of interview

Mental health	Men		Women		Total	
	No.	*%*	*No.*	*%*	*No.*	*%*
No reported or apparent problem	63	41	7	11	70	32
Reported problem[1]: no treatment	19	12	4	6	23	11
Reported problem[1]: having treatment	11	7	7	11	18	8
Unreported but apparent problem[2]	62	40	46	72	108	49
Total known	155	100	64	100	219	100
Not known	4		2		6	
Total subjects	159		66		215	

[1] Self-reports of depression or schizophrenia
[2] Symptoms of a psychotic illness and/or memory problems

mental health problems, but psychotic symptoms or memory problems were observed. Some expressed persecutory ideas commonly associated with royalty, politicians or neighbours, some were hallucinating and responding to imaginary voices, while others were disorientated and confused and produced seriously inconsistent responses to questions. The women were more likely than the men to have mental health problems and to have unreported problems. The sex differences were statistically significant. Those over the age of 65 years were more likely than those aged 55–64 years to have unreported problems (58 and 38 per cent, respectively). Although mental health problems were common, less than one-tenth were receiving psychiatric medication. Similarly, many older homeless men in New York City had mental health problems but were receiving no treatment (Cohen and Sokolovsky 1989).

Those sleeping rough were exceptionally likely (75 per cent) to have unreported problems (Table 9.3). Older men sleeping rough in New York City were also found to have higher rates of depression and severe psychotic symptoms than those in shelters (Cohen and Sokolovsky 1989)

For some older homeless people, mental health problems prevent them from providing realistic information about their circumstances. In Chicago, some subjects were extremely confused when contacted and were unable to give details as to why they had become homeless. Attention had been drawn to their situation because they were found on the streets wandering or displaying disturbed behaviour (Kutza 1987). Similarly, in the Four-City Study, one man was interviewed ten times, was deluded at each interview, and could not provide realistic information. He stated that he was 100 years old (this was incorrect), then later said he was 30,000 years old as he was from the moon. When asked about his family, he said he had a son but 'I'm not sure if I'm the father or grandfather because all my family are 90 years old and they are from the moon'. One woman repeatedly expressed delusions about death, giants and space. She described how 'monsters with machinery inside them are sending out laser rays to attack me, . . . freezing gas is coming up

Table 9.3   Mental health of the Four-City Study subjects by type of accommodation

Mental health problems	Sleeping rough		In temporary accommodation		In permanent housing	
	No.	%	No.	%	No.	%
No reported or apparent problem	15	22	38	39	17	33
Reported problem[1]: no treatment	2	3	13	13	8	15
Reported problem[1]: having treatment	0	0	13	13	5	10
Unreported but apparent problem[2]	52	75	34	35	22	42
Total known	69	100	98	100	52	100
Not known	2		4		0	
Total subjects	71		102		52	

[1] Depression or schizophrenia
[2] Symptoms of a psychotic illness and/or memory problems

from the ground and it will choke me, . . . blood and urine is coming out of the food'. When asked where she was born, she replied: 'I was hurled from a star'.

For some older rough sleepers, a mental illness distorts their perceptions of reality, and influences their capacity to seek and accept services, and thus helps to sustain homelessness. Out-reach workers in London and New York City have found that this group are the most difficult to engage and some persistently refuse help (Crane and Warnes 1998; Cohen *et al.* 1992). In the Four-City Study, one elderly woman had been sleeping rough for years and had severe memory problems. She repeatedly said that she wanted accommodation but refused offers of help because she believed that 'a friend' was finding her somewhere to live. A man aged in his sixties had been sleeping rough for seven years and was extremely paranoid. He refused to access day centres or soup kitchens because he believed that the staff were terrorists: 'they are killing people; they cut off your legs so you cannot escape and cut off your arms so that you cannot write or phone for help'. Mental health problems also contribute to transience among some older homeless men, who never stay in one town long enough to benefit from services (see Chapter 8).

Complex syndromes: mental illness and alcoholism

Since the late 1980s, there has been increasing attention to the problem of coincident severe chronic mental illness and substance abuse (alcohol or drugs) among homeless people. American reports suggest that 10–25 per cent of homeless people are chronically mentally ill and dependent on alcohol or drugs (Breakey 1996; Wright 1989; Koegel *et al.* 1988). In Britain, 38 per cent of 440 residents of cold-weather shelters in 1996–97 were so classified (O'Leary 1997). Likewise, 59 per cent of mentally ill homeless people in contact with the **Homeless Mentally Ill Initiative** (HMII) teams[1] in

London regularly abused alcohol or drugs (Craig 1995). Those with combined problems tend to be men, sleeping rough, with long histories of homelessness. Their lifestyle is often described as 'extremely disorganized' and 'chaotic', many have poor everyday living skills, and are particularly difficult to help. Among 547 mentally ill homeless people seen by the HMII teams in London, 19 per cent also had a history of violence (Craig 1995).

Several European studies have demonstrated a link between schizophrenia and problem drinking among housed populations, with 22–43 per cent of schizophrenics also drinking heavily or misusing drugs (Johnson 1997). It is believed that some psychotic people, regardless of their housing status, use alcohol as a form of self-medication, as a way of gaining access to a social group, as a relief from boredom and inactivity, and as a means of coping with stressful relationships and situations (Rosenthal 1994). The problems are generally interlinked. At the Lancefield Street Centre, one elderly woman was deluded, believed that the air contained gases which would harm her, and drank heavily because she was distressed by these ideas. Another resident drank heavily which induced psychotic thoughts and disturbed behaviour. His symptoms subsided when he was admitted to hospital and stopped drinking. Several people in the Four-City Study associated heavy drinking with 'bad nerves'. One man said: 'I suffer from hallucinations and depression; when I'm sober I think people are watching me and talking about me. When I drink I become insensitive to people and what they're thinking.'

Drug abuse is rare among older homeless people (Rich *et al.* 1995; Fischer and Breakey 1991; Wright 1989). But in the Four-City Study sample, 9 per cent of the women and 25 per cent of the men were both mentally ill and heavy drinkers. Those with dual problems tended to be sleeping rough (34 per cent of rough sleepers compared to 18 per cent of hostel residents) and relatively young (28 per cent aged 55–64 years compared to 14 per cent aged 65 years or more). Almost half (48 per cent) had been homeless for at least ten years, and 26 per cent for more than 20 years. At the Lancefield Street Centre, a small proportion of older homeless men with histories of heavy drinking and mental illness have displayed severe behavioural problems and have been evicted for violence, sexual misdemeanours, and for starting fires.

Physical health problems

Homelessness increases the prevalence of physical health problems. It may cause health problems or aggravate existing illnesses: 'risks to health are likely to increase the further a homeless person gets from being in adequate housing. The risks of infectious disease rise as soon as accommodation is cramped, overcrowded or insanitary, and the risks to physical health are likely to be at their most extreme when people are living on the streets' (Pleace and Quilgars 1996: 35, 42). More than one ill-health condition was reported by approximately 58 per cent of those sleeping rough who used day centres or soup kitchens, by 38 per cent of homeless people in hostels and bed-and-breakfast hotels, and by only 24 per cent of the general population in the 1991 British Household Panel Survey (Bines 1994).

Health problems among older homeless people are exacerbated by age, their lifestyle and lack of treatment. Those who sleep rough are at risk of exposure, hypothermia and frostbite. Hypothermia is more common among older people and it often occurs in association with other pre-existing medical conditions such as alcoholism (Balazs 1993). Although some older rough sleepers wear several layers of clothing and use blankets, sleeping bags and cardboard to keep warm, others are inadequately dressed and lack bedding. One man said: 'I have sometimes woken up frozen and my mind seems to be in one place and my body in another; it makes me feel deranged.' Another said that on waking in winter he has been covered in ice and as he has moved, 'I've heard the ice cracking over my body; I've been so numb, it took hours before I got going'. Another elderly man who had slept rough for years was admitted to hospital with frostbite and gangrene; both his feet needed to be amputated.

Older homeless people, particularly those who sleep rough, often live in cold, damp insanitary conditions, some eat food from litter bins and have poor diets, and a few use crowded and badly ventilated soup kitchens and day centres. Infections are widespread and they are susceptible to diseases such as gastro-enteritis and tuberculosis, and to malnutrition and skin infestations, notably scabies and lice (Connelly and Crown 1994; Jahiel 1992; Brickner *et al*. 1986). Poor nutrition increases the risk of infections, such as tuberculosis, and may lead to cognitive disabilities, loss of energy, apathy and retardation (Balazs 1993; Belcher and DiBlasio 1990; Winick 1985). Older rough sleepers often have inadequate sleep, are faced daily with the problems of acquiring food and shelter, and are at risk of assault. One elderly man said: 'on the streets you have to live like a deer; always be on the alert'. Severe stress can aggravate conditions such as hypertension among those who are genetically predisposed (Wright, 1990).

Some older homeless people walk miles each day to street handouts, are often 'moved on' if they occupy seats at railway stations or in cafés, and wander around the streets at night for fear of being attacked if they rest. Prolonged standing and persistent walking, sometimes in ill-fitting shoes, provokes circulatory problems such as leg ulcers, oedema and cellulitis, and foot problems such as blisters and corns. Alcohol abuse is linked to high rates of physical illnesses and early mortality (Fischer and Breakey 1991; Struening and Padgett 1990; Wright 1989; Morgan *et al*. 1985). It leads to nutritional deficiencies, particularly of the vitamin B group, upper respiratory infections, active tuberculosis, neurological disorders including Korsakoff's syndrome, seizures, cirrhosis of the liver, gastro-intestinal and pancreatic disorders, cardiac problems, hypertension, peripheral vascular disease, and eye problems. Older homeless people who drink heavily tend to be in poorer physical health (Crane and Warnes 1998; Cohen and Sokolovsky 1989).

Physical illnesses

Homeless people experience higher levels of physical illness than housed people, across a broad range of conditions. They are more likely than the general population to suffer from neurological disorders, particularly epilepsy, gastro-intestinal problems, musculoskeletal disorders, and from respiratory disorders, particularly pneumococcal pneumonia, chronic obstructive airways disease and tuberculosis (Connelly and Crown 1994; Wright 1990). The self-reported health problems of 1,786 single homeless people in Britain in 1991 were compared with those of 10,264 housed people in the British Household Panel Survey in 1991, and the data were standardized by age and gender (Table 9.4). The prevalence of health problems was higher among homeless people than among the general population for all problems except heart conditions, and was particularly high among rough sleepers. The survey of single homeless people only included rough sleepers who used day centres and soup runs and were therefore amenable to accept help. Many older rough sleepers do not use services, have untreated physical health problems, and it can be assumed that the prevalence of physical health problems will be even higher among this group.

Common physical health problems among older homeless people include bronchitis and pneumonia, chronic obstructive airways disease, hypertension, arthritis, peripheral vascular diseases such as leg ulcers and cellulitis, diabetes, gastro-intestinal problems, neurological disorders, and infestations (Gelberg *et al.* 1990; Douglass *et al.* 1988). In Chicago, 66 per cent of older homeless men and 74 per cent of older homeless women were in poor health

Table 9.4 Standardized morbidity rates[1] of health problems among homeless people

Health problem	In hostels/bed-and-breakfast hotels	Sleeping rough	
		Seen at day centres	Seen at soup runs
Musculoskeletal problems	153	185	221
Wounds, skin ulcers, skin complaints	105	189	298
Chronic chest or breathing problems	183	259	365
Heart problems	54	64	66
Digestive problems	183	244	265
Fits or loss of consciousness[2]	651	2,109	1,892
Frequent headaches	264	338	365
Depression, anxiety, nerves	785	1,072	1,152
Number in sample	1,280	351	155

Sources: Bines (1997: Table 9.3), using Single Homeless People Survey data (1991) and British Household Panel Survey (BHPS) data (1991)

[1] Standardized by age and gender. The figures should be interpreted as follows: a value of 100 indicates no difference between the rate of health problems among single homeless people and the general population; a value above 100 indicates that the health of single homeless people is worse than that of the general population; and a value below 100 indicates that their health is better. For example, a value of 500 would mean that the health of homeless people is five times as bad as that of the general population

[2] Different definitions were used: the survey of single homeless people used 'fits or loss of consciousness', while the BHPS used the term 'epilepsy'

(Kutza 1987). In New York City, 35 per cent of older homeless street men compared to only 12 per cent of elderly men in the general population had been in hospital in one year (Cohen and Sokolovsky 1989).

In the early 1990s, high rates of active tuberculosis were reported among homeless people in London, the most vulnerable being middle-aged and elderly men who were heavy drinkers and slept rough or stayed in hostels. Of 114 homeless people over the age of 60 years, 5 per cent had active tuberculosis. In contrast, the reported incidence of tuberculosis in the general population of England and Wales in 1993 was just 0.01 per cent (Citron *et al.* 1995). The incidence of tuberculosis is reported to be rising in the USA and in Denmark, Norway, Italy, Ireland, and England and Wales (Connelly and Crown 1994). Homeless people are susceptible to the disease and to old lesions becoming reactivated because of their general ill health and poor diet, poor compliance with treatment, and because early detection and treatment is rare. For some, tuberculosis infections are drug-resistant because either they have failed to comply with treatment or they have been infected with resistant organisms by others who were not treated properly.

Many older rough sleepers have severe physical health problems which become apparent when they accept hostel residency or are in contact with services. On admission to the hostel at Lancefield Street, many had been sleeping rough and drinking heavily for years, and 76 per cent had physical health problems. One-third had major physical illnesses which required hospital treatment, including advanced carcinomas, internal haemorrhaging, tuberculosis, jaundice and ascites from liver and renal failure, severe anaemia (requiring blood transfusion), and uncontrolled epileptic seizures (Crane and Warnes 1998). Others had chronic problems, such as arthritis and bronchitis, for which they needed medication.

Injury from accidents and assault

Injury from accidents and assaults is common among homeless street people (Brickner *et al.* 1986; Kelly 1985). They are reported to be 50 times more likely than the general population to be fatally assaulted, and twice as likely to die in an accident (Grenier 1996). Those who are older are exceptionally vulnerable to violence and accidents if they are frail, have poor mobility, and their senses are impaired by lack of sleep, heavy drinking or mental illness. Some sleep in derelict buildings to avoid being attacked. But these sites may be structurally unsafe and dangerous. One elderly man in the Four-City Study slept in woods, had no sleeping bag or blankets, and lit a fire for warmth. While asleep one night, he rolled onto the fire and burned his clothing and hands. A second man lost an eye after being kicked in the face while asleep in a doorway. Another was set alight and suffered severe burns while sleeping in a derelict building. In New York City, more than one-third of older Bowery men compared to only 2 per cent of elderly men in the general population had been attacked and injured in one year (Cohen and Sokolovsky 1989). Similarly, one-third of older homeless people in Detroit had been attacked and injured in a year, and those over the age of 65 years were most likely to have been assaulted (Douglass *et al.* 1988).

Mortality rates

Mortality rates among homeless people are high compared with the overall population; the average age of death of people who are recorded as homeless when they die (from coroners' reports) is variously reported between 42 and 53 years (Grenier 1996; Keyes and Kennedy 1992; Alstrom *et al.* 1975). Among 30,000 homeless people in the National Health Care for the Homeless Program in 16 American cities, the average age of death of 88 subjects was 53 years, and the conclusion was that homeless men die some 20 or so years earlier than normal (Wright 1989). The suggestion is therefore that many long-term homeless people die before they reach old age, and that older homeless people are either a minority of survivors or those who became homeless late in life. But there have only been a few studies of mortality among homeless people, they have generally produced limited information, and they have not examined the relationship between duration of homelessness and age of death.

Mortality patterns among 78 homeless men who had resided in large lodging-houses in Manchester and who had died between 1977 and 1981 have been analysed by Shanks (1984). Homeless men were found to be more likely than the general population to die from tuberculosis, bronchitis, emphysema, asthma and malignant disease, but less likely to die from heart and cerebrovascular diseases. In Stockholm, mortality rates among 6,032 homeless men registered at the Bureau for Homeless Men (social welfare department) were monitored between 1969 and 1971, and the deaths of 327 subjects were compared with those of the general male population (Alstrom *et al.* 1975). The mortality rate among homeless men aged 50–59 years was four times as high as that among the general male population: 89 died instead of an expected 23. Among those aged 60 years and over, 123 homeless men died instead of an expected 49. Mortality rates were higher among homeless people than among the general male population for all causes of death, including respiratory diseases, mainly pneumonia (28 observed deaths was seven times higher than an expected 4 deaths), cirrhosis of the liver (26 observed deaths was six times higher than an expected 4.2 deaths), diseases of the circulatory system (90 observed deaths was three times higher than an expected 34.7 deaths), diseases of the digestive system (19 observed deaths was seven times higher than an expected 2.6 deaths), and accidents and assault (65 observed deaths was 12 times higher than an expected 5.5 deaths). Alcoholism was identified as the cause of death among 36 homeless men, and an important contributory factor for many others.

Two British studies have recently investigated mortality among homeless people. The first examined the deaths of 86 rough sleepers in London between 1991 and 1992, and found that 17 per cent had been due to natural causes, 13 per cent to pneumonia or hypothermia, 26 per cent to accidents or assault, 23 per cent to suicide, and 18 per cent to drugs or alcohol (Keyes and Kennedy 1992). The second study examined the deaths of 74 rough sleepers in London, Manchester and Bristol in 1995–96, found that 34 per cent had been due to natural causes, 14 per cent to pneumonia or hypothermia, 8 per cent to accidents or assault, 22 per cent to suicide, and 19 per cent to drugs or alcohol, and concluded that rough sleepers are 35 times more likely than the general population to commit suicide (Grenier 1996). The findings have to be treated cautiously. The two studies excluded hostel residents although the majority of homeless people are so housed, and the records of death were inconsistent as some used an address of a relative or a hostel for ex-rough sleepers.

Problems of accessing and delivering health-care

Although physical health problems are common among older homeless people, many do not receive appropriate treatment for several reasons. Many general practitioners are reluctant to register homeless people, particularly those sleeping rough, because they tend to have multiple health problems and are thus expensive patients, they often do not keep appointments and comply with treatment, and they are likely to move around and not stay in one area (Pleace and Quilgars 1996; Williams and Avebury 1995; Fisher and Collins 1993; Williams and Allen 1989). Some general practitioners will accept hostel residents only as temporary patients. This arrangement means that medical records are not transferred from the previous GP, and it is thus difficult to provide continuity of care (Connelly and Crown 1994).

Many homeless people do not have a general practitioner. In Sheffield in the late 1980s, one-third of homeless people in hostels and bed-and-break-fast hotels were not registered with a general practitioner (George *et al.* 1991). In London, 65 per cent of rough sleepers at one project and 76 per cent of rough sleepers and hostel residents at a second project were not registered with a general practitioner (Balazs 1993; Fisher and Collins 1993). In 1987, only one-third of homeless people over the age of 65 years at a health-care project in Camden, London, and only 55 per cent at an east London project, were registered with a general practitioner (Williams and Allen 1989). At the Lancefield Street Centre, the staff have experienced difficulties in obtaining primary health-care services for residents. Most local general practitioners were unwilling to register the residents, and most residents were without a general practitioner from September to December 1997 (Crane and Warnes 1998).

Instead of accessing general practitioners, homeless people sometimes use hospital accident and emergency departments when physically ill. Nearly three-quarters of older homeless men in New York City primarily used hospitals for medical care, and less than one in 13 used a local doctor (Cohen *et al.* 1988). Some hospital staff, however, regard homeless people as 'problem patients' using hospital emergency services inappropriately for minor ailments or chronic problems, or as people whose health problems are self-inflicted, for example due to heavy drinking (Pleace and Quilgars 1996; Williams and Allen 1989). The outcome is that homeless people are sometimes stigmatized, kept waiting many hours before being seen by a doctor, given cursory treatment, and inappropriately discharged with serious problems but no adequate follow-up care. An older homeless man was turned away untreated from a London hospital casualty department twice because he was considered to be drunk. He soon after died of a brain haemorrhage on the streets (Fisher and Collins 1993). Some reports indicate that only a small proportion of homeless attenders use hospital emergency services inappropriately (Hinton 1992; Maitra 1982). In contrast, at the Accident and Emergency Department of the University College Hospital, London, in 1992, 57 per cent of 3,489 visits by homeless people were deemed inappropriate; most of this group, however, were not registered with a general practitioner (North *et al.* 1996).

The reluctance of general practitioners to register homeless people is compounded by the attitude of many homeless people who perceive their health as a low priority, expect to be refused registration, and do not seek medical care. Those sleeping rough sometimes 'suffer from poor physical health which remains untreated until the disease has reached an advanced state' (Fisher and Collins 1993: 41). Many older homeless people do not seek medical help when they are ill, a finding in both London and New York City (Crane and Warnes 1998; Cohen *et al.* 1988). On admission to the Lancefield Street Centre, several older street people had severe problems yet had not sought medical care. One man had a carcinoma of the mouth, and another had cataracts in both eyes and was nearly blind. There were several reasons why they had not sought help. Some did not recognize the severity of their illness; some could not manage the 'bureaucracy' of doctors' surgeries with appointment systems and busy waiting-areas, and feared being stigmatized by staff; while others were depressed, had low self-esteem, feared illness and mistrusted doctors.

Many older homeless people need supervision with health-care once they are in contact with services. At the Lancefield Street Centre, some residents were unmotivated or unable to self-medicate, some had to be encouraged to have treatments such as dressings, and doctors' appointments had to be arranged for them. The staff had to escort some residents to medical and hospital appointments. The Three Boroughs Primary Health Care Team works with homeless people in hostels and day centres in the London boroughs of Lambeth, Southwark and Lewisham. Its nurses have found that they also have to escort some older clients to hospitals and clinics as many would not keep appointments if unescorted. Some are confused and forgetful, while others have low self-esteem and fear being stigmatized by health-care workers. Some older homeless people refuse to comply with medical care. Some hostel residents at Lancefield Street refused to attend medical appointments or allow nurses to dress infected leg ulcers. A few were admitted to hospital but discharged themselves before treatment was completed. Similar problems of non-compliance were noted in Chicago, particularly among older homeless men (Kutza 1987).

There are particular problems in treating people who are homeless when they become ill. There are problems of providing continuity of care for those with acute and chronic illnesses who require medication or other treatment but move around. On admission to the Lancefield Street Centre, several residents should have been taking medication for illnesses yet had no tablets and had not seen a doctor for some time. There are also problems in providing care for homeless people who are ill or recovering from an operation or an injury yet do not need to be in hospital. Many have no choice but to recuperate in unsuitable hostel accommodation or on the streets.

Conclusions

Compared to the general older population, homeless older people are in poor mental and physical health, and they have higher morbidity rates for most illnesses except heart conditions. Psychological problems are common and range from generalized feelings of depression and demoralization to heavy drinking, mental illness, and complex syndromes of alcoholism and mental illness. Health problems are interlinked. Demoralization and feelings of hopelessness lead to heavy drinking and clinical depression, and heavy drinking provokes mental and physical illnesses. There are sex differences. Many older homeless women, particularly those sleeping rough, have mental health problems and display disturbed behaviour, but only a minority are heavy drinkers. In contrast, heavy drinking is common among some men, and a small proportion are both heavy drinkers and mentally ill.

Health problems among older homeless people are exacerbated by age, the lifestyle, low self-esteem and morale, and their inability or unwillingness to access services and comply with treatment. As psychological problems intensify and people become more depressed and demoralized or psychotic, some drink heavily, they do not eat, their personal care deteriorates, their physical health problems become exacerbated, and their need for help is more acute. It is at this stage, however, that they are often less amenable to accepting services and are difficult to engage and maintain in treatment programmes. As a result, some die on the streets. An elderly man died in the doorway of a Pizza Hut restaurant in west London, having 'lived' there for at least one year (Penhale 1997). Others are only admitted to hospital when illnesses have become so severe that they require drastic treatment, as with a man whose feet needed to be amputated because of frostbite and gangrene. Some are so depressed and demoralized that they continue to drink alcohol even though they know that it is severely damaging their health.

In New York City, the Homeless Emergency Liaison Project functions as a mobile out-reach unit providing crisis medical and psychiatric services to rough sleepers who are mentally ill, resistant to services, and at risk of physical harm (Marcos *et al.* 1990). It transports people, many aged over 50 years, to hospital, against their will if necessary. Such measures are essential if a person is seriously disabled with mental illness and needs urgent care and attention (Lamb 1990; Susser *et al.* 1990). Belcher (1988b: 398) suggested that 'service providers need to weigh client rights to self-determination against immediate survival needs and the potential mental restoration that could be provided through commitment to a psychiatric hospital'.

Health problems among older homeless people are compounded by the attitudes of many health-care workers who are reluctant to work with the client group, and by the difficulties that homeless people face in accessing health services. Older homeless people have multiple problems and are thus expensive patients. Yet they are likely to be the most needy group in terms of health-care services. Some hostel staff experience difficulties in obtaining health-care for the residents. The problem is likely to be intensified for older homeless people who have low self-esteem and do not know how to access bureaucratic services. As a result, many do not seek help when they become ill. They only come to the attention of services when a disease has reached an advanced stage and their plight is apparent to an out-reach worker, to hostel staff, or to a concerned member of the public.

Note

1 The HMII was set up in 1990 and funded by the Department of Health and the Mental Health Foundation to work with mentally ill rough sleepers (see Chapter 11).

10

Sub-groups of older homeless people and their problems

> *My father was an alcoholic and he died when I was 15. I joined the army soon after. It was nerve-racking and I hated it. I was with a boy named Barry in the army. He was only 19 years old. A huge piece of shrapnel flew past us, slashed him in the neck, and killed him. He died screaming to death. I stood there helpless and could do nothing. I only did three years in the army but it put 10 years on me.*
>
> *(Cyril, homeless since leaving the army in 1947)*

Homeless people are reported to become 'entrenched' or 'engulfed' in homelessness with time (Snow and Anderson 1993; Grigsby *et al*. 1990). They become increasingly detached from conventional social relationships and roles, health and substance abuse problems are exacerbated, and some become increasingly isolated and dysfunctional, while others integrate with homeless people and learn ways of surviving on the streets (Winkleby and White 1992). But the problems and needs of older homeless people differ, and this has implications for the development of services and interventions to help them. Some are in contact with hostels and day centres and thus demonstrate their willingness to accept help, while others are hostile and difficult to engage. Some need treatment for a mental illness, while others require counselling for an unresolved grief or support for an alcohol addiction. Others do not have these problems but need help to settle after having integrated in the homeless community for years and having become accustomed to the lifestyle. This short chapter synthesizes the characteristics, behaviours and problems of older homeless people in the form of a typology. It identifies subgroups with different behaviours, problems and needs. There has previously been little attempt to classify sub-groups of older homeless people with distinct behaviours and needs, although the device is likely to be helpful in the planning and provision of effective services.

Older homeless people differ by whether they regularly sleep rough or use hostels, whether they are isolated or use day centres, soup kitchens and socialize with homeless people, whether they have mental health problems or are heavy drinkers, whether they remain in one town or are transient, whether or not they are in receipt of benefits, whether they have been rehoused since first becoming homeless, and whether they engage in marginal occupations during the day. By first dividing the subjects in the Four-City and the Lancefield Street Centre studies according to their sleeping arrangements, it was possible to chart their characteristics, behaviours and problems. The dimensions examined were sex, experience of rough sleeping, use of hostels and other temporary accommodation, use of day centres and soup kitchens, peer-group contacts, reports of transience, mental health states, drinking habits, daily activities, whether in receipt of benefits, and experiences of rehousing (Table 10.1).

From these dimensions, it was possible to identify salient characteristics and combinations of circumstances, problems and needs, and develop categories of older homeless people with different patterns. For example, some who slept rough were isolated, had mental health problems and never used day centres; others were heavy drinkers, socialized with other homeless drinkers, and sometimes used day centres; yet a third group were isolated but had neither mental health problems nor were heavy drinkers. Using these categories, it was then possible to develop a typology of older homeless people. It was not possible to recognize distinct patterns for all subjects, but 207 in the Four-City Study and 65 in the Lancefield Street Centre Study were categorized into seven sub-groups, each containing distinct features and behaviours (Table 10.2).

The first sub-group of *withdrawn rough sleepers* consisted of 28 men and 22 women who regularly slept rough in isolated spots, and were often hidden, elusive and hostile. Over one-third of the women were so classified. Many had a poor standard of hygiene and dirty clothing, and 16 (five men and 11 women) were typical bag people who hoarded rubbish in luggage-trolleys and old carrier bags. The majority had apparent yet unreported mental health problems, and some displayed disturbed behaviour. They tended to remain in one area, seldom used soup kitchens or day centres, and rejected help. They often had long histories of homelessness and rough sleeping and only one person had ever been rehoused. Because they seldom used soup kitchens, they were not in contact with services which might have been able to help them. Most were not in receipt of welfare benefits. Their mental health problems influenced their ability to seek and accept services. Therefore they remained homeless and isolated on the streets.

Convivial rough sleepers were a group of 47 men and just three women who were heavy drinkers. They tended to congregate in busy public areas and were easily visible. Many socialized with other drinkers and 14 used soup kitchens occasionally. A few drank alone. They slept rough most of the time, although 29 intermittently stayed in hostels. They tended to remain in one town. Eighteen had marked memory difficulties, possibly related to heavy drinking over many years. They had long histories of homelessness and sleeping rough. Six had been rehoused but soon became homeless again. Their reports suggested that loneliness and heavy drinking contributed to failed resettlement.

Active rough sleepers were a small group of 18 men and one woman, mostly under 65 years of age, who stayed in one town. They sometimes worked casually or made money in marginal occupations such as trading phone-cards and

Table 10.1 Dominant sub-groups of older homeless people[1]

Sub-group	Sex	Sleeps rough	Uses hostels[2]	Uses day centres	Works casually[3]	Socializes[4]	Mental illness	Heavy drinking	Transient[5]	Receipt of benefits	Rehousing attempts
I Withdrawn rough sleeper	M + F	Yes	No	No	No	No	Yes	No	No	Rare	No
II Convivial rough sleeper	M	Yes	Some	Some	No	Yes	Some	Yes	No	Some	Rare
III Active rough sleeper	M	Yes	No	Some	Yes	No	No	Rare	No	Yes	Some
IV Transient rough sleeper	M	Yes	Some	No	No	No	Some	Some	Yes	Some	Yes
V Settled hostel resident	M + F	No	Yes	No	No	Some	Some	Some	No	Yes	No
VI Recently homeless	M + F	Some	Some	No	Some	No	Some	Some	Some	Some	No
VII Symptomatically homeless	M + F	No	No	Yes	No	Yes	Some	Some	No	Yes	Yes

[1] Includes housed people displaying homelessness behaviours
[2] Includes former resettlement units
[3] Includes occupations renumerated by gratuities, e.g. collecting luggage-trolleys at railway stations
[4] With homeless people
[5] Frequently moves from town to town

Table 10.2 The frequency of older male and female homeless sub-groups

Sub-group	Men		Women		Total	
	No.	%	No.	%	No.	%
I Withdrawn rough sleeper	28	13	22	35	50	18
II Convivial rough sleeper	47	22	3	5	50	18
III Active rough sleeper	18	9	1	2	19	7
IV Transient rough sleeper	30	14	0	0	30	11
V Passive hostel resident	22	10	12	19	34	13
VI Recently homeless	29	14	8	13	37	14
VII Symptomatically homeless	36	17	16	26	52	19
Total grouped	210		62		272	
Not grouped	17		10		27	
Total subjects	227		72		299	

collecting luggage-trolleys at railway stations. They slept in hidden and in-accessible locations, such as in sheds, which they locked at night for safety reasons, and went to great lengths to protect themselves. Eleven used soup kitchens. Mental health problems were not common, but a few were binge drinkers. Five had been rehoused in the past. In all cases, they had themselves found either private rented or tied accommodation or they had cohabited, suggesting the independent and relatively capable traits manifested by this group.

Transient rough sleepers were a group of 30 men who frequently moved around the country staying in different towns. They slept rough and all except two booked into resettlement units and hostels for brief spells. They were estranged, seldom mixed with homeless people or congregated in public places, and travelled alone. They rarely used soup kitchens. Twelve were heavy drinkers and a further six had been so in the past. Ten said that they had suffered from depression for years. They were difficult to trace except when they booked into temporary accommodation. Seventeen had been rehoused, mostly in shared houses or in accommodation on their own, but soon became homeless again. Some had been resettled on several occasions.

Passive hostel residents consisted of 22 men and 12 women who had stayed in hostels for years. Most women (ten) and four men were mentally ill, and nine men were heavy drinkers. They generally did not use soup kitchens. Some integrated with residents, while others were isolated. They had 'settled' in a hostel and only four had been rehoused for a short time.

The sixth group, the *recently homeless*, consisted of 29 men and eight women who had been homeless for less than 12 months. Some used hostels, others slept rough. Thirteen had mental health problems, and eight were heavy drinkers. None had as yet been resettled. Possibly because of their 'newness' to homelessness, they tended to be isolated from homeless people and did not use soup kitchens.

The seventh group, the *symptomatically homeless*, consisted of 36 men and 16 women. They had permanent housing, but were estranged from their family and regularly used soup kitchens and congregated on the streets with homeless people. Thirty-five reported or had apparent mental health problems, and ten were heavy drinkers. The majority had once been homeless. They were living alone, and said that they were lonely, unsettled in their accommodation, and were finding it difficult to manage at home. Generally, they were willing to use services and make known their health, welfare and housing needs.

This typology prompts several observations. Homelessness among older people is often a hidden problem, and the older people who are seen at soup kitchens or on the streets with homeless people are often not themselves homeless. Apart from those who are heavy drinkers and are visible in public areas, those sleeping rough are not readily found. They remain in hidden locations or frequently move between towns; both are behaviours which maximize detachment and anonymity. There are sex differences. Many men who sleep rough are heavy drinkers who integrate with homeless people, while some are transient. The women who sleep rough are generally isolated, have mental health problems, and are rarely transient.

Only certain groups of older homeless people have ever been resettled, and this is not necessarily related to their contact with services. The majority of withdrawn rough sleepers and convivial rough sleepers had never been rehoused. This might be attributed to their poor contact with hostels and day centres. But passive hostel residents had also rarely been rehoused. By virtue of being in a hostel, they were continuously in contact with services.

Different services are needed for different groups of older homeless people. Withdrawn rough sleepers are isolated, elusive, reluctant to use services, and the majority have mental health problems. Street out-reach workers are required to seek out this difficult client group, build trust, and encourage them to accept help. Convivial rough sleepers are heavy drinkers who occasionally book into hostels. Once again, street out-reach workers are required to persuade the group to use hostels. The group also require encouragement and help by out-reach workers and hostel staff to reduce or control their drinking, and possibly counselling for unresolved traumas. Active rough sleepers are fairly independent and self-reliant. Street out-reach workers need to find out what type of help and support this group are willing to accept, and to develop effective **rehabilitation** and resettlement programmes.

Transient rough sleepers are isolated and frequently move from town to town. Out-reach workers and hostel staff need to develop effective ways to build trust with the group, and to persuade them to remain in one location, accept basic services such as food and temporary accommodation, and treatment and support for problems. Passive hostel residents have been in hostels for years. Depending on their problems and needs, this group require individualized rehabilitation and resettlement programmes to rehouse them in more appropriate accommodation. To prevent their becoming chronically homeless, recently homeless people need prompt assessments of their problems and needs, treatment and rehabilitation programmes, and resettlement and rehousing packages.

Symptomatically homeless people have permanent housing but display

The problems and needs of older homeless people differ

homelessness behaviours. There needs to be an assessment of their problems and needs by day centre staff and street out-reach workers. Effective monitoring and support need to be developed to enable them to cope at home and prevent homelessness recurring.

The next chapter examines the development of policies and services for homeless people and highlights the ways in which present practices are effectively addressing the needs of older homeless people.

11

British policies and services to address homelessness

I never use day centres and street handouts. They are supposed to be for home-less people but we do not benefit from them. They are dangerous places. Most people who use them are young, have flats, and are aggressive. The real home-less people are the street people but they are too scared to use the centres . . . We live out of litter bins, have nowhere to wash our clothes, and have to urinate in public. We are thrown out of public toilets and launderettes. We are treated worse than dogs.

(Maisie, aged 64, sleeping rough for nearly 10 years)

The development of policies and services for homeless people is complex. Policy-making reflects an understanding of the problem which is a mixture of presumptions and research findings. Services for homeless people compete for scarce resources alongside health- and social care, and older homeless people's needs vie for attention with those of younger homeless people. Policies and services are complicated by different conceptions and understandings of homelessness. At times, homelessness is regarded as crim-inal or antisocial behaviour and produces policies of restraint. A welfarist perspective underpins the policies which marshal help and support, some-times reflecting a social welfare and medical construction that stimulate treatment and rehabilitation programmes, and sometimes focusing on improving the availability of low-cost housing. Homelessness is also seen as a moral problem, and some religious bodies have developed services with salvation in mind.

This chapter reviews how policies and services for homeless people have developed in Britain over the years. It summarizes how policies have been implemented through time, opening with a brief historical review but con-centrating on those which have evolved since the mid-1970s. The develop-ment of services for homeless people during the twentieth century is examined. Particular attention is given to the marked change since the 1970s from services which 'contain' the problem of homelessness to practices which aim at resettling homeless people, and to the 1990s, when the need for ser-vices dedicated to *older* homeless people was recognized.

Evolving policies in relation to homelessness

Policies through the centuries

Legal and humanitarian interventions to address the problem of homelessness in Britain have an exceptionally long history. Policies to control vagrancy date back to the fourteenth century when, following the disestablishment of the monasteries and the Black Death, a large number of people became transient and resorted to begging (Gillin 1929). The first English vagrancy statute was passed in 1349, giving powers to place vagrants in stocks and return them to their parish in carts (Chambliss 1964; Ribton Turner 1887). This was found to be no deterrent, however, as the cart provided free welcome transport and was 'in complete consonance with the wandering habits of vagrants' (George 1966: 359, writing in 1925). Punishments became more severe in the sixteenth and seventeenth centuries, and vagrants were tied naked to a cart and whipped, they were branded and had their ears cut off, while repeated offenders were sentenced to death. Under the Vagrancy Act 1597, some vagrants were banished overseas to the East and West Indies, France, Germany and Spain, and later to the American colonies and Australia (Jütte 1994). Over the years, vagrancy laws and statutes have changed but the Vagrancy Act 1824, amended in 1935, is extant (Home Office 1974). The Vagrancy Act 1824 abandoned the requirement that vagrants should be returned to their place of settlement and instead favoured imprisonment with hard labour (Joseph 1996). Corporal punishment for vagrancy was rarely used after 1900 (Rose 1988).

Although vagrancy and destitution were made criminal offences, it was also recognized that some people were vulnerable, needy, and deserved help. The Elizabethan Poor Law statute was passed in 1601, parishes imposed a tax to meet the needs of their destitute and homeless families, the able-bodied were given 'outdoor relief' while they sought work, and the sick and the old were looked after in residential houses or given licences to beg (Lowe 1997; Burnett 1994; Ribton Turner 1887). The Law of Settlement and Removal 1662, however, allowed parishes to exclude from relief anyone who could not prove a local connection or some right of settlement. From 1722, parishes opened 'workhouses' for those destitute. Growing demands on the Poor Law system prompted the Poor Law Amendment Act 1834, which aimed to end outdoor relief and organize assistance through workhouses. Vagrants could obtain food and shelter in the casual wards attached to workhouses. This only applied in England and Wales. In Scotland, vagrants were unofficially provided with food and shelter in police station cells (Rose 1988; Berry 1978).

While the accommodation at casual wards was free, there were often no beds, the men had to sleep on the floor, and the rules governed by the Pauper Inmates Discharge Act 1871 and the Casual Poor Act 1882 discouraged use. The men had to leave the next day after a compulsory work task, and they were not allowed to stay in any one casual ward more than one night in any month (Rose 1988; Orwell 1949, writing in 1933). The work tasks were similar to those allocated to British prisoners and involved breaking half a ton of stones or picking four pounds of oakum[1] (Brunton 1995; Berry 1978).

Oakum-picking was painful work, for the fingers became raw and would bleed. It was abolished in prisons by 1924 and in casual wards by 1926 (Rose 1988). Those who tried to book into a casual ward more frequently or refused to do the allocated work task were punished, received extra work tasks, and were detained at the workhouses or received 7 or 14 days' imprisonment (Southerton 1993). Work tasks and detention remained 'the theoretical foundation of casual ward discipline and deterrence' until the welfare state became responsible for homelessness in 1948 (Rose 1988: 83–4).

In 1904, the government appointed an Inter-Departmental Committee on Vagrancy which recommended that casual wards should be replaced by labour colonies, or developed as labour exchanges to prevent men tramping around Britain to find work (see Chapter 5). At the time, labour and detention colonies operated in Belgium, Switzerland and Germany. The former accepted vagrants who voluntarily committed themselves to rehabilitation and training, the latter were for those convicted by the courts. The belief was that rehabiliation in labour colonies followed by emigration was the answer to Britain's vagrancy problem (Rose 1988). The Salvation Army had already established a labour colony in Hadleigh, Essex; others were developed, but they were unsuccessful and only lasted a few years.

Policies from 1948 to mid-1970s

In 1948 the Poor Law was replaced by the National Assistance Act and the responsibility for homelessness was allocated to local authority welfare departments. They had a duty to provide 'temporary accommodation for persons who are in urgent need thereof' (cited in Clapham *et al*. 1990: 116). This included homeless women with dependent children but not able-bodied single homeless people. Husbands were excluded from the accommodation, and mothers were expected to have found housing in three months or else they were evicted and their children taken into care. The Act also placed an emphasis on resettling vagrants. Casual wards became the responsibility of the National Assistance Board and known as reception centres, with a duty 'to make provision whereby persons without a settled way of living may be influenced to lead more settled lives' (National Assistance Board 1966: 263), and vagrants became entitled to welfare benefit payments.

During the 1960s and early 1970s, there were marked changes in attitudes to homelessness, instigated by official reports and the concern of voluntary organizations and the public. Concern had been aroused by the increasing number of people sleeping rough in central London, and by the film *Cathy Come Home* in 1966 which depicted the squalid conditions of local authority hostels (Archard 1979). The number of homeless people placed in these hostels had risen substantially, demand outstripped supply, and local authorities were forced to accommodate homeless people in bed-and-breakfast hotels (Rose 1988). Various committees were set up and produced reports on housing and social services, such as the Seebohm Report (Department of Health and Social Security 1969), and the Cullingworth Report (Ministry of Housing & Local Government 1969). Their reports asserted that homelessness was essentially a housing rather than a welfare problem, and that statutory responsibility for homelessness should be transferred to housing departments, which should provide permanent rather than temporary housing to prevent homeless families being separated.

There was also concern about the rising prevalence of mental health and alcohol problems among single homeless people who slept rough or stayed in hostels, lodging-houses and reception centres. The process of deinstitutionalization of mentally ill people had been in progress since 1954, and involved the closure of psychiatric hospitals and the discharge of patients into the community (Timms 1993). This concern prompted a National Survey of Single Homeless People in 1965, and the setting up of working parties in the early 1970s (National Assistance Board 1966). Many single homeless people were reported to be socially inadequate, chronic alcoholics or mentally ill, and recommendations were that help and treatment should be provided by psychiatric and social services through rehabilitation, therapy, specialized hostels, and detoxification centres (Archard 1979; Cook 1979; Home Office 1974).

Policies in the late 1970s and 1980s

Rising concerns about homelessness in the 1960s and 1970s prompted new policies and interventions to address the growing problem. Homelessness was constructed as a housing problem, and its responsibility was transferred by the Housing (Homeless Persons) Act 1977 from local authority social services departments to their housing departments. The Act placed a duty on the latter to secure accommodation for homeless people in priority need, provided that they had not made themselves intentionally homeless (Chapter 2). Those in priority need included people who were vulnerable because of old age, and those who were mentally or physically ill. Most single homeless people were excluded. This legislation echoes the Poor Law principles and was reused in the Housing Act 1985.

The transfer of homelessness responsibility occurred at a time of high unemployment and of pervasive changes in housing provision. From the late 1890s until 1979, local authorities played an important and growing role in the provision of low-cost rented housing, particularly for low-income families (Malpass and Murie, 1994). Although the elaboration of their role had been uneven, they nevertheless had become major providers of accommodation. The Conservative government programme from 1979 diminished the role of local authorities, and housing associations became a key provider of rented housing. At the same time, home ownership was encouraged, council house tenants became eligible to buy their homes, and there was a virtual cessation in housing investment by local authorities.

Organizations established in the 1970s, such as the Campaign for the Homeless and Rootless (CHAR), campaigned for improved housing conditions on behalf of homeless people (Rose 1988). The large traditional hostels and the resettlement units (former reception centres) were castigated as institutional settings with poor standards of privacy and cleanliness, they had a low rate of resettlement, and promoted a 'circuit of homelessnessness' circumscribed to temporary accommodation and the streets (Deacon *et al.* 1993:

4; CHAR 1985; Consortium Joint Planning Group 1981). In 1980 the Hostels Initiative was launched by the government to replace the traditional hostels with smaller, special-needs housing units and hostels (Drake 1989).

Policies in the 1990s

During the late 1980s, there was an increasing number of young homeless people on the streets in central London, an escalating demand for services, and neither voluntary organizations nor the local authorities had the resources to tackle the problem (DoE *et al.* 1995; Randall and Brown 1993). There was little secure, long-term accommodation for resettling homeless people, and the declining number of hostel beds were 'blocked' and unavailable for new homeless people (Spaull and Rowe 1992; Eardley 1989). A social security reform in the late 1980s was reported to have exacerbated the situation, for board-and-lodging allowances were replaced by income support and housing benefit, income support decreased for those under the age of 25 years, and those younger than 18 years were disentitled to benefits (Hutson and Liddiard 1994; Malpass and Murie 1994).

In response to the situation, the Conservative government launched the Rough Sleepers Initiative (RSI) in 1990 with the objective of 'making it unnecessary to have to sleep rough in central London' (DoE *et al.* 1995: 5). The first phase lasted three years, and £96 million was allocated for temporary and permanent accommodation, cold-weather shelters, and out-reach and resettlement workers to help people sleeping rough in central London (Randall and Brown 1993). The RSI was extended in London to March 1996 with an additional £86 million. There was heightened attention on long-term rough sleepers, out-reach and resettlement work, and on forming consortia of voluntary and statutory agencies (Randall and Brown 1996). The aim was to return housing responsibility for rough sleepers to local authorities at the conclusion of its second phase (DoE *et al.* 1995).

In June 1995, the White Paper, *Our Future Homes: Opportunity, Choice, Responsibility* (DoE and Welsh Office 1995), reported on the government's commitment to continue the RSI in London after March 1996, and to extend it to other areas where rough sleeping was a problem (DoE *et al.* 1995). The RSI has been extended to 1999, £73 million has been made available to provide services for people sleeping rough, and it has been extended to 28 other towns and cities, including Bristol, Brighton, Southampton and Nottingham, mainly to fund out-reach and resettlement workers (DoE 1996; DoE *et al.* 1996). The RSI is a radical change in Britain's response to homelessness, for the first time placing the control of targeted funds with central government. The DETR (formerly the DoE) invites non-statutory organizations to submit project bids which have been approved by the local authorities.

In 1990, the Mental Health Foundation and the Department of Health launched the Homeless Mentally Ill Initiative to coincide with the RSI, and in response to concerns about the increasing number of mentally ill people sleeping rough in central London (Craig 1995). The policy of deinstitutionalization and the closure of psychiatric hospitals had continued since the 1950s, the number of psychiatric beds had halved since 1954, and some psychiatrists believed that the process should be halted (Craig and Timms 1992; Weller 1989). The HMII's objective was to provide short-term accommodation and services for homeless mentally ill people sleeping rough in London, until they could be resettled in conventional or supported housing and receive care from health services and local authority social services. Over £20 million was made available for out-reach teams and specialist hostel places (Craig 1995; Department of Health 1992; 1990). The HMII has been extended in partnership with the third phase of the RSI, with nearly £2 million until 1999 (DoE 1996).

The DETR allocates a further £8 million a year to voluntary sector organizations through Section 180 of the Housing Act 1996, to fund projects which help prevent homelessness among single people, such as emergency accommodation schemes and resettlement and after-care projects. The Department of Health funds services to help rough sleepers who are substance abusers through their Drug and Alcohol Specific Grant. In 1997–98, the sum of £720,000 was allocated to 20 schemes. The money cannot, however, be used unless local authorities provide 30 per cent of the total cost. Through a resettlement programme, the Department of Social Security funds approximately 4,300 beds in hostels and move-on accommodation, costing about £18 million a year (Social Exclusion Unit 1998).

Since 1996, there have been two major policy developments in relation to homeless people. The Housing Act 1996 became operative in January 1997. Under the Housing Acts 1977 and 1985 local authorities generally allocated permanent accommodation to statutory homeless people. To avoid homeless people having preferential treatment over non-homeless people on housing waiting lists, under the Housing Act 1996 local authorities have a duty to provide only temporary accommodation to statutory homeless people in priority need for two years, with discretion to continue if the applicant still meets the criteria (Lowe 1997; Niner 1997). If suitable private rented housing or hostels are available in the area, local authorities need only advise and assist homeless people to secure that accommodation. The definition of those in priority need remains unchanged.

The Labour government was elected in May 1997, set up a Social Exclusion Unit in December 1997, and launched a report in July 1998 on strategies to tackle rough sleeping (Social Exclusion Unit 1998). The government's objective is to reduce rough sleeping to as near zero as possible, by reducing the number of people sleeping rough to one-third of its current level by the year 2002. It intends to fund programmes to prevent homelessness, and to set up a new coordinating body in London. The latter would be responsible for rough sleeping in the capital, manage as a single budget the funds which are currently provided for services to help homeless people by different central government initiatives, and link the work of central government departments, the local authorities and voluntary organizations. Outside London, local authority housing departments would coordinate services for rough sleepers.

The report's main objective is to clear London's streets of rough sleepers, and there is little mention of the much larger number of homeless people who are in hostels and other temporary shelters. It does not clarify whether currently RSI-funded towns and cities outside London would continue to receive targeted funds, or would only receive funds through Section 180 grants. Unlike previous reports in the 1990s on rough sleeping, it indicates that coercion may be used to tackle the problem. The power to insist that rough sleepers accept hostel beds will be considered if needed (Social Exclusion Unit 1998: Section 4.23), and the possibility of restricting hostel places only to people who are willing to participate in an employment or training programme may be considered (Social Exclusion Unit 1998: Section 4.27). The report focuses on the circumstances of young homeless people and ways of supporting their return to employment. Little attention is paid to older homeless people and to the particular difficulties of helping those with complex problems and needs.

Implementing policies and developing services

Services to 'contain' the problem of homelessness: 1900–70

During the nineteenth century a few charitable night-shelters and soup kitchens existed for homeless people in cities such as London, Liverpool and Manchester (Rose 1988; Ribton Turner 1887). The Houseless Poor Asylum in Cripplegate, founded in 1819, was the first charitable night-shelter in London. Elsewhere, homeless people booked into common lodging-houses, stayed in casual wards, or slept rough. In 1848, there were an estimated 115,108 vagrants in England and Wales, of whom 13,547 stayed in casual wards, 81,213 in lodging-houses, and 20,348 in barns and tents (Mayhew 1968: 397, writing in 1861).

By the first decade of the twentieth century, voluntary and religious organizations, notably the Salvation Army, local authorities and philanthropists provided large hostels for homeless men (Rose 1988). Lord Rowton built five lodging-houses in London for around 5,000 men, the largest being Arlington House in Camden Town which offered 1,100 cubicle places (Richardson 1991). Other charitable organizations accommodated homeless people in crypts of churches and in warehouses. Many people slept rough at the Embankment, in London, and the area became a focus for soup runs. Casual wards were also frequently used. In the 1930s, there were over 300 in England and Wales, used by approximately 17,000 men each night. They were generally 15–20 miles apart, and homeless men walked from one to the next (Berry 1978). The introduction of old age pensions in Britain in 1908 meant that some elderly destitute people could afford to stay in lodging-houses instead of relying on casual wards, although in 1911 one-quarter of single men over the age of 65 years still lived in casual wards of workhouses (Townsend [1964], cited in Lowe 1997).

In 1948, when the National Assistance Act was introduced, homelessness was not a visible problem, religious organizations provided hostels, and few men were using casual wards. Therefore many casual wards were closed and only 17 were converted to reception centres (Rose 1988; National Assistance Board 1966). The emphasis was now on resettling itinerants, and men were able to stay in the centres for several weeks providing that they were working or looking for work (O'Connor 1963). The rule remained that those not seeking work could stay for only one night. The remaining centres were up to 60 miles apart, making it difficult for men to reach the next one before nightfall. In the 1960s, just 1,200 people used the reception centres nightly; many had mental health and alcohol problems and were unable to sustain jobs (Rose 1988). By this time, the Salvation Army had become the major service provider among religious organizations, with 62 hostels and just over 8,000 bed-spaces nation-wide (National Assistance Board 1966).

In the early twentieth century, the Vagrancy Act 1824 was widely implemented. Sleeping rough in a barn, deserted building or in the open air was a criminal offence if a person was unable to give an account of himself (Home Office 1974). In 1905, over 12,000 people were prosecuted for sleeping rough, and in February of that year three-tenths of male prisoners and 14 per cent of female prisoners were vagrants (Rose 1988). One 57-year-old man was found 'lodging' in a shed and sent to Reading Gaol in 1910 for seven days' hard labour (Southerton 1993). The belief was that some vagrants deliberately incurred short-term prison sentences because prison conditions were more favourable than those in casual wards. In 1901, over 5,000 vagrants who received prison sentences for failing to comply with work tasks imposed at the casual wards, were found in prison to be medically unfit for such work.

By the early 1960s, the number of prosecutions for vagrancy had reduced to just under 800 a year, and by the 1970s to fewer than 400. The amended Vagrancy Act 1935 made it necessary to prove that the person arrested for vagrancy had refused the offer of free accommodation. But since the National Assistance Board had taken over the casual wards in 1948, the assumption that free accommodation was available was no longer realistic. In 1974 a working party on vagrancy and street offences recommended that sleeping rough should no longer be a criminal offence, provided that such persons were not filthy, verminous or causing a nuisance (Home Office 1974). Their recommendation was never implemented.

Until the mid-1970s, rough sleeping was 'contained' to some extent by religious organizations and at reception centres. Successful resettlement programmes were rare and the policies and services of the time may have done more to maintain than to reduce homelessness. The reception centres encouraged transience and unsettledness by forcing at least some men to move on each night, a pattern which was sustained by employers who used them to contact casual workers. Many centres were situated in former Royal Air Force and miners' camps and anti-aircraft gun sites, several miles from towns and populated areas (Rose 1988; CHAR 1985). The Fazakerley Reception Centre, 6 miles from Liverpool city centre, housed 121 men in Nissen huts; Winterbourne was 8 miles from Bristol city centre; and Walkden 7 miles from central Manchester. The most notorious, the Camberwell 'spike' in south London, accommodated 900 men in 'a large, austere and antiquated institution' (Consortium Joint Planning Group 1981: Section 1.1).

Hostels are likely to have encouraged dependency by accommodating people in primitive, institutional conditions for years with few opportunities for rehabilitation and rehousing. A national survey of 679 hostels and lodging houses in 1972 found that 85 per cent had been built before 1914, and that establishments with 100 or more beds provided 56 per cent of the total 31,253 beds (Digby 1976). Most were owned by the Salvation Army and local authorities, many had large dormitories or cubicles, and only a quarter of the beds were in single rooms. Two-thirds failed to meet the DoE's standards for washing and toilet facilities. The residents often had little opportunity to practise domestic skills, and the belief is that they became progressively 'deskilled' and less and less able to cope with life outside a hostel. The hostels 'created the problem they were supposed to solve . . . [they] all but imposed a transient lifestyle upon many of their residents, only for that lifestyle to be then cited as evidence of an individual pathology which required and justified the retention of such hostels' (Vincent *et al.* 1995: 2).

Towards rehabilitation and resettlement: 1970–90

From the mid-1970s, several changes in services for homeless people were introduced. The social welfare consensus had turned away from the custodial care of vulnerable people in institutions such as mental hospitals, and favoured individualized interventions, rehabilitation, and care in the community (Rogers and Pilgrim 1996). There was a growth in the housing association movement stimulated by the creation of the Housing Corporation in 1964, financial support from local authorities such as the Greater London Council to rehabilitate and convert existing properties, and the Housing Act 1974 which introduced a range of capital and revenue social housing subsidies, the most important being the Housing Association Grant (Lund 1996; Malpass and Murie 1994). Voluntary organizations offering long-term shared housing could register as housing associations (HAs) and obtain capital and revenue funding. Organizations such as the Carr-Gomm Society, founded in 1964, developed shared housing schemes nation-wide offering support to lonely people and those discharged from specialist long-stay hospitals (Cooper *et al.* 1994).

A new generation of homeless sector voluntary bodies grew up. Housing associations, such as St Anne's Shelter and Housing Action (known simply as St Anne's) in Leeds, and the St Mungo Community HA (known as St Mungo's), were founded in the late 1960s and early 1970s to work with single homeless people. They generally started as a single hostel or a day centre to meet overt local needs, and progressively developed special-needs hostels and supported housing schemes. Some have idiosyncratic roots. In Lowestoft, after the collapse of the fishing industry in the early 1970s, many men were unemployed or working casually, drinking heavily, and sleeping on the streets and the beach when they could not afford to stay at the local seamen's mission. Following a count by local postmen of 60 men sleeping rough, a night-shelter staffed by volunteers was opened in 1975, and subsequently the St John's Housing Trust developed. In Glasgow, the Talbot Association was founded in 1970 by a local man, Vincent Buchanan, and a few friends, and started as a night-shelter in the Gorbals where 'men lay on newspapers on the floor' (Talbot Association 1995: 3).

By the 1980s, conditions in many large hostels and lodging-houses had deteriorated. Some were due for closure or redevelopment and so had been neglected (Rose 1988). In 1980, Tony Wilkinson, a BBC journalist, described

Bruce House, a hostel in London for more than 400 men and owned by West-minster Council, as in a condition of 'squalor, danger and neglect' (Wilkinson 1981: 78). When he visited, the accommodation was small open-topped cubicles, and the corridor and toilet floors were awash with urine. According to the staff eight years later, only men 'who could stand the bad, physical environment' were admitted to the hostel (Crane 1990: 17). In 1988, Tooley Street, in the London Borough of Southwark, accommodated 165 men in cubicles, with no dining or lounge facilities, and only two staff on duty. The Salvation Army hostel at Great Peter Street, central London, accommodated men in large dormitories, and had just two baths and six showers for 260 men (Crane 1990). Conditions in the Rowton Houses had also deteriorated. In the early 1980s, Arlington House in Camden Town had a ratio of one bath to 62 residents, the toilets were all in the basement of a five-storey block, men slept in cubicles measuring 7 feet by 5 feet, and they were fined £7 for wetting their beds (Richardson 1991; Rose 1988).

During the late 1970s and in the 1980s, there were moves to close large hostels, develop smaller, special-needs housing units and hostels, and rehouse hostel residents. The reception centres became the responsibility of the Department of Health and Social Services in 1976 and were renamed re-settlement units, and the plan was to replace the units with small therapeutic hostels managed by voluntary organizations. Schemes began to rehouse hostel residents through designated teams or local authority social services and housing departments (Duncan *et al.* 1983). The Joint Assessment and Resettlement Team was established in 1979 to rehouse the residents of London's resettlement units, as was the Leeds Shaftesbury Project in 1981 to rehouse hostel residents in Leeds (Dant and Deacon 1989; Duncan and Downey 1985). The latter was funded through inner city programmes and Leeds City Council had an important role in its establishment. St Mungo's set up a specialist resettlement team in 1981.

Services and interventions in the 1990s

Temporary accommodation

Many large old hostels and resettlement units have been replaced by small hostels with single rooms, adequate bathing facilities, kitchens, and spacious and attractive communal areas. Some hostels accommodate people with special needs, including heavy drinkers or those who are mentally ill. Some allow drinking on the premises, making it possible to begin work with home-less people who have alcohol problems and who would otherwise stay on the streets. Since the early-1990s, RSI-funded cold-weather shelters in London, Cambridge and Bristol have provided accommodation from December to March. Because the shelters are free, easily accessible, and make few demands, they attract people with long histories of homelessness, mental illness and heavy drinking. They are important 'contact facilities' and a useful first step off the streets for those who are not ready for permanent housing or who are wary of accepting help (Randall and Brown 1995; Consortium Joint Planning Group 1981).

But some large hostels remain and substandard accommodation and poor facilities are still found. Hostels and night-shelters exist in London, Cardiff, Nottingham and Bournemouth which require the residents (of all ages) to leave in the morning. The residents have no option but to circulate the streets, soup kitchens and day centres. The Consortium Joint Planning Group (1981), which reported on the closure of Camberwell Reception Centre, recommended that temporary accommodation should be in units for no more than 30 people in single rooms. Yet London still has 12 hostels with more than 100 beds, including Arlington House which now houses nearly 400 men, and Glasgow has eight hostels with more than 100 beds (Crockett *et al.* 1997; Glasgow Council for the Single Homeless 1996). Only half of the 2,588 beds in direct-access hostels in London are in single rooms (Harrison 1996). Bondway Nightshelter, in London, accommodates 95 men, many of whom are aged in their fifties, in three dormitories divided into cubicles (Crockett *et al.* 1997). Until 1994, older homeless men were living in very poor conditions at the privately owned Great Eastern Hotel in Glasgow, a former lodging-house (Gilchrist and Clark 1994). When the hotel was taken over by the Loretto HA in August 1994, the men were housed in cubicles, the basement was covered in sewage, and pigeons and rats were inside the building.

As recently as 1995, Crisis developed an 'Open House' programme which offered emergency accommodation to people sleeping rough. The aim was to develop up to 14 projects by converting existing buildings at a low capital cost, and to partially fund each for up to three years (Pleace 1998). Of the first five projects, one was established in the basement of a church in Cambridge, one in portakabins in Crawley which had been used as offices while the Channel Tunnel was constructed, and one in a former office building in Doncaster. At four projects, the residents had to leave the premises in the morning and could not return until the evening despite three being in areas where there were no day centres for homeless people. All projects had low staff levels and two were reliant on volunteers to provide staff cover. Apart from the project managers, most staff 'were not trained in medical care, support or in other fields' (Pleace 1998: 53), and stress among staff was a serious issue with up to 16-hour shifts being worked. A two-year evaluation of the Open House programme found that the projects had little success in resettling homeless people or referring them to housing, social services and health services. Nearly two-thirds of residents left with no known destination and less than one-tenth had accommodation on departure. At all the projects, the residents were concerned about the lack of privacy and some felt that 'being in a desperate situation meant that they had to take whatever there was available and be grateful for it' (Pleace 1998: 65).

There is a lack of temporary accommodation with adequate facilities in many cities. In London, there had been a loss of almost 8,000 hostel beds from 1981 to 1994, and in February 1996 an estimated 87 people each day were turned away from hostels because they were full (Harrison 1996; Single Homelessness in London (SHiL) 1995). Many hostels have inadequate resources and staff untrained to cope with people who are mentally ill or heavy drinkers, and so operate exclusion policies (Ham 1996; Harrison 1996; DoE *et al.* 1995). Older men have been evicted from hostels in Liverpool,

Arlington House, a former Rowton House, now accommodates neary 400 men, many of them elderly

Glasgow and London hostels because of disruptive behaviour associated with heavy drinking and mental illness (Crane and Warnes 1998; 1997a). They therefore move from hostel to hostel or sleep rough, without settling and receiving consistent care and treatment. In Oxford, all local hostels have 'no drink' rules so heavy drinkers have to stay in bed-and-breakfast hotels (Carter 1997).

Rehabilitation and resettlement programmes

Some hostels have self-catering facilities, rehabilitation and resettlement programmes, and residents have the opportunity to practise household and budgeting tasks, and 'acquire the skills necessary to maintain an independent life in self-contained accommodation' (Harrison 1996; Consortium Joint Planning Group 1981: Section 4d). A few hostels in London have clustered flats within the hostel, each accommodating four to eight residents, and each with its own kitchen. The residents cook for themselves, receive help from staff with daily living skills and budgeting, and prepare to move into independent accommodation. Resettlement workers are employed to assess the housing needs of clients, refer to housing providers, and help the clients when they move to accommodation.

Other hostels lack such programmes, provide no opportunity for residents to practise or learn household skills, and either rehouse homeless people unaware of their ability to manage independent living or allow them to become long-term dependent residents. Of 35 direct-access hostels for people of all ages listed in the *London Hostels Directory 1997*, only seven provided self-catering facilities where residents had access to a kitchen which was shared by fewer than ten people (Crockett *et al.* 1997). Some hostels do not employ resettlement workers and expect generalist hostel staff to carry out such duties (Randall and Brown 1995). But hostel staff have only limited time for such work, and it is particularly difficult for them to provide sufficient follow-up support once people have been rehoused, as priority has to be given to current hostel residents. It is costly to employ resettlement workers and time-consuming to prepare residents for tenured accommodation, and there may be a perverse financial incentive for hostels to retain instead of resettle stable residents so as to minimize vacancies. According to Donnison, writing in 1991 (cited in Vincent *et al.* 1995: 2), 'by confining people to institutional life, and so preventing them from learning housekeeping skills, hostels create a permanent demand for their own services'.

Permanent accommodation

Various supported housing options have been developed for homeless people in the 1980s and 1990s, by housing associations, and local authority housing and social service departments. These include shared houses, independent accommodation with support, and **high-care homes**. In London, beds in such schemes increased by nearly 4,700 between 1985 and 1994, but demand outstrips supply, and people who need support remain in temporary hostels (DoE *et al.* 1996; Craig 1995; SHiL 1995; Spaull and Rowe 1992; Eardley 1989). In shared houses, three or four people live together, they have their own bedroom, a communal kitchen and sitting room, and a support worker visits daily. In some, the tenants are provided with a meal each day, and are taught to budget and cook. In Beeston, Leeds, three terraced houses were taken over by St Anne's in 1993 and used to rehouse ten older homeless men. Some had for years lived in hostels or been transient and had moved around Britain, and it was their first experience of having a tenancy.

Shared housing offers support, social contacts, and enables some tenants to develop skills and confidence before moving to independent accommodation (Cooper *et al.* 1994). But sharing a house requires more interdependence and trust than living in hostels and some people prefer to be alone, others have mental health or alcohol problems and disruptive behaviour and are unsuited for communal accommodation, and conflicts arise among tenants who are expected to 'live' with people they do not know or like, or in instances where one tenant avoids responsibilities in the home (Crane and Warnes 1997b; O'Leary 1997; Morrish 1996; Dant and Deacon 1989).

For those who need support but prefer to live alone, Thames Reach HA and Bridge HA have developed in London self-contained flats adjacent to a hostel or a group home, with the tenants in the flats receiving support from the attached project (Crane and Warnes 1997b; O'Leary 1997). Bridge HA's scheme is specifically for older homeless men and women, and comprises a 25-bed group home and adjacent flats for 13 men and women. Tenants from the flats have access to the home's dining room and communal facilities. Another solution, developed by St Anne's, has been to accommodate homeless people in grouped self-contained flats. The organization has 93 such flats: two clusters with six and 12 flats are specifically for older people (Crane and Warnes 1997b). The tenants receive help from housing support workers employed by St Anne's.

Several organizations in London, Glasgow, Nottingham and other cities have developed small high-care group homes (with 20 to 30 beds) for homeless people with severe mental health and alcohol-related problems, who are unable to live independently and need 24-hour support. Instead of providing separate homes, some organizations in London have established a high-care unit within an existing large hostel, such as Bridge HA at Arlington House and the Salvation Army at Booth House. However, the image and stigma of being attached to a large institutional setting remains. High-care schemes are registered with local authority social services departments which fund the care of the residents. Problems arise because some social services departments are unwilling to fund homeless people in **high-care homes** who have chronic alcohol problems and are unable to live independently (Crane and Warnes 1998; Randall and Brown 1995).

Out-reach work on the streets

In some cities, street out-reach workers have been employed to engage with people who are sleeping rough and not accessing services. It is easier to persuade people to accept help when they first become homeless, although it has been demonstrated that it is possible to help some long-term rough sleepers who have complex needs and who resist services through persistent and intensive street out-reach work (Craig 1995; Randall and Brown 1995; Sheridan *et al.* 1993; Wasylenki *et al.* 1993; Marcos *et al.* 1990). Cities such as London and Manchester have out-reach teams who work on the streets daily, but in other places, such as Glasgow, these services are limited (Crane and Warnes 1997a). Much of the RSI funding outside London has been earmarked for out-reach work in cities such as Birmingham, Canterbury, Plymouth and Portsmouth.

Day centres and soup kitchens

Day centres for homeless people have multiplied rapidly throughout Britain: only seven existed before 1970, but there are now over 250 and they are used by approximately 10,000 people daily (Cooper 1997; Llewellin and Murdoch 1996). Some began and continue as soup kitchens, providing only food, clothing and showers, depend heavily on volunteers, and are in crypts of churches. Others have salaried and trained staff who provide rehabilitation, group therapies, resettlement programmes and health-care. They support homeless people, those who have been rehoused but remain vulnerable, those with mental health and substance abuse problems, and others who have 'lost contact with the community care system or never found access to it in the first place' (Llewellin and Murdoch 1996: 5). An increase in the number of users is reported to have contributed to overcrowded conditions and increased violence (Waters 1992).

Their evolution has, however, been 'subject to individual whims and quirks

Small high-care group home for 19 residents, St Mungo's HA, London

and funding availability', and generally has paid little attention to supply and need (Waters 1992: 7). There are 37 listed day centres for single homeless people in London, and a further 46 drop-in centres (Jacobs *et al.* 1998). The majority of the latter are linked to churches and provide free food and beverages. Day centres exist in remote places such as Boston in Lincolnshire, but there are few in Wales, and towns, such as Lowestoft, Gloucester and Stevenage have recognized problems of homelessness but no day centres. The majority of day centres are only open during the day and there is little provision for rough sleepers in the evening. One exception is Glasgow, where two centres stay open until late evening. In London, there are six day centres for young homeless people (up to 25 years of age) but none specifically for older homeless people.

Primary health-care services

Because many homeless people do not access mainstream health-care services, several towns and cities have developed specialist primary health-care services for homeless people. The services are flexible and easily accessible. People neither require appointments nor need to be registered with a doctor to receive treatment. Teams of peripatetic nurses, doctors and other workers provide health-care to homeless people at hostels, day centres and drop-in centres. The Three Boroughs Primary Health Care Team in London, for example, established in 1992, includes a dental practitioner, tuberculosis screening workers, and chiropodists (see also Chapter 9). A few 'walk-in' medical clinics, staffed by nurses, doctors and other professionals, have been developed in London, Oxford and Newcastle upon Tyne. Wytham Hall, in London, was established in 1984 as a sick-bay for ten homeless men. It is staffed by resident medical students and doctors, and provides temporary accommodation, treatment, convalescent care and rehabilitation for those who are ill but do not require hospital admission. Its service is, however, unique.

Services for homeless people with mental health and alcohol problems

Specialist services to help homeless people with mental health or alcohol problems have been developed. Through the Homeless Mentally Ill Initiative, five teams of psychiatrists, community mental health nurses and housing workers have been set up in London to work with mentally ill rough sleepers who are not accessing mainstream services. The teams encourage people to move to hostels and eventually resettle them in long-term housing. The workers have experienced difficulties in getting psychiatric services and social services to take over responsibility for providing long-term support to the clients once they are resettled. Many require high levels of care to enable them to sustain tenancies, yet 'mainstream agencies are unable to maintain the level of contact achieved by the teams, which facilitated the resettlement in the first place' (Craig 1995: 122). Mental health teams for homeless people have also been established in Birmingham, Nottingham and some other cities.

Detoxification units, rehabilitation programmes and counselling services have been set up to work with homeless people who are heavy drinkers, although some areas lack such services. Local authority social services departments fund admissions to detoxification units, but are sometimes reluctant if a person has no local connection (Pleace and Quilgars 1996). Homeless people with both mental health and alcohol problems are particularly difficult to help, and are especially vulnerable to slipping through the net of service provision. Services usually target either mentally ill people or substance abusers, and few offer integrated treatment (Pleace and Quilgars 1996; Wright 1989; Koegel *et al.* 1988). Many clients contacted by the HMII teams had combined problems, yet 'none of the teams were equipped to provide specialist interventions for substance dependency' (Craig 1995: 73). The importance of integrated treatment for such clients has been reported in America, where it is acknowledged that the disorders cannot be treated independent of each other (Rosenheck *et al.* 1998; Drake *et al.* 1997).

The development of current services

The move towards treatment, rehabilitation and resettlement for homeless people has intensified in the 1990s, although services are unevenly developed and there is much local variation. Services have stemmed from diverse initiatives by government, voluntary and religious organizations, statutory agencies and individuals. Many housing associations have extended their range of provision over time. St Anne's started as a day centre for homeless people in 1971, founded the first community-based detoxification centre in Britain in 1976, and has developed more than 80 supported housing schemes around west Yorkshire. St Mungo's, established in 1969 to provide accommodation for rough sleepers in London, now manages over 50 projects and accommodates over a thousand people every night in temporary hostels, supported housing schemes and high-care registered homes. Some services have developed through inter-agency partnerships. The Joseph Cowen Healthcare Centre, Newcastle upon Tyne, is a partnership between Byker Bridge HA, Newcastle City Health Care NHS Trust, and Newcastle and North Tyneside Health Authority. Hopkinson House in London, opened in 1998, provides supported housing, health-care and resettlement to street drinkers. Its partnership includes Look Ahead HA, the Drink Crisis Centre, City of Westminster Social Services, and Kensington & Chelsea and Westminster Health Authority.

Some recent innovations have been instigated through the enthusiasm and efforts of local individuals and organizations. Centrepoint Outreach in Boston, Lincolnshire, was initiated through the town's Methodist Church which, having recognized that some local people were lonely, arranged a weekly coffee evening. It soon became apparent that some attenders had social and housing problems and were sleeping in sheds and cars or on railway embankments. After a meeting with other churches, Centrepoint Outreach was formed in 1992 as a drop-in and advice centre for homeless and vulnerably housed people. Services have often been established and elaborated in response to a perceived local problem. Whatever the starting point, they tend to develop a common range involving out-reach work on the streets, temporary accommodation, day centres, services to combat health problems and heavy drinking, resettlement programmes, several permanent housing options, and continuing support for those rehoused.

Services dedicated to older homeless people

Since the early 1990s, it has been recognized that many existing services for homeless people in Britain are inadequately meeting the needs of *older* people. Day centres, hostels, and out-reach and resettlement workers provide services for homeless people of any age but the services are often dominated by younger homeless people, and there are problems in mixing age-groups (Ham 1996; Waters 1992). Many older people dislike the noise and overcrowded conditions in hostels and day centres, and they fear violence and intimidation from young users (Crane and Warnes 1997a). Some who do patronize the services are unassertive and their needs tend to be overshadowed by those of younger users who are often more demanding. Similar problems are reported in America (Cohen and Sokolovsky 1989; Douglass *et al.* 1988; Doolin 1986; Coalition for the Homeless 1984).

Many older rough sleepers are isolated, extremely hard to find, and more difficult than younger homeless people to persuade to accept services (Crane and Warnes 1998). Street out-reach workers in Richmond, Virginia, noted that 'many elderly persons were likely to avoid contact with both service providers for the homeless and other homeless persons. Their extreme isolation, in a population that is generally fearful and withdrawn, required a longer and more persistent period of engagement and relationship building than was needed with most younger clients' (Sheridan *et al.* 1993: 414). Generic out-reach workers may not have the time and resources to seek out and engage older entrenched rough sleepers.

While elderly people have priority rights to housing and community care through the Housing Act 1996 and the National Health Service and Community Care Act 1990, they can only access these rights by presenting themselves to local authorities or health- and social care professionals, so declaring themselves as homeless and in need. Few statutory services reach out to older homeless people on the streets. Because of their reluctance to use 'normal' health, social and housing services, and their unwillingness to use general homeless services, a few organizations have responded by developing services dedicated to *older* homeless people (Table 11.1). In central London, St Martin-in-the-Fields, North Lambeth, The Passage and St Giles Trust day centres have introduced designated workers and sessions once or twice every week for this group. The workers 'seek out' older users, assess their needs and help them utilize services.

Short-stay hostels for older rough sleepers have been set up by Focus Housing Group in Birmingham, and since 1996 St Mungo's has managed an older persons' cold-weather shelter each winter in London. In January 1997, an experimental centre for rough sleepers over the age of 50 years opened at Lancefield Street, west London, to help those who are isolated and not accessing services. It provides an out-reach service, a 24-hour drop-in centre, temporary or 'first-stage' accommodation for 33 homeless men and women, and a resettlement service (Crane and Warnes 1998). Many of its residents have rejected all-age hostels in the past yet have accepted residency at Lancefield Street.

Projects to rehabilitate older homeless people and help them build (or rebuild) daily living skills and prepare them for a move to permanent housing have been established. Grangetown PREP (Project for the Rehabilitation of Elderly People), Cardiff, of the South Wales Federated HA (now the United Welsh HA), started in 1992 as a short-stay rehabilitation and resettlement project for older homeless people because several in the group were refusing to use the city's large direct-access hostels and the resettlement needs of those who did were being overshadowed by those of younger residents (Crane and Warnes 1997b). It houses four residents who are responsible for self-care, cooking and cleaning. The staff provide help with budgeting, shopping and accessing local facilities. Since its inception, the project has worked with 45 older people and over half have been rehoused in independent accommodation. A similar unit in London accommodates six older homeless Asian men and women. Plans are under way to develop a rehabilitation house in Birmingham for 16 older men. Such units promote independence, rehabilitation and resettlement, and help to build confidence and self-esteem.

Programmes dedicated to resettlement have been instituted. The Over 55s Accommodation Project, at St Anne's Day Centre, Leeds, was established in 1991 by St Anne's to resettle older homeless people. The staff develop care packages and resettlement plans with clients, refer them to housing providers, and help them move into accommodation. They support clients once they are resettled until their housing situation has stabilized, and statutory agencies

Table 11.1 Examples of dedicated services for older homeless people, Great Britain, 1990s

Name of project and (organization)	Year began	OR	TA	DC	RS	SP	GP	DW
Lancefield Street Centre, Westbourne Park, London (St Mungo's Community HA)	1997	•	•	•	•	•[1]	•[1]	•
St Martin-in-the-Fields Day Centre, Trafalgar Square, London (St Martin-in-the-Fields Social Care Unit)	1995	◊[2]	•		◊[2]	◊[2]		•
St Giles Day Centre, Camberwell, London (St Giles Trust)	1995			•	•	•		•
North Lambeth Day Centre, Waterloo, London	1995			•	•	•		•
Passage Day Centre, Victoria, London	1996			•	•	•		•
Older homeless Asian people project, Cricklewood, London (Paddington Churches Housing Group)	1982	•			•	•		•
Zambesi and allied temporary housing projects, Sparkbrook, Birmingham (Focus Housing Group)	1987	•				•		•
Grangetown PREP (Preparation for resettlement scheme), Cardiff (United Welsh HA)	1992	•			•	•		•
Over 55s Accommodation Project, Leeds (St Anne's Shelter & Housing Action)	1991			◊[2]	•	•		•
Arlington Road/Mary Terrace project, London (Bridge HA)	1996				•	•		•
Sandringham Road supported housing, Lowestoft (Suffolk Heritage HA)	1996					•		•
Older Homeless Persons' Advocacy Scheme, London (Arlington Care Association)	1996							•

Key to services: OR: Street out-reach workers. TA: Temporary (hostel) accommodation. DC: Day or drop-in centres. RS: Resettlement preparation and planning. SP: Continuing support for independent tenants. GP: Group housing schemes. DW: Workers dedicated to older people.
[1] Enlisting of other St Mungo's provision
[2] None exclusively for older people

are involved if needed. The project has rehoused over 300 people, some with long histories of homelessness complicated by mental health and alcohol problems, in independent accommodation, sheltered flats and shared houses.

In America and Australia, there are also age-segregated services for older homeless people. Project Rescue, adjacent to the Bowery, New York City, was established in 1985 as a day centre for people aged 60 years and over who are sleeping rough or living in shelters and flop-houses. It provides meals, showers, clothing, medical and psychiatric care, alcohol counselling, and help to claim financial entitlements and secure housing (Cohen *et al.* 1993; 1992). A similar centre for older homeless people, the Cardinal Medeiros Day Centre, opened in Boston, Massachusetts, in 1984 (Doolin 1986). Valley Lodge, in New York City, provides temporary accommodation for 92 homeless people over the age of 50 years who have been living in public shelters. The residents receive help with mental health and alcohol problems, are taught (or relearn) daily living skills such as shopping, cooking and budgeting, and are prepared to move to independent accommodation. The staff support former residents once they are resettled (Lipmann 1995).

In cities such as New York, Chicago and Washington, some SRO hotels have been renovated into single, self-contained apartments for older homeless people. There are communal dining and social facilities, and social workers on site arrange social activities and provide a range of services from counselling to financial management. One scheme in Washington, known as Sarah's Circle, is specifically for older women. It has a daily activities programme to which residents of the local neighbourhood are invited, and thus links tenants to the local community (Lipmann 1995). In Melbourne, Australia, Wintringham Hostels provide permanent accommodation and care services for frail elderly homeless people. By 1995, they were supporting 48 residents in independent tenancies, and 129 in two hostels. Although referred to as 'hostels', each person has a bungalow with its own entrance, kitchen, living room and verandah, and communal facilities are on site (Wintringham Hostels 1995–96).

Only a few services exist in Britain specifically for older homeless people, and they have generally developed through the initiative of local organizations who have recognized an unmet need. There has been no national programme to address the problem. Some local authorities, such as Eastbourne and Bradford, have developed single homelessness strategies for young people, but few exist for older homeless people (McCluskey 1997). An exception is Birmingham, where the Sparkbrook Forum was established in 1997 through concern for older local people living in poor-standard, private rented accommodation. It was instigated by the social services department, and its members include the local authority housing department, Age Concern, the staff of the Zambesi project (a local temporary hostel for older homeless people), and mental health workers (Crane and Warnes 1997b).

In the 1990s, organizations such as Help the Aged and Age Concern London have shown an interest in the problems and needs of older homeless people. In 1997, Help the Aged launched a national appeal for funds to support projects working with the group. In mid-1998, Help the Aged, the Housing Associations Charitable Trust and Crisis formed a three-year partnership to raise funds and support projects nationally that are working with older homeless people.

Conclusions

This review has highlighted the diverse and ambivalent attitudes, policies and services that have developed over the years in Britain to tackle the problem of homelessness. Since the Elizabethan Poor Law, homeless people have been treated as both needy and deserving of help, and as criminals and undeserving members of society. The casual wards were established to help those with an unsettled lifestyle, yet users were treated similarly to prisoners with compulsory work tasks and punishments, the difference being only that prisoners were detained while the casual ward users were forced to keep on the move. Similar to mental illness, homelessness was a problem diverted and concealed through the provision of minimal accommodation in large and formidable institutions such as hostels, lodging-houses, casual wards and the crypts of churches.

Only since the late 1970s have there been dramatic changes in the approach to homeless people. Many large hostels have been replaced by smaller units with adequate facilities, and there has been an emphasis on resettling homeless people instead of merely containing the problem. These changes have been instigated by several parallel changes in society. Since the 1950s, the social welfare consensus has turned away from the custodial care of vulnerable people in large institutions, in favour of the provision of intensive and individually oriented services and rehabilitation programmes to support and sustain people in the community. Unskilled and casual manual work has also declined substantially. It sustained transient lifestyles and a male workforce who were accustomed to minimal shelter in barrack-like accommodation. Hence, the disapprobation of large hostels and resettlement units was partly because of their poor privacy and amenity standards, and partly because they were an inappropriate setting in which to rebuild conventional living skills, social relationships and roles.

Another associated change is in the frameworks of provision. A generation ago, statutory and religious organizations took the major role in provision and to a large extent worked to a national template. This was partly for historical reasons, but also evinced the prevailing model of universalist, state-managed services and was partly a 'default' solution – for no other independent agencies were active in the field. Over the last two decades, an 'agency approach' and competitive 'market' to homeless services have developed. The state and charities provide funding, and provision is determined by the enterprise, initiative and (to an extent) good management exhibited by local organizations, mostly in the voluntary sector.

Different attitudes towards homeless people remain, however, and practices of exclusion and stigmatization still exist. Under the Housing Act 1996, local authority housing departments have a responsibility towards only certain groups of homeless people in priority need. Statutory and health-care services are oriented towards people who are housed and who can demonstrate a local connection. The multiple problems of many homeless people, among them mental illness and alcohol dependency, do not easily fit into the single categories constructed by many service providers. Recent policies on homelessness indicate a return to the principles and practices seen in the first half of the twentieth century. The government's Social Exclusion Unit (1998) report hints that London's rough sleepers may be coerced to move into hostels and to participate in employment and training programmes, echoing the practices of former casual wards. Since the Housing Act 1996, local authority housing departments have had a duty to find only temporary accommodation for homeless people in priority need, reverting to practices of 1948–77.

Services for homeless people have often been established locally in response to a perceived need without a detailed assessment of that need and appraisal of the effectiveness of present services. As a result, services are unevenly developed and there is much local variation. Services are duplicated in some towns and cities yet are lacking in other areas. Some are effectively meeting the needs of homeless people, while others are ineffective, have low resettlement rates or other incentives than that of resettlement, and thus inadvertently help to sustain homelessness. The latter includes hostels which allow long-term residency to minimize vacancies, and missions which only provide help if a person first attends a religious service.

The type of help that a homeless person receives and the likelihood of that person being rehoused depend on: (i) the availability and appropriateness of local services such as out-reach workers to seek out those who are isolated; (ii) the experience of the service providers and their connectedness, which governs the extent to which they effectively identify and manage problems and refer clients to other agencies; (iii) the attitude of the service providers and the extent to which they encourage rehabilitation and resettlement or have other motives for providing services; and (iv) the continuity and stability of services. Projects take time to develop effective ways of working and to fit into a spectrum of local provision. A great deal of provision currently relies on short-term funding and is therefore insecure, an arrangement which sits uneasily with the time requirements of the progressive rehabilitation and 'reskilling' of vulnerable homeless people.

The circumstances of many contemporary older homeless people can be related to past policies and services. A small proportion of men are transient and have been travelling around Britain for years, behaviour which was insti- tuted (or at least reinforced) by the reception centres. Many older men and women have remained in hostels and temporary shelters for more than 25 years and have thus become dependent and institutionalized. In addition, the circumstances of many can be related to present policies and services. Some first became homeless because their vulnerability was not recognized or was ignored by community care services. Some remain in hostels without inten- sive resettlement programmes being instituted. A number with mental health and alcohol problems have been evicted from hostels because of inadequate resources and untrained staff, while others stay in shelters that they have to vacate during the day. Both situations are likely to increase instability and unsettledness. The final chapter looks at how the situation can be changed.

Note

1 Pieces of old rope shredded and used for jobs such as caulking between the wooden seams of ships' deck planking.

12

Resettling older homeless people

Life is strange. You see people and they have money, houses and flash cars, and the next minute they are dressed in rags, filthy dirty, and homeless. Look at me.

(John, aged 68 years, homeless for more than 15 years)

Many older people have been homeless intermittently or consistently for years. Some have deep-seated behavioural, morale, mental health and social problems, and are difficult to find, engage and help. Evidence from Britain and America, however, demonstrates that older homeless people can be helped but the service response must involve more than simple housing provision. It has to include treatment for health and psychological problems, individualized rehabilitation packages, and intensive resettlement programmes and long-term support if needed. A few innovatory schemes have been established in Britain in the 1990s and have successfully rehabilitated and resettled older homeless people who have been on the streets or in hostels for years.

Many older homeless people are motivated and *want* to be resettled. Twenty-five younger men were resettled from Arlington House into supported housing, yet 78 older men expressed an interest to be included in the scheme (Crane and Warnes 1997b). Several long-term rough sleepers said that age and ill health made them want to settle. One 66-year-old man who slept rough for years before being rehoused explained: 'I have heart problems . . . I was scared that I would be found dead on the streets one day.' It has been suggested that people adapt to homelessness within three weeks, become 'deskilled', and find difficulty in reintegrating with mainstream society (Keyes and Kennedy 1992). Although this is now cited in British reports such as that by the Social Exclusion Unit (1998), there is little by way of longitudinal data to support the idea and there is contrasting evidence from the experiences of many older homeless people.

This final chapter examines the process of resettling older homeless people and the experiences of those who are resettled. Although few evaluations exist, likely factors in the success and failure of resettlement are discussed. The chapter draws on the experiences of the subjects in the Four-City Study and on early findings of the longitudinal study of the resettlement of older homeless people in the Lancefield Street Centre Study.

The process of resettlement

Resettlement involves the planned move of a person to tenured accommodation, usually with an unrestricted period of residence and with the provision of personal and social support if needed. The DETR has defined the role of RSI-funded resettlement workers as 'to secure access for homeless people with a history of sleeping rough to long term accommodation which best suits their needs and reasonable preferences, and to ensure that they do not subsequently lose it or move to less suitable accommodation' (DoE *et al.* 1996: 6). Resettlement is not an easy process. Many former homeless people experience problems with adjusting to settled living, sorting out finances and claiming benefits, and with loneliness and boredom (Pleace 1995; Randall and Brown 1994b). There is a high rate of tenancy breakdown in the first two years, particularly in the first six months (Craig 1995; Randall and Bown 1994b; Deacon *et al.* 1993; Dant and Deacon 1989; Duncan and Downey 1985). This equally applies to older homeless people. One-quarter of those over the age of 60 years rehoused by the City of Glasgow District Council between 1983 and 1993 gave up their tenancies within two years (Wilson 1997a). Eighty-six people in the Four-City Study had been rehoused since first becoming homeless, but 49 became homeless for a second time, and 16 for a third time (Figure 3.1). Two-thirds stayed housed for less than two years. More than one-half of hostel residents at the Lancefield Street Centre had been rehoused since first becoming homeless but had become homeless again (Crane and Warnes 1998).

Resettlement has four stages: (i) assessment of the client's problems, competences, motivations and requirements for resettlement; (ii) the preparation of the client; (iii) finding a suitable housing vacancy and planning the move; and (iv) supporting the adjustment to settled and (more) independent living. For many older and some younger homeless people, a pre-phase to resettlement involves making contact with a rough sleeper and persuading that person to use services. These stages are examined in relation to older homeless people.

Contacting older rough sleepers

The first step is to make contact with older people sleeping rough, gain their trust and encourage them to accept services. This can often be achieved through persistent out-reach work on the streets. In London, two out-reach workers have been employed at the Lancefield Street Centre since January 1997 to work specifically with older rough sleepers. Through intensive work over many months, they have built relationships of trust with the group and have persuaded some to accept help and move into accommodation. A vehicle is attached to the project and the out-reach workers are able to transport older people from the streets to the centre. Street out-reach work is also conducted from Project Rescue, the centre for older homeless people in New

An older homeless man arriving at the Lancefield Street Centre with an out-reach worker

York City, and an estimated 90 per cent of contacts finally use the centre (see Chapter 11).

Drop-in centres and temporary shelters where few demands are placed on people are important 'contact facilities' for those older rough sleepers who are initially unsettled, distrustful and reluctant to accept services. The Lancefield Street drop-in centre functions as a 'stepping-stone' to the hostel and eventual rehousing (Figure 12.1). In the 20 months to September 1998, 57 older rough sleepers first used the drop-in centre and were then persuaded to accept a hostel place. In some cases, the transition occurred after a few days, but others were exceptionally wary and it took weeks. Two drop-in centres in New York City for homeless people over the age of 40 years, the Moravian Church Coffee Pot (transferred to Peter's Place) and the Antonio Olivieri Center, have attracted and gained the trust of elderly, chronically homeless people, including older bag ladies (Coalition for the Homeless 1984; Schwam 1979).

Assessment of the clients' problems and needs

Once an older homeless person is supported by services, the next stage involves careful assessments of their problems and needs. Information is

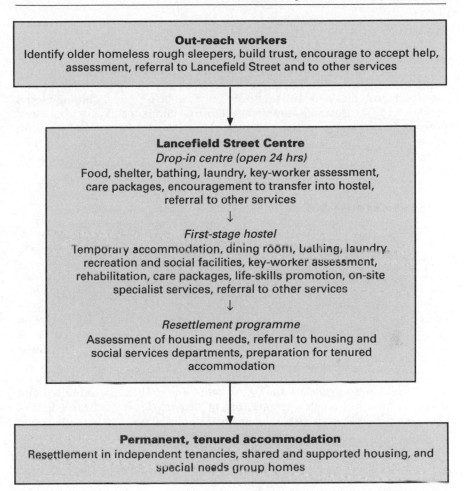

Out-reach workers
Identify older homeless rough sleepers, build trust, encourage to accept help,
assessment, referral to Lancefield Street and to other services

Lancefield Street Centre
Drop-in centre (open 24 hrs)
Food, shelter, bathing, laundry, key-worker assessment,
care packages, encouragement to transfer into hostel,
referral to other services

↓

First-stage hostel
Temporary accommodation, dining room, bathing, laundry,
recreation and social facilities, key-worker assessment,
rehabilitation, care packages, life-skills promotion, on-site
specialist services, referral to other services

↓

Resettlement programme
Assessment of housing needs, referral to housing and
social services departments, preparation for tenured
accommodation

Permanent, tenured accommodation
Resettlement in independent tenancies, shared and supported housing, and
special needs group homes

Figure 12.1 *Pathways from the streets to resettlement, the Lancefield Street Centre, London*

required about the person's mental and physical health states, benefit entitlements and claims, drinking habits, housing history, the reasons for homelessness and experiences of resettlement, social contacts, motivation to be resettled, housing preferences, and personal care and daily living skills, that is, their ability to look after their personal appearance and hygiene, to cook, to shop, to budget, to pay bills and to manage a home. It can take several weeks to build trust and compile a person's history, and may require contact with other agencies.

Before resettlement can be contemplated, many are likely to require treatment for physical or mental illnesses, and some may need help to control drinking such as an admission to a detoxification unit or a controlled drinking programme, help to claim welfare benefits, and retraining in personal care skills. Some are likely to need time to settle in accommodation, particularly if they have long histories of transience. One man who travelled around for 30 years and now has ill health, said: 'I have to settle down but the question is where do I settle. I've moved around for years; I don't belong anywhere.' Some may require counselling and support for psychological problems and unresolved traumas and stresses before they can be resettled, although some may prefer to settle in accommodation before tackling such experiences. Once pressing health and personal care issues have been addressed and a person has become accustomed to staying in accommodation, assessments can then be made of a person's competences, motivation and requirements for long-term housing.

The preparation of the client

At this stage, the objective is to ensure that the older person has the means, skills and attitudes to settle in the intended accommodation. Some of those who have never managed a home, or have not had a tenancy for years, are likely to need rehabilitation if they are to be resettled in tenancies where they will be responsible for paying bills and managing household tasks. Rehabilitation involves training to build or to restore personal care and household skills to enable a person to function at a level needed in the intended accommodation. Where such programmes have been implemented, as at Grangetown PREP in Cardiff, and at Valley Lodge in New York City, these have proved successful (see Chapter 11).

Being resettled is a major step for many older homeless people, particularly if they have been homeless for years. Some are afraid to be rehoused and leave the familiar homeless community, make considerable adjustments and changes to their lifestyle, and take on the responsibilities of a tenancy. A few residents at the Lancefield Street Centre returned to the streets when appointments were made to view housing or when accommodation became available. Others became anxious in the weeks before they moved, neglected their appearance, isolated themselves and drank heavily. People therefore need to be prepared psychologically as well as practically to move. Regular discussions need to take place between the staff and the clients to explain the process of moving and possible problems or issues which may arise and how these can be overcome or managed. This will help to allay fears and worries and boost the morale and confidence of the clients.

The preparation may extend over many months. In two British schemes, which have successfully rehoused older homeless people who had lived in direct-access hostels for years, the preparation lasted 8 and 18 months, respectively. The first resettled 25 residents over the age of 60 years from Arlington House, in London, into a purpose-built supported group home nearby. Most had lived in the hostel at Arlington House for more than 20 years. The second, in Lowestoft, resettled six men over the age of 60 years from the Fyffe Centre into a purpose-built, supported group of flats nearby at Sandringham Road. In both schemes, regular discussions about moving took place between the staff and the men, and the men visited the new projects frequently and were involved in selecting the furnishings and furniture (Crane and Warnes 1997b).

Finding a suitable housing vacancy and planning the move

Resettlement requires the careful selection of suitable housing to meet a person's preferences and needs. An inappropriate move can be extremely stressful and demoralizing for a person. Older homeless people are rehoused in various types of long-term accommodation, including fully independent, conventional tenancies, sheltered accommodation with assistance from wardens, shared houses with non-residential daily support workers, and group homes which are staffed 24 hours a day. For some, resettlement entails several moves to progressively less supported housing. Some move from a hostel to a shared house, before acquiring the skills and confidence to manage in independent accommodation.

For those older homeless people who can manage in independent or supported housing schemes, referrals are made to housing associations and local authority housing departments. For those who are unable to live alone, referrals are made to local authority social services departments, which make their own assessments of care needs, and fund suitable long-term placements in high-care group homes. Unlike most housed older people who have furniture, furnishings, kitchen utensils and possessions which they have accumulated over years and often have family who help if they move, homeless older people often have no belongings to start a home and no relatives to assist with a move. The resettlement worker therefore has a key role when an offer has been made. He or she accompanies the client on a visit to view the accommodation, assesses its suitability, and helps make other preparations once the offer is accepted.

If a person is moving to an independent flat or an unfurnished tenancy, the resettlement worker helps with applying for a community care grant, purchasing furniture and furnishings, and making the connection arrangements for gas, electricity and other utilities. Community care grants are available from the Department of Social Security to help people on low income (income support or jobseeker's allowance claimants) who are moving out of institutional and residential settings to establish a home in the community (George *et al.* 1997). The grants are discretionary, no stipulated amount is paid, and claims can be made for furniture, furnishings, household equipment, connection charges and moving expenses. Some people who are ineligible for a community care grant are entitled to a loan from the Department of Social Security. In several cities, there are projects or charities which supply free or cheap second-hand furniture and furnishings to homeless people who acquire tenancies.

Supporting the adjustment to settled living

The final stage involves monitoring and assisting a person once they are rehoused while they adjust to settled living and their new home. This is usually undertaken by resettlement workers or specially employed housing support workers. Helping with the initial adjustment involves ensuring that gas and electricity are connected and that the person understands how to use a token meter or pay through a budget scheme; ensuring that the person is receiving a pension or benefit entitlements and that rent or housing benefit is being paid to the landlord; training in tasks such as budgeting and paying bills; ensuring that support services such as a home-help are involved if needed; and helping the person to get to know the local shops and post office, and to register with a local general practitioner.

Rehousing often involves moving to a new area and possibly losing social and support networks at hostels and on the streets. Many older homeless people have minimal contact with relatives and have few friends, and their isolation may be compounded when they move because some find it difficult to socialize and will therefore find it hard to become acquainted with neighbours or to access community facilities. Once they are rehoused, an important role of the housing support workers is to assist the person to socialize and to provide emotional support. The Leeds Shaftesbury Project, which resettled hostel residents in Leeds, found that for many clients after about eight weeks, 'the pleasure of a new home may be replaced by apprehension at managing greater or more complex financial responsibilities, or people may be at a loss as to how to spend their time . . . the transition between lifestyles is often accompanied by an emotional low' (Leeds Shaftesbury Project 1986, cited in Dant and Deacon 1989: 35).

The long-term adjustment to settled living involves accepting the accommodation as 'home', and ceasing to use day centres for homeless people and integrating with homeless people on the streets. It also involves rebuilding a socially integrated and purposeful life, depending on a person's circumstances, competences, motivation and preferences. Returning to work may be a feasible objective for some older people who have been homeless for just a few months, are aged in their fifties, and have worked until recently. Organizations, such as St Mungo's, have employment and training schemes to help homeless people to return to work. Because of age, ill health or long-term unemployment, many older people will not return to work. They can, however, be encouraged to access community centres and libraries, develop or renew interests and activities, and form new social relationships and roles or restore estranged kin ties.

The experience of being resettled

There are indications that older homeless people benefit by living in conventional housing rather than hostels. In Lowestoft and London, older men who had lived in direct-access hostels for years were rehoused into supported housing. Since moving, most men have become more motivated and confident, are drinking less and eating better, and are taking better care of their personal appearance and rooms (Crane and Warnes 1997b). Similarly, in Seattle, ten older men were rehoused from a temporary shelter into supported accommodation. The staff noted: 'the most dramatic impact of residence at this facility was on self-perceptions, an impact reflected in an improvement in hygiene and other aspects of self-care, [and in] utilization of health services' (Elias and Inui 1993: 400). In Melbourne, Australia, 36 older homeless men were rehoused from an old barracks-style shelter which closed in 1993 into independent flats, supported houses and high-care homes. Some had been at the shelter for up to 20 years. Since moving, many of the men have become more sociable, have renewed contact with relatives, and some have gained confidence and independence. One man, who has purchased a motor-scooter, said that he wished he had moved from the shelter years earlier but 'no one ever suggested it [and I] didn't think about it' (Hallebone 1997: 82).

The resettlement experiences of older people in the Lancefield Street Centre Study are varied. Those who have been homeless for a short while have tended to settle quickly in permanent accommodation, form social networks, and become involved in activities. Some with long histories of homelessness have also settled in accommodation within six months, have shown improvements in their behaviour such as reduced drinking, and have developed interests. One 62-year-old Irish man was rehoused in shared accommodation, having been homeless and a heavy drinker for more than 30 years. He has had no contact with his family for 26 years. When interviewed six months later, he had written to the address where he last knew his sister was living, and hoped to trace her and restore contact, he had reduced his alcohol intake, and had made enquiries about taking a holiday in Ireland for the first time in 20 years.

Another 56-year-old man has been rehoused in a shared house, having been homeless for just four months. He has started a computer course at the Bridge Resource Centre in west London. The Centre provides computer training, employment opportunities and job-hunting facilities to homeless people. He hopes to move eventually to independent accommodation and to return to work. Some older homeless people who have been long-term heavy drinkers were rehoused in high-care group homes as they were unable to manage on their own. Their weekly income is greatly reduced after rent and service charges are deducted, and this seems inadvertently to help them. Their drinking is controlled and reduced because they have limited funds to spend on alcohol. As a result, their appetite has improved, they report feeling better physically and less depressed, and they are more sociable.

According to their reports, older homeless people face three main difficulties when they are resettled. The first is adjusting to living in accommodation and having responsibilities. Several commented: 'when you move in, you experience pressures you never had on the streets; it doesn't take much to put you back on the streets'. Another man explained: 'it is hard for people who have been homeless when they move to accommodation; we have to work hard to make it work, to prove that we can manage, and to gain the respectability of neighbours'. For some, it takes months to adjust to being housed. One man had been rehoused for six months but still expressed uncertainty: 'I don't know if I can adjust to my flat. I miss my street-friends. I've kept my sleeping bag so that I can go back on the streets at any time.' Minor incidents can unsettle some. One man had considered abandoning his tenancy after a warden had spoken abruptly to him. Another had thought similarly when there were delays in transferring his pension to a nearby post office.

Another common problem faced by some who are rehoused in accommodation on their own is loneliness and boredom. One 68-year-old man,

The home of a man aged in his sixties: he slept rough for many years and was successfully rehoused in 1997

resettled in sheltered accommodation, said: 'I find it hard to mix with the other tenants . . . I've slept rough for 15 years and have been on my own so long that I'm now a loner.' Loneliness and boredom were commonly reported reasons why some rehoused older people in the Four-City Study ceded tenancies and others continued to use soup kitchens and linger on the streets with homeless people. One man had been rehoused twice in council accommodation but evicted on both occasions because he was lonely, allowed drinkers to stay in his flat, and they caused a disturbance.

The third difficulty relates to managing household chores and sorting out finances. One man was rehoused from a hostel where no rehabilitation programme existed. He said: 'I slept rough for 12 years and would have liked the opportunity to practise shopping and cooking before I moved into my flat. I was petrified when I first went into a supermarket and I ran out; I did not know where to start with shopping. I helped my wife with the cooking and cleaning before she died. Unlike many homeless men, I had that experience to draw on when I moved.' Another explained: 'I'm no good at shopping or cooking; I always had a woman looking after me; I had my mother, and then my landlady.' Another man's flat had central heating to which he was unaccustomed. He left it on continuously and had a huge quarterly bill. He explained: 'I've always lived in places which had gas fires; I could see the fire and remembered to turn it off.'

Several in the Lancefield Street Centre Study experienced problems with obtaining welfare benefits and sorting out rent, council tax and other bills in the early months after being rehoused. One man had been rehoused for three months when interviewed yet his housing benefit had not been sorted out. He was extremely worried as his rent book showed that he owed over £1,300, and he was contemplating leaving his home. Another had been waiting for nearly ten months for his benefits to be sorted out. In London, the majority of homeless people rehoused by resettlement agencies in the early 1990s experienced problems with paying bills, budgeting and sorting out grants and housing benefit payments, and one-third (of 117 subjects) had rent arrears when interviewed (Randall and Brown 1994b).

Factors in the success or failure of resettlement

Formal resettlement programmes are growing in the homeless sector but as yet have rarely been evaluated (Randall and Brown 1994b). There is little evidence of the direct outcomes of the resettlement of homeless people such as the number who remain housed after several months, and even less on the factors which increase success. One recent 'enhanced' study in New York City found that mentally ill men who were given additional support when rehoused from a temporary shelter were less likely to become homeless than those who received the usual community support: the benefit continued even after the enhanced support ceased (Susser *et al.* 1997). Only a few studies have contacted former homeless people who have been rehoused (Dant and Deacon 1989; Duncan and Downey 1985; Duncan *et al.* 1983).

Among 72 hostel residents rehoused by the Leeds Shaftesbury Project, 28 left their tenancy within two years, but there was no connection between whether a person stayed and their experience of managing household chores and paying bills, and their contact with relatives and friends (Dant and Deacon 1989). Resettlement tended to be least successful for those who had been in the city for less than six months. Among the Four-City Study sample, older men with long histories of transience and resettlement unit usage were more likely than those who had stayed in one city and never used resettlement units to have been rehoused, but they were also likely to have become homeless again. Other studies have noted that resettlement unit users generally have long histories of institutional living, sleeping rough and transience, and have proved more difficult to resettle than other hostel residents (Vincent *et al.* 1995).

Heavy drinking and mental health problems are likely to be important factors which influence the success of resettlement, particularly if people with such problems are rehoused in independent accommodation without adequate support. Reports from the Four-City Study sample suggest that loneliness and coping difficulties aggravated and intensified problems for some who were mentally ill or heavy drinkers. Some lost tenancies because they drank excessively and did not pay rent. One man, rehoused alone in a council flat, became lonely and depressed, drank heavily, and abandoned the flat after seven months. He was rehoused again two years later, but experienced the same problems and left the flat after nine months. Another man was resettled in a warden-assisted flat but ceded his tenancy after 13 days. While in the flat, he drank heavily, became deluded, and believed that people were trying to harm him. He described his flat as 'a death trap'. Before being resettled, there was no evidence to suggest that he was a heavy drinker or mentally ill.

Among the Four-City Study subjects who were housed when interviewed but displaying homelessness behaviours, two-thirds had mental health problems (Table 9.3). Some were receiving no treatment and stayed on the streets at night because they believed that neighbours or terrorists would harm them if they returned home. One woman, rehoused in sheltered accommodation, believed that her warden was plotting against her. She had refused to pay rent and was taken to the rent tribunal. She explained: 'I did not pay rent because I do not want to live there; there are 21 surveillance cameras watching me at home.' Another woman had a council flat but stayed on the streets several nights each week. She believed that her neighbours were trying to harm her, and did not feel safe at home. The out-reach workers at the Lancefield Street Centre have found that some older formerly homeless people stay on the streets at night because they have severe memory problems and forget that they have been rehoused (Crane and Warnes 1998).

Adequate preparation and planning for moving are important features. Some older people in the Four-City and the Lancefield Street Centre studies who were rehoused without adequate preparation and planning have ceded tenancies shortly afterwards. One man regularly used a day centre and was rehoused into a local authority tenancy. Although he was in contact with services, he received no help with resettlement and when he moved into his flat he had neither furniture, bedding, curtains nor carpets. The first night he slept on the floor covered by his overcoat. An elderly neighbour arranged for him to obtain some second-hand furniture. He left the flat after a few weeks. Another 62-year-old man was rehoused into a flat from a hostel. He had a history of homelessness and depression dating back 30 years, had suffered two heart attacks, and 15 months earlier had had a heart operation. He received little help from the hostel staff with preparing to move, and when he moved to his flat, it was filthy, damp, and had no heating. He had a bed and chair, but no cooker or fridge; and no arrangements had been made for him to take over the electricity account. When visited at home ten days later, he still had no heating, he was wearing several layers of clothing because his flat was cold, and he had stopped taking his medication for depression. He abandoned his flat just four weeks after moving in. Another investigation also found that many single homeless people were rehoused in unfurnished council tenancies but lacked basic household goods such as a cooker and fridge (Pleace 1995).

Effective monitoring and support once a person is rehoused are important. The Homeless Mentally Ill Initiative teams found that most tenancy breakdowns among clients occurred shortly after the teams withdrew support (Craig 1995). Practices among organizations vary. Many provide support only for the first 6–12 months after a person has been rehoused. Others offer long-term support. St Martin-in-the-Fields Day Centre has a 'resettlement group' which meets every two weeks and there is no limit on the length of time people can attend. It offers support to those who are rehoused, advice if needed, and the opportunity for people to share experiences. Similarly, the Over 55s Accommodation Project in Leeds has a monthly luncheon club for older people who have been rehoused. The clients have the opportunity to seek help and advice, and the staff are able to monitor their progress.

Although at an early stage, there are indications from the resettlement study and from the Four-City Study that older people with long histories of homelessness and heavy drinking or mental illness who need supported housing, find it easier to settle in accommodation specifically for the group than in conventional sheltered housing and high-care group homes for older people. Among the homeless population, the group requiring such accommodation consists typically of men who have very different backgrounds from the majority of older tenants in mainstream supported accommodation, who are predominantly women. One man in the Lancefield Street Centre Study has been rehoused in conventional sheltered housing. He feels uncomfortable in the accommodation as the other tenants are mainly women, he is reluctant to use the communal lounge, and his feelings have been exacerbated by the hostility of some residents who have become aware that he has slept rough for years. Another man has experienced similar problems in a conventional residential home.

Several evaluations have been undertaken of the resettlement from long-stay hospitals of mentally ill people and of those with learning disabilities (Etherington *et al.* 1995; Higgins and Richardson 1994; Pickard *et al.* 1991; Malin 1983), and of the cost-effectiveness of such moves (Dockrell *et al.* 1995; Knapp *et al.* 1994). The progress of those resettled has been monitored for up to five years (Trieman *et al.* 1998; Cambridge *et al.* 1994; Francis *et al.* 1994; Craig and Timms 1992). The longer experience of resettlement in work with other vulnerable and disadvantaged groups could be drawn upon when planning resettlement for homeless people.

The way forward

Resettlement services for homeless people are multiplying but are uncoordinated and unevenly developed. They are provided both by generalist hostel and day centre staff, and by specialist, designated teams. Schemes differ according to the experience and qualifications of staff and the range of interventions. Some hostels have rehabilitation programmes and resettlement workers who prepare the residents for resettlement and effectively liaise with other agencies and housing providers. But others lack such programmes, provide no opportunity for residents to practise or learn independent living skills, and do not encourage residents to move. Schemes also differ according to the type and intensity of support which homeless people receive once they are rehoused. Some offer no follow-up support. In others, resettlement or community-housing support workers continue to monitor the client's progress at home, and a few offer long-term support.

Resettlement should be the ultimate goal of all service providers working with older homeless people. It is a process and requires a continuum of services from the streets, to temporary accommodation, and to permanent tenured housing (Figure 12.1). Temporary accommodation with 24-hour shelter and services – more than a bed at night – is therefore needed, and intensive, sensitive, carefully planned and individualized assessment, treatment, rehabilitation and resettlement programmes. There is also a need for staff trained in and dedicated to rehabilitation and resettlement, who are able to prepare clients to move into permanent accommodation and who are able to develop information networks and cross-referral paths with complementary providers, particularly with local housing organizations. Because of the reluctance of many older homeless people to use services for homeless people of all ages, and because hostels and day centres are often dominated by younger homeless people, services and workers dedicated to older homeless people are required.

A range of permanent housing is required to provide varying levels of independence, companionship and support, including independent housing with support, shared housing schemes, and small high-care group homes. Effective monitoring and support are also needed once an older homeless person is rehoused. Procedures and practices which enable this require: (i) reliable ways of keeping in contact with those who are rehoused; (ii) flexibility in the frequency and intensity of monitoring; (iii) ways of assessing and adjusting counselling and instrumental support; (iv) approaches and instruments which reliably detect critical levels of 'residential distress', loneliness and morale; and (v) regular liaison between the resettlement agency, the landlord and the support services.

There is a need for comprehensive local strategies for older homeless people through consortia of voluntary and statutory organizations, to monitor the scale and nature of homelessness among older people locally, to regulate the establishment of services so that resources are targeted efficiently into high-quality and effective service provision, to ensure better coordination of services, and to identify gaps in service provision. In London, for example, the need for a centre to be established for older formerly homeless people which is open during the day and evening, and which provides social contacts and purposeful activities should be explored. At present, many of the group still linger on the streets and circulate around the day centres and soup kitchens once they are rehoused.

There is a strong case for building evaluation programmes into services and programmes so that lessons learned from innovations and good practice can be disseminated, providers learn more and more about effective and ineffective care, and scarce resources can be targeted at efficient high-quality services. There is little longitudinal evidence of factors which enhance resettlement, the outcomes of resettlement, and the number of people who remain housed after several months. Thus different approaches are opportunistically adopted. The DoE (now DETR) has developed performance indicators, a support needs index, and targets for out-reach and resettlement work (DoE *et al.* 1996; Randall and Brown 1995). Many service providers are now keen to set working standards and goals, and to develop models of good practice. The National Homeless Alliance launched in August 1997 a National Resettlement Project to develop good practice, and in 1998 they published the Resettlement Handbook that describes practice (National Homeless Alliance 1997).

There are no simple remedies for homelessness and there is 'an unabated flow of people (young and old) finding themselves homeless on the streets' in Britain (Williamson 1993: 75; Crane and Warnes 1998). During the 1990s, the need for services dedicated to older homeless people has been increasingly realized and acted upon. The innovative services have demonstrated that it is possible successfully to help and resettle older homeless people. But the problem is still a long way from being resolved or minimized. Specialist interventions and services are needed nation-wide to prevent older people from becoming homeless and to help those on the streets and in hostels to resettle back into the community. This is long overdue.

Afterwords

Note

by Paul Potts

My dreams
Watching me said
One to the other
This life has let us down.

First published in 1944. From *Instead of a Sonnet* (Paul Potts, 1978, Tuba Press, London).

This man's home is on his back

Appendix A: Glossary

Bag people: typically older people who sleep rough, are isolated, rummage through litter bins, and hoard old food, newspapers and garbage in carrier bags and shopping-trolleys. Many have mental health problems.

Cold-weather shelters: shelters which are funded through the Rough Sleepers Initiative and are open between December and March.

Detoxification units: units which attempt to help people reduce excess consumption of alcohol. Many admit people for short, intensive periods of treatment and withdrawal from alcohol.

Direct-access hostels: hostels for single homeless people which offer immediate accommodation, and accept referrals from any agency, including self-referrals.

Entrenched homelessness: the state of acceptance, nihilism and lack of hope for a better housed state that is found among long-term rough sleepers.

Flop-houses: in America, lodging houses which consist of small cubicles measuring 4 feet by 7 feet. The cubicles are separated by a thin wall that extends part way to the ceiling and the space is filled by chicken wire (Cohen and Sokolovsky 1989).

High-care homes: a term employed in social housing and the homelessness sector for accommodation which is registered with social services and has 24-hour coverage of staff to provide psychological and personal care support.

Homeless Mentally Ill Initiative: launched in 1990 by the Department of Health and the Mental Health Foundation to provide services for mentally ill people sleeping on the streets in London.

Homelessness behaviours: in this book, a term used to describe the distinctive behaviour of people who congregate on the streets with homeless people and regularly use day centres and soup kitchens for homeless people. In its extreme form the behaviour may also include sleeping on the streets, drinking alcohol in doorways, rummaging through litter bins, hoarding rubbish in shopping-trolleys and begging, observed among some housed people.

Indigent homeless people: in this study, a term used to describe homeless people who sleep rough or stay in hostels and night-shelters, and who are not statutory homeless, that is, officially registered as homeless with local authority housing departments.

Out-reach workers: workers on the streets whose objectives are to make contact with people sleeping rough and persuade them to accept help and to move into accommodation.

Rehabilitation: training to build or to restore personal care, household or other skills to enable a person to function at a level needed in the intended situation.

Resettlement: the planned move of a person to tenured accommodation, usually with an unrestricted period of residence and with the provision of personal and social support if needed.

Resettlement Units: former reception centres (or spikes) which became the responsibility of the Department of Health and Social Services in 1976. They originated from the casual wards, became the responsibility of the National Assistance Board in 1948, and were sometimes referred to as 'spikes' (which referred to the splitting iron used in stone-breaking). They have either now closed or are managed mainly by voluntary organizations.

Rough Sleepers Initiative (RSI):   launched in 1990 by the Conservative government to provide services for people sleeping on the streets in inner London zones. Extended in 1996 to other towns and cities in England where sleeping rough is a problem.

Shared houses: tenured accommodation for homeless people with non-residential support workers. Three to six people live together, they have their own bedroom but share kitchen and bathroom facilities.

Skid row: an area of a city predominantly inhabited by homeless men, and which offers cheap lodgings in missions, flop-houses, single-room occupancy hotels, and services such as cheap bars and cafés, second-hand clothing stores and pawnshops. Originated in Seattle as 'Skid Road', and referred to a street lined with cheap hotels, taverns and restaurants used by Henry Yesler, a local lumberman, to roll or 'skid' logs to his sawmill on the waterfront. Implies downward social mobility, as in 'being on the skids' (Hoch and Slayton 1989; Cohen and Sokolovsky 1989).

Skippering: term used by homeless people to describe sleeping in open or public places at night.

Sleeping rough: primary night-time residence is in the streets, in doorways, railway stations and bus terminals, public plazas and parks, subways, abandoned buildings, loading docks, disused cars and other hidden street sites (Baxter and Hopper 1981: 6–7).

SRO hotels: in America, Single-Room Occupancy Hotels originally designed as accommodation for poor transient workers. The hotels were designed in a way to maximize density and provide for the minimal needs of the migrants (Hoch and Slayton 1989).

Statutory homeless people: people who are registered with British local authority housing departments as homeless. They are included in official statistics of homelessness.

Street sites: in this book, a term used to refer to recognized street locations where homeless people sleep and where handouts of food and clothing are distributed.

Transience: in this book, a term used to refer to the frequent movement from town to town of some homeless people.

Vagrants: homeless people who are unsettled, wander from place to place, sleep rough, are destitute, and scavenge. Vagrancy is a term recognized by English statutes for six centuries.

Appendix B: The methodology of the empirical studies

The Four-City Study

The Four-City Study, conducted for a doctoral thesis, is an ethnographic field study of 159 men and 66 women aged 55 years and over. It lasted for 15 months from June 1994. Brief details of the study design and methodology are described. Further details are available in Crane (1997).

The population studied

Of the 225 subjects, 145 were interviewed in London, 32 in Sheffield, 34 in Leeds and 14 in Manchester. When first interviewed, 71 subjects were sleeping rough, 102 were in hostels, resettlement units or night-shelters, and 52 had permanent accommodation but displayed homelessness behaviours. All except nine of the latter group had been homeless. It was a convenience sample and does not claim to be representative of all older homeless people. Homelessness is a transient state, many older homeless people are hidden and not registered with a general practitioner, and the prevalence of homelessness among the group is unknown. It is therefore impossible to construct a sampling frame and to obtain a representative sample of older homeless people. Considerable efforts were made, however, to include as diverse a group as possible within the capacity constraints of a single researcher. The sample will have been dependent upon the balance of time spent at different settings. Sampling will also have been affected because access into some women's hostels was refused, and some hostel residents were excluded because they had severe mental health problems and could not provide information.

Locating the subjects

Just over 1,540 hours were spent conducting field-work. Nearly half of the time was spent on the streets, one-third in day centres and soup kitchens, and one-fifth in hostels and resettlement units. This partly reflects the amount of time needed to 'search' for and develop trust with isolated rough sleepers. The field-work began in London, Sheffield and Leeds, and Manchester was included in the final three months of the study to supplement the numbers of female respondents and people sleeping rough in the North of England. All hostels in Leeds and Sheffield and all women's hostels in London were contacted. Because of the large number of men's hostels in London, initially three which were known to have large numbers of older residents were selected. As interviews were completed at these facilities, others were contacted. By the end of the field-work, 19 hostels and 11 day centres and soup kitchens had been involved in the study. These offered a diverse range of services and included direct-access hostels, a probation hostel, and hostels for people who have mental health and drink problems.

Three methods were used to make contact with older rough sleepers who did not use services. Regular visits were made to 'street sites' where homeless people congregate and where handouts of food are distributed. Many hours were spent in the evening and at night 'searching' in subways, abandoned buildings and other hidden sites for isolated older homeless people. Time was also spent at railway and bus stations, and in public squares, observing and waiting for the appearance of older homeless people who move around a city looking for food.

Interviewing strategies

It was not appropriate to use a fully structured questionnaire with this subject group, and therefore a schedule of required information was designed, piloted and used as a framework in interviews. Interviews were conducted in a flexible, semi-structured procedure which allowed for detailed information to be collected while the interviews were paced and the questions sequenced to meet individual reactions, needs and abilities. Older homeless people are often suspicious and uncooperative if taping interviews is suggested. Permission was not therefore sought for interviews to be taped but the subjects were asked if notes could be made during the interview. The majority agreed to this. Two-fifths were interviewed just once, 35 per cent had at least five interviews, and a few were interviewed up to ten times. The number of times a person was interviewed, the length of each interview, and the extent of information depended on several factors, including whether the person could be relocated, their cooperation, and their ability to provide details. Because of mental health problems, it was particularly difficult to interview and collect information from some rough sleepers, particularly older women.

The quality of the data

Detailed histories were collected from 157 subjects, partial information from 48 subjects, and minimal details from 20 subjects. The reliability and validity of the data were checked wherever possible. Reported facts were checked for internal consistency. After each interview, histories were recorded in a chronological order and facts compared to determine their plausibility and accuracy. Wherever possible, the subjects were interviewed on several occasions. This allowed checks for reliability and discrepancies and ambiguities to be verified. Through repeated questioning and probing during the interviews, it was sometimes possible to identify misconceptions and elicit more accurate details. The observed behaviour of the subjects, such as signs of anger or distress when discussing traumatic events, suggested (although it did not confirm) the plausibility of the information.

The field-work was conducted in several settings, and therefore contact was made with some respondents in more than one location. This enabled their behaviour to be observed in different settings and at different times of the day and night. Having contact with a person intermittently over months increased the likelihood of observing unreported problems. Wherever possible, information about the subjects was collected from the staff at hostels and day centres, and compared with that reported by the subjects. Information was compared between subjects and its plausibility strengthened by external consistency. For example, men who had been itinerant workers and were unknown to each other, described similar work and accommodation experiences.

The Lancefield Street Centre Study

The Lancefield Street Centre Study started in February 1997 at a 24-hour drop-in centre and hostel for older homeless people, in Lancefield Street, west London, and is still in progress in August 1998. The research has two elements. It combines a monitoring study of the Lancefield Street Centre residents with a longitudinal study of the resettlement of older homeless people. Brief details of the studies are described. Further details are available in Crane and Warnes (1998).

A monitoring study of the Lancefield Street Centre residents

The aim of this study is to monitor the progress of older homeless people who are admitted to the Lancefield Street Centre. A questionnaire has been piloted and is administered to all residents who stay in the centre for more than seven days, and who agree to participate in the study. The questionnaire has three parts which collect from the subjects: (i) their personal details and circumstances in the last five years; (ii) their history of homelessness and resettlement experiences; and (iii) details about their morale, and future aspirations and plans. The subjects who remain in the hostel are re-interviewed every four months, and information is collected about changes in their physical and mental health, morale, behaviour, daily activities, social contacts and personal care, and about interventions and services which they have received. By August 1998, 70 subjects were involved in the study.

A longitudinal study of the resettlement of older homeless people

A longitudinal study of the resettlement of clients from the Lancefield Street Centre has been designed and implementation begun. The eligible subjects are those rehoused in permanent accommodation, including high-care group homes. Two questionnaires have been developed. The first collects information about the client's rehabilitation and resettlement programme, and the move to accommodation. It is completed when the client is about to be rehoused. The second collects information from the client at three-monthly intervals once they are rehoused. The resettlement study has been extended to the Over 55s Accommodation Project in Leeds, and to the St Martin-in-the-Fields Day Centre in central London. By August 1998, there were 36 subjects in the study.

References

Abramson, L., Seligman, M. and Teasdale, J. (1978) Learned helplessness in humans: critique and reformulation, *Journal of Abnormal Psychology*, 87(1), 49–74.

Alloy, L., Abramson, L., Metalsky, G. and Hartlage, S. (1988) The hopelessness theory of depression: attributional aspects, *British Journal of Clinical Psychology*, 27, 5–21.

Allsop, K. (1967) *Hard Travellin': The Story of the Migrant Worker*. London, Pimlico.

Alstrom, C., Lindelius, R. and Salum, I. (1975) Mortality among homeless men, *British Journal of Addiction*, 70, 245–52.

Anderson, E. (1978) *A Place on the Corner*. Chicago, University of Chicago Press.

Anderson, N. (1923) *The Hobo: The Sociology of the Homeless Man*. Chicago, University of Chicago Press.

Anderson, I., Kemp, P. and Quilgars, D. (1993) *Single Homeless People: A Report for the Department of the Environment*. London, Her Majesty's Stationery Office.

Anon. (1998) 9718 (PP): Supporting a National Priority to Eliminate Homelessness. Policy Statements Adopted by the Governing Council of the American Public Health Association, November 12, 1997, *American Journal of Public Health*, 88(3), 518–21.

Archard, P. (1979) *Vagrancy, Alcoholism and Social Control*. London, Macmillan Press.

Argyle, M. and Henderson, M. (1985) *The Anatomy of Relationships: and the Rules and Skills Needed to Manage Them Successfully*. London, Penguin.

Audit Commission (1989) *Housing the Homeless: The Local Authority Role*. London, Her Majesty's Stationery Office.

Audit Commission (1998) *Home Alone: The Role of Housing in Community Care*. London, Audit Commission.

Avramov, D. (1995) *Homelessness in the European Union: Social and Legal Context of Housing Exclusion in the 1990s*. Fourth Research Report of the European Observatory on Homelessness. Brussels, FEANTSA.

Bachrach, L. (1987) Geographic mobility and the homeless mentally ill, *Hospital and Community Psychiatry*, 38(1), 27–8.

Bachrach, L. (1992) What we know about homelessness among mentally ill persons: an analytical review and commentary, *Hospital and Community Psychiatry*, 43(5), 453–64.

Bahr, H. (1967) Drinking, interaction, and identification: Notes on socialization into Skid Row, *Journal of Health and Social Behaviour,* 8, 272–85.

Bahr, H. and Caplow, T. (1974) *Old Men Drunk and Sober.* New York, New York University Press.

Bahr, H. and Garrett, G. (1976) *Women Alone: The Disaffiliation of Urban Females.* Lexington, MA, Lexington Books.

Balazs, J. (1993) Health care for single homeless people. In K. Fisher and J. Collins (eds), *Homelessness, Health Care and Welfare Provision.* London, Routledge, pp. 51–93.

Baum, A. and Burnes, D. (1993) *A Nation in Denial: The Truth about Homelessness.* Boulder, CO, Westview Press.

Baxter, E. and Hopper, K. (1981) *Private Lives/Public Spaces: Homeless Adults on the Streets of New York City.* New York, Community Service Society, Institute for Social Welfare Research.

Baxter, E. and Hopper, K. (1982) The new mendicancy: Homeless in New York City, *American Journal of Orthopsychiatry,* 52(3), 393–408.

Belcher, J. (1988a) Are jails replacing the mental health system for the homeless mentally ill? *Community Mental Health Journal,* 24(3), 185–95.

Belcher, J. (1988b) Right versus needs of homeless mentally ill persons. *Social Work USA,* 33, 398–402.

Belcher, J. and DiBlasio, F. (1990) The needs of depressed homeless persons: designing appropriate services, *Community Mental Health Journal,* 26(3), 255–66.

Bengston, V., Burgess, E. and Parrott, T. (1997) Theory, explanation, and a third generation of theoretical development in social gerontology, *Journal of Gerontology: Social Sciences,* 52(2), S72–88.

Bennett, A. (1997) *Writing Home.* London, Faber and Faber.

Bennett, N., Jarvis, L., Rowlands, O., Singleton, N. and Haselden, L. (1996) *Living in Britain: Results from the 1994 General Household Survey.* London, Her Majesty's Stationery Office.

Berry, C.A. (1978) *Gentleman of the Road.* London, Constable.

Bines, W. (1994) *The Health of Single Homeless People.* York, Centre for Housing Policy, University of York.

Bines, W. (1997) The health of single homeless people. In R. Burrows, N. Pleace and D. Quilgars (eds), *Homelessness and Social Policy.* London, Routledge, pp. 132–48.

Blumberg, L., Hoffman, F., LoCicero, V. *et al.* (1960) *The Men on Skid Row: A Study of Philadelphia's Homeless Man Population.* Philadelphia, Temple University School of Medicine.

Bogue, D. (1963) *Skid Row in American Cities,* Chicago, University of Chicago Press.

Bramley, G. (1994) *Homelessness in Rural England: Statistical Update to 1992/93.* Salisbury, Rural Development Commission.

Bramley, G., Doogan, K., Leather, P., Murie, A. and Watson, E. (1988) *Homelessness and the London Housing Market.* Bristol, School for Advanced Urban Studies.

Breakey, W. (1996) Clinical work with homeless people in the USA. In D. Bhugra (ed.), *Homelessness and Mental Health.* Melbourne, Cambridge University Press, pp. 110–32.

Brickner, P., Scanlan, B., Conanan, B. *et al.* (1986) Homeless persons and health care, *Annals of Internal Medicine,* 104, 405–9.

Brunton, A. (1995) *Bodmin Gaol, Cornwall.* Terry Gilhooly, Bodmin Gaol, Bodmin, Cornwall.

Buchanan, A. and Brinke, J. (1997) *What happened When They Were Grown Up? Outcomes from Parenting Experiences.* York, Joseph Rowntree Foundation.

Bull, J. (1993) *Housing Consequences of Relationship Breakdown.* London, Her Majesty's Stationery Office.

Burnett, J. (1994) *Idle Hands: The Experience of Unemployment, 1790–1990.* London, Routledge.

Burrows, R. (1997) The social distribution of the experience of homelessness. In R. Burrows, N. Pleace and D. Quilgars (eds), *Homelessness and Social Policy*. London, Routledge, pp. 50–68.

Burt, M. (1992) *Over the Edge: The Growth of Homelessness in the 1980s*. New York, Russell Sage Foundation.

Burt, M. (1995) Critical factors in counting the homeless: An invited commentary, *Amercian Journal of Orthopsychiatry*, 65(3), 334–9.

Burt, M. and Cohen, B. (1989) Differences among homeless single women, women with children, and single men, *Social Problems*, 36(5), 508–24.

Calsyn, R. and Morse, G. (1991) Correlates of problem drinking among homeless men, *Hospital and Community Psychiatry*, 42(7), 721–5.

Cambridge, P., Hayes, L., Knapp, M., Gould, E. and Fenyo, A. (1994) *Care in the Community: Five Years On*. Aldershot, Ashgate.

Campaign for the Homeless and Rootless (1985) *The Future of Resettlement Units*. Occasional Papers 4. London, CHAR.

Caplow, T. (1940) Transiency as a cultural pattern, *American Sociological Review*, 5, 731–9.

Caplow, T., Bahr, H. and Sternberg, D. (1968) 'Homelessness' In D. Stills (ed.), *International Encyclopaedia of the Social Sciences*. New York, Macmillan, pp. 494–9.

Carlisle, J. (1996) *The Housing Needs of Ex-prisoners*. Housing Research 178. York, Joseph Rowntree Foundation.

Carlisle, J. (1997) The housing needs of ex-prisoners. In R. Burrows, N. Pleace and D. Quilgars (eds), *Homelessness and Social Policy*. London, Routledge, pp. 123–31.

Carter, M. (1997) *The Last Resort: Living in Bed and Breakfast in the 1990's*. London, Shelter.

Cavell, I. (1993) Plots, counter plots and pecking orders, *New Statesman and Society: Gimme Shelter*, 2 April, pp. 12–13.

Chambliss, W. (1964) A sociological analysis of the law of vagrancy, *Social Problems*, 12, 67–77.

Citron, K., Southern, A. and Dixon, M. (1995) *Out of the Shadow: Detecting and Treating Tuberculosis amongst Single Homeless People*. London, Crisis.

Clapham, D., Kemp, P. and Smith, S. (1990) *Housing and Social Policy*. Basingstoke, Macmillan.

Clark, A., Mankikan, G. and Gray, I. (1975) Diogenes Syndrome: A clinical study of gross neglect in old age. *Lancet*, 15 February 1975, 366–8.

Clement, P.F. (1984) The transformation of the wandering poor in nineteenth century Philadelphia. In E. Monkkonen (ed.), *Walking to Work: Tramps in America, 1790–1935*. Lincoln, University of Nebraska Press, pp. 56–84.

Cloward, R. and Ohlin, L. (1960) *Delinquency and Opportunity: A Theory of Delinquent Gangs*. London, Routledge and Kegan Paul.

Coalition for the Homeless (1984) *Crowded Out: Homelessness and the Elderly Poor in New York City*. New York, Coalition for the Homeless.

Cobain, I. (1998) Hobo of the House: MPs mourn tragic tramp who lobbied them for 35 years, *Daily Mail*, 16 January, p. 26.

Cohen, C. and Sokolovsky, J. (1983) Toward a concept of homelessness among aged men, *Journal of Gerontology*, 38(1), 81–9.

Cohen, C. and Sokolovsky, J. (1989) *Old Men of the Bowery: Strategies for Survival Among the Homeless*. New York, Guilford Press.

Cohen, C., Teresi, J. and Holmes, D. (1988) The physical well-being of old homeless men, *Journal of Gerontology*, 43(4), S121–8.

Cohen, C., Onserud, H. and Monaco, C. (1992) Project Rescue: Serving the homeless and marginally housed elderly, *The Gerontologist*, 32(4), 466–71.

Cohen, C., Onserud, H. and Monaco, C. (1993) Outcomes for the mentally ill in a program for older homeless persons. *Hospital and Community Psychiatry*, 44(7), 650–6.

Cohen, C., Ramirez, M., Teresi, J., Gallagher, M. and Sokolovsky, J. (1997) Predictors of becoming redomiciled among older homeless women, *The Gerontologist*, 37(1), 67–74.

Coleman, D. and Salt, J. (1992) *The British Population: Patterns, Trends, and Processes*. New York, Oxford University Press.

Coleman, T. (1965) *The Railway Navvies: A History of the Men Who Made the Railways*. Harmondsworth, Penguin.

Connelly, J. and Crown, J. (1994) *Homelessness and Ill Health: Report of a Working Party of the Royal College of Physicians*. London, Royal College of Physicians.

Consortium Joint Planning Group (1981) *The Proposed Closure of Camberwell Reception Centre and Its Implications for Services in S.E. London: A Report from the Consortium Planning Group*. Camberwell, London, S.E. London Consortium.

Cook, T. (1979) *Vagrancy: Some New Perspectives*. London, Academic Press.

Cooper, A. (1997) *All in a Day's Work: A Guide to Good Practice in Day Centres Working with Homeless People*. London, CHAR.

Cooper, R., Watson, L. and Allan, G. (1994) *Shared Living: Social Relations in Supported Housing*. Sheffield, Joint Unit for Social Services Research, University of Sheffield.

Coston, C. (1989) The original designer label: Prototypes of New York City's shopping-bag ladies, *Deviant Behaviour*, 10, 157–72.

Craig, T. (1995) *The Homeless Mentally Ill Initiative: An Evaluation of Four Clinical Teams*. London, Department of Health.

Craig, T. and Timms, P. (1992) Out of the wards and onto the streets? Deinstitutionalization and homelessness in Britain, *Journal of Mental Health*, 1, 265–75.

Craig, T., Hodson, S., Woodward, S. and Richardson, S. (1996) *Off to a Bad Start: A Longitudinal Study of Homeless Young People in London*. London, The Mental Health Foundation.

Crane, M. (1990) *Elderly Homeless People in Central London*. London, Age Concern England and Age Concern Greater London.

Crane, M. (1993) *Elderly People Sleeping on the Streets in Inner London: An Exploratory Study*. London, Age Concern Institute of Gerontology, King's College.

Crane, M. (1994) The mental health problems of elderly people living on London's streets, *International Journal of Geriatric Psychiatry*, 9, 87–95.

Crane, M. (1997) Pathways to later life homelessness. Ph.D. thesis, University of Sheffield, Sheffield.

Crane, M. and Warnes, A. (1997a) *Homeless Truths: Challenging the Myths about Older Homeless People*. London, Help the Aged and Crisis.

Crane, M. and Warnes, A. (1997b) *Coming Home: A Guide to Good Practice by Projects Helping Older Homeless People*. London, Help the Aged.

Crane, M. and Warnes, A. (1998) *The Lancefield Street Centre: An Experimental Project for Older Homeless People in London*. Report to the King's Fund. Sheffield, University of Sheffield.

Crockett, N. and Spicker, P. (1994) *Discharged: Homelessness among Psychiatric Patients in Scotland*. Edinburgh, Shelter Scotland.

Crockett, T., Watson, P., Chandler, R., Harrison, M. and Taylor, V. (1997) *London Hostels Directory 1997*. London, Resource Information Service.

Crocq, L. (1997) The emotional consequences of war 50 years on: a psychiatrist's perspective. In L. Hunt, M. Marshall and C. Rowlings (eds), *Past Trauma in Late Life: European Perspectives on Therapeutic Work with Older People*. London, Jessica Kingsley, pp. 39–48.

Crystal, S. (1984) Homeless men and homeless women: The gender gap, *Urban and Social Change Review*, 17, 2–6.

Cumming, E. and Henry, W. (1961) *Growing Old: The Process of Disengagement*. New York, Basic Books.

Currie, H. and Pawson, H. (1996) *Temporary Accommodation for Homeless Households in Scotland: A Study of Local Policies and Provision*. Edinburgh, Shelter Scotland.

Daly, G. (1996) *Homeless: Policies, Strategies, and Lives on the Streets*. London, Routledge.

Daly, M. (1992) *European Homelessness: The Rising Tide*. First Report of the European Observatory on Homelessness. Brussels, FEANTSA.

Daly, M. (1993) *Abandoned: Profile of Europe's Homeless People*. Second Report of the European Observatory on Homelessness. Brussels, FEANTSA.

Damrosch, S. and Strasser, J. (1988) The homeless elderly in America, *Journal of Gerontological Nursing*, 14(10), 26–9.

Dant, T. and Deacon, A. (1989) *Hostels to Homes? The Rehousing of Homeless Single People*. Aldershot, Avebury.

Davies, S. and Leat, M. (1997) The Western approach. *Roof*, September/October, 32–3.

Deacon, A., Vincent, J. and Walker, R. (1993) *The Closure of Alvaston Resettlement Unit: Summary Report*. Loughborough, Centre for Research in Social Policy, Department of Social Sciences, Loughborough University.

DeMallie, D., North, C. and Smith, E. (1997) Psychiatric disorders among the homeless: a comparison of older and younger groups. *The Gerontologist*, 37(1), 61–6.

Department of the Environment (1996) *Government provides further help for rough sleepers*. Press release 454/96, 31 October.

Department of the Environment and Welsh Office (1995) *Our Future Homes: Opportunity, Choice, Responsibility*. Cm 2901. London, The Stationery Office.

Department of the Environment, Department of Health and Welsh Office (1994) *Homelessness Code of Guidance for Local Authorities: Revised Third Edition*. London, Her Majesty's Stationery Office.

Department of the Environment, Department of Health, Department of Social Security, Home Office and Department for Education and Employment (1995) *Rough Sleepers Initiative: Future Plans*. Consultation Paper, October. London, DoE.

Department of the Environment, Department of Health, Department of Social Security, Home Office and Department for Education and Employment (1996) *Rough Sleepers Initiative: The Next Challenge*. Strategy Paper, March. London, DoE.

Department of the Environment, Transport and the Regions (1998) Statistics of local authority activities under the homelessness legislation: England. Information Bulletin 194, 13 March.

Department of Health (1990) Stephen Dorrell announces new scheme to help homeless and mentally ill people in London. Press release 90/352, 12 July.

Department of Health (1992) More money to help mentally ill people sleeping rough. Press release H92/31, January.

Department of Health and Social Security (1969) Report of the Committee on Local Authority and Allied Personal Social Services (Seebohm Report). London, Her Majesty's Stationery Office.

D'Ercole, A. and Struening, E. (1990) Victimization among homeless women: Implications for service delivery, *Journal of Community Psychology*, 18, 141–52.

Digby, P.W. (1976) *Hostels and Lodgings for Single People*. London, Her Majesty's Stationery Office.

Dittmar, H. (1992) *The Social Psychology of Material Possessions: To Have Is To Be*. Hemel Hempstead, Harvester Wheatsheaf.

Dockrell, J., Gaskell, G., Normand, C. and Rehman, H. (1995) An economic analysis of the resettlement of people with mild learning disabilities and challenging behaviour. *Social Science and Medicine*, 40(7), 895–901.

Doolin, J. (1986) Planning for the special needs of the homeless elderly, *The Gerontologist*, 26, 229–31.

Douglas, A., MacDonald, C. and Taylor, M. (1998) *Living Independently with Support: Service Users' Perspective on 'Floating Support'*. Bristol, Policy Press.

Douglass, R., Atchison, B., Lofton, W. *et al.* (1988) *Aged, Adrift and Alone: Detroit's Elderly*

Homeless. Final Report to the Detroit Area Agency on Aging. Ypsilanti, Department of Associated Health Professions, Eastern Michigan University.

Downing-Orr, K. (1996) *Alienation and Social Support: A Social Psychological Study of Homelessness in London and Sydney*. Aldershot, Avebury.

Drake, M. (1989) Fifteen years of homelessness in the UK, *Housing Studies*, 4(2), 119–27.

Drake, R., Yovetich, N., Bebout, R., Harris, M. and McHugo, G. (1997) Integrated treatment for dually diagnosed homeless adults. *Journal of Nervous and Mental Disease*, 185, 298–305.

Duck, S. (1992) *Human Relationships*, 2nd edn. London, Sage.

Duncan, S., Downey, P. and Finch, H. (1983) *A Home of Their Own: A Survey of Rehoused Hostel Residents*. London, Her Majesty's Stationery Office.

Duncan, S. and Downey, P. (1985) *Settling Down: A Study of the Rehousing of Users of DHSS Resettlement Units*. London, Her Majesty's Stationery Office.

Durkheim, E. (1984) *The Division of Labour in Society*, translated by W.D. Halls. London, Macmillan. First published in 1893.

Eardley, T. (1989) *Move-On Housing: The Permanent Housing Needs of Residents of Hostels and Special Needs Housing Projects in London*. London, National Federation of Housing Associations.

Eckert, J. (1980) *The Unseen Elderly: A Study of Marginally Subsistent Hotel Dwellers*. San Diego, CA, Campanile Press, San Diego State University.

Edwards, G., Williamson, V., Hawker, A. and Hensman, C. (1966) London's Skid Row. *The Lancet*, 29 January, 249–52.

Elam, G. (1992) *Survey of Admissions to London Resettlement Units*. Department of Social Security: Research Report No.12. London, Her Majesty's Stationery Office.

Elder, G. and Clipp, E. (1988) Combat experience, comradeship, and psychological health. In J. Wilson, Z. Harel and B. Kahana (eds), *Human Adaptation to Extreme Stress: From the Holocaust to Vietnam*. New York, Plenum Press, pp. 131–56.

Elias, C. and Inui, T. (1993) When a house is not a home: exploring the meaning of shelter among chronically homeless older men, *The Gerontologist*, 33(3), 396–402.

Elliott, M. and Krivo, L. (1991) Structural determinants of homelessness in the United States, *Social Problems*, 38(1), 113–31.

Erikson, E. (1965) *Childhood and Society*. Harmondsworth, Penguin.

Erikson, E. (1982) *The Life Cycle Completed: A Review*. New York, W.W. Norton.

Etherington, A., Stocker, B. and Whittaker, A. (1995) *Outside but not Inside*. London, People First.

Farr, R., Koegel, P. and Burnam, A. (1986) *A Study of Homelessness and Mental Illness in the Skid Row Area of Los Angeles*. Los Angeles, Los Angeles County Department of Mental Health.

Fennell, G., Phillipson, C. and Evers, H. (1988) *The Sociology of Old Age*. Milton Keynes, Open University Press.

Fine, G. and Kleinman, S. (1979) Rethinking subculture: an interactionist analysis, *American Journal of Sociology*, 85(1), 1–20.

Fischer, C. (1976) Alienation: trying to bridge the chasm, *British Journal of Sociology*, 27(1), 35–49.

Fischer, P. and Breakey, W. (1986) Homelessness and mental health: an overview, *International Journal of Mental Health*, 14(4), 6–41.

Fischer, P. and Breakey, W. (1991) The epidemiology of alcohol, drug, and mental disorders among homeless persons, *American Psychologist*, 46(11), 1115–28.

Fisher, K. and Collins, J. (1993) Access to health care. In K. Fisher and J. Collins (eds), *Homelessness, Health Care and Welfare Provision*. London, Routledge, pp. 32–50.

Fisher, N., Turner, S., Pugh, R. and Taylor, C. (1994) Estimating numbers of homeless and homeless mentally ill people in North East Westminster by using capture-recapture analysis, *British Medical Journal*, 308, 27–30.

Francis, V., Vesey, P. and Lowe, G. (1994) The closure of a long-stay psychiatric hospital: a longitudinal study of patients' behaviour. *Social Psychiatry and Psychiatric Epidemiology*, 29(4), 184–9.

Gallagher, D., Thompson, L. and Peterson, J. (1981–82) Psychosocial factors affecting adaptation to bereavement in the elderly, *International Journal of Aging and Human Development*, 14(2), 79–95.

Garside, P., Grimshaw, R. and Ward, F. (1990) *No Place Like Home: The Hostels Experience*. London, Her Majesty's Stationery Office.

Gelberg, L., Linn, L. and Mayer-Oakes, S.A. (1990) Differences in health status between older and younger homeless adults, *Journal of the American Geriatrics Society*, 38, 1220–9.

Gelles, R. (1979) *Family Violence*. London, Sage.

George, C., Simmons, D., Thurley, D. and Wright, S. (1997) *National Welfare Benefits Handbook*, 27th edn. London, Child Poverty Action Group.

George, M.D. (1966) *London Life in the Eighteenth Century*. London, Peregrine. First published in 1925.

George, S., Shanks, N. and Westlake, L. (1991) Census of single homeless people in Sheffield, *British Medical Journal*, 302, 1387–9.

Gibinu, B. (1994) Phil duuli, aetting gone, *Journal of Social Distress and the Homeless*, 3(2), 203–6.

Giddens, A. (1989) *Sociology*. Cambridge, Polity Press.

Gilchrist, A. and Clark, G. (1994) Hell hostel. *The Big Issue*, 91, 18–19.

Gillin, J.L. (1929) Vagrancy and begging. *American Journal of Sociology*, 35, 424–32.

Glasgow Council for Single Homeless (1996) *Homelessness: A Directory of Key Services in Glasgow 1996*. Glasgow, Glasgow Council for Single Homeless.

Glaser, B. and Strauss, A. (1967) *The Discovery of Grounded Theory: Strategies for Qualitative Research*. New York, Aldine de Gruyter.

Glasser, I. (1988) *More Than Bread: Ethnography of a Soup Kitchen*. Tuscaloosa, University of Alabama Press.

Goffman, E. (1959) *The Presentation of Self in Everyday Life*. London, Penguin.

Goffman, E. (1961) *Asylums: Essays on the Social Situation of Mental Patients and Other Inmates*. London, Penguin.

Goffman, E. (1963) *Stigma: Notes on the Management of Spoiled Identity*. Englewood Cliffs, NJ, Prentice Hall.

Goodman, L., Saxe, L. and Harvey, M. (1991) Homelessness as psychological trauma, *American Psychologist*, 46(11), 1219–25.

Grenier, P. (1996) *Still Dying for a Home*. London, Crisis.

Greve, J. (1991) *Homelessness in Britain*. York, Joseph Rowntree Foundation.

Grigsby, C., Baumann, D., Gregorich, S. and Roberts-Gray, C. (1990) Disaffiliation to entrenchment: a model for understanding homelessness, *Journal of Social Issues*, 46(4), 141–55.

Gunner, G. and Knott, H. (1997) *Homeless on Civvy Street: Survey of Homelessness amongst Ex-servicemen in London 1997*. London, Sir Oswald Stoll Foundation.

Gurland, B. and Fogel, B. (1992) Functional mental disorders of the elderly. In J. Brocklehurst, R. Tallis and H. Fillit (eds), *Textbook of Geriatric Medicine and Gerontology*. 4th edn. New York, Churchill Livingstone, pp. 349–64.

Hagan, J. and McCarthy, B. (1997) *Mean Streets: Youth Crime and Homelessness*. Cambridge, Cambridge University Press.

Hagestad, G. and Smyer, M. (1982) Dissolving longterm relationships: patterns of divorcing in middle age. In S. Duck (ed.), *Personal Relationships 4: Dissolving Personal Relationships*. London, Academic Press.

Hallebone, E. (1997) Homelessness and marginality in Australia: Young and old people excluded from independence. In M. Huth and T. Wright (eds), *International Critical Perspectives on Homelessness*. Westport, CT, Praeger, pp. 69–103.

Ham, J. (1996) *Steps from the Street: A Report on Direct Access Provision*. London, CHAR and Crisis.

Hand, J. (1983) Shopping-bag women: aging deviants in the city. In E. Markson (ed.), *Older Women*. Lexington, MA, Lexington Books, pp. 155–77.

Harrison, M. (1996) *Emergency Hostels: Direct Access Accommodation in London 1996*. London, Single Homelessness in London and the London Borough Grants Committee.

Havighurst, R. (1963) Successful ageing. In R. Williams, C. Tibbitts and W. Donahue (eds), *Processes of Ageing, Volume 1*. New York, Atherton, pp. 299–320.

Hayward, D. (1975) Home as an environmental and psychological concept, *Landscape*, 20, 2–9.

Herman, D., Susser, E., Struening, E. and Link, B. (1997) Adverse childhood experiences: are they risk factors for adult homelessness? *American Journal of Public Health*, 87(2), 249–55.

Hertz, E. and Hutheesing, O. (1975) At the edge of society: the nominal culture of urban hotel isolates, *Urban Anthropology*, 4, 317–32.

Higgins, R. and Richardson, A. (1994) Into the community: a comparison of care management and traditional approaches to resettlement. *Social Policy and Administration*, 28(3), 221–350.

Hill, R. and Stamey, M. (1990) The homeless in America: an examination of possessions and consumption behaviours, *Journal of Consumer Research*, 17, 303–21.

Hinton, T. (1992) *Health and Homelessness in Hackney*. London, The Medical Campaign Project.

Hirschi, T. (1969) *Causes of Delinquency*. Los Angeles, University of California Press.

Hoch, C. (1991) The spatial organization of the urban homeless: a case study of Chicago, *Urban Geography*, 12(2), 137–54.

Hoch, C. and Slayton, R. (1989) *New Homeless and Old: Community and the Skid Row Hotel*, Philadelphia, Temple University Press.

Holden, N. (1987) Late paraphrenia or the paraphrenias? A descriptive study with a 10-year follow up. *British Journal of Psychiatry*, 150, 635–9.

Holmes, R. (1985) *Firing Line*. London, Pimlico.

Holmes, T. and Rahe, R. (1967) The social readjustment rating scale, *Journal of Psychosomatic Research*, 11, 213–18.

Home Office (1974) *Working Party on Vagrancy and Street Offences Working Paper*. London, Her Majesty's Stationery Office.

Homeless Network (1995) *Central London Street Monitor: November 16th 1995*. London, Homeless Network.

Homeless Network (1996) *Central London Street Monitor: May 23rd 1996*. London, Homeless Network.

Hooker, K., Frazier, L. and Monahan, D. (1994) Personality and coping among caregivers of spouses with dementia. *The Gerontologist*, 34(3), 386–92.

Hunt, A. (1978) *The Elderly at Home: A Study of People Aged Sixty Five and Over Living in the Community in England in 1976*. London, Her Majesty's Stationery Office.

Hunter, E. (1988) The psychological effects of being a prisoner of war. In J. Wilson, Z. Harel and B. Kahana (eds), *Human Adaptation to Extreme Stress: From the Holocaust to Vietnam*. New York, Plenum Press, pp. 157–70.

Hutson, S. and Liddiard, M. (1994) *Youth Homelessness: The Construction of a Social Issue*, Basingstoke, Macmillan.

Inside Housing (1998) Motor home. *Inside Housing*, 21 August 1998, 4.

Jackson, J. (1963) *The Irish in Britain*, London, Routledge & Kegan Paul.

Jackson, J. and Connor, R. (1953) The Skid Row alcoholic. *Quarterly Journal of Studies on Alcohol*, 14, 468–86.

Jaco, E.G. (1954) The social isolation hypothesis and schizophrenia, *American Sociological Review*, 19, 567–77.

Jacobs, C., Woods, N. and Crockett, T. (1998) *London Day Centres Directory: Services for Homeless People*, 3rd edn. London, Resource Information Service.

Jahiel, R. (1992) Health and health care of homeless people. In M. Robertson and M. Greenblatt (eds), *Homelessness: A National Perspective*. New York, Plenum Press, pp. 133–63.

Jarvik, L., Lavretsky, E. and Neshkes, R. (1992) Dementia and delirium in old age. In J. Brocklehurst, R. Tallis and H. Fillit (eds), *Textbook of Geriatric Medicine and Gerontology*, 4th edn. New York, Churchill Livingstone, pp. 326–48.

Jencks, C. (1994) *The Homeless*. Cambridge, MA, Harvard University Press.

Johnson, S. (1997) Dual diagnosis of severe mental illness and substance misuse: a case for specialist services? *British Journal of Psychiatry*, 171, 205–8.

Jones, E., Farina, A., Hastorf, A. *et al.* (1984) *Social Stigma: The Psychology of Marked Relationships*. New York, W.H. Freeman.

Joseph, P. (1996) Homelessness and criminality. In D. Bhugra (ed.), *Homelessness and Mental Health*. Cambridge, Cambridge University Press, pp. 78–95.

Jütte, R. (1994) *Poverty and Deviance in Early Modern Europe: New Approaches to European History*. Cambridge, Cambridge University Press.

Kahana, E., Kahana, B. and Kinney, J. (1990) Coping among vulnerable elders. In Z. Harel, P. Ehrlich and R. Hubbard (eds), *The Vulnerable Aged: People, Services and Policies*, New York, Springer, pp. 64–85.

Kay, D. and Roth, M. (1961) Environmental and hereditary factors in the schizophrenias of old age ('late paraphrenia') and their bearing on the general problem of causation in schizophrenia, *Journal of Mental Science*, 107, 649–81.

Keigher, S., Berman, R. and Greenblatt, S. (1989) *Relocation, Residence and Risk: A Study of Housing Risks and the Causes of Homelessness among the Urban Elderly*. Chicago, Metropolitan Chicago Coalition of Aging.

Kelly, J. (1985) Trauma: with the example of San Francisco's shelter programs. In P. Brickner, L. Scharer, B. Conanan, A. Elvy and M. Savarese (eds), *Health Care of Homeless People*, New York, Springer, pp. 77–91.

Keniston, K. (1972) The varieties of alienation: an attempt at definition. In A. Finifter (ed.), *Alienation and the Social System*, New York, Wiley, pp. 32–54.

Keyes, S. and Kennedy, M. (1992) *Sick to Death of Homelessness: An Investigation into the Links between Homelessness, Health and Mortality*. London, Crisis.

Kirby, P. (1994) *A Word from the Street: Young People Who Leave Care and Become Homeless*, London, Centrepoint.

Knapp, M., Cambridge, P., Thomason, C. *et al.* (1994) Residential care as an alternative to long-stay hospital: a cost-effectiveness evaluation of two pilot projects. *International Journal of Geriatric Psychiatry*, 9, 297–304.

Koegel, P. (1992) Through a different lens: an anthropological perspective on the homeless mentally ill, *Culture, Medicine and Psychiatry*, 16, 1–22.

Koegel, P. and Burnam, A. (1988) Alcoholism among homeless adults in the inner city of Los Angeles, *Archives of General Psychiatry*, 45, 1011–18.

Koegel, P. and Burnam, A. (1992) Problems in the assessment of mental illness among the homeless: an empirical approach. In M. Robertson and M. Greenblatt (eds), *Homelessness: A National Perspective*, New York, Plenum Press, pp. 77–99.

Koegel, P., Burnam, A. and Farr, R. (1988) The prevalence of specific psychiatric disorders among homeless individuals in the inner city of Los Angeles, *Archives of General Psychiatry*, 45, 1085–92.

Koegel, P., Melamid, E. and Burnam, A. (1995) Childhood risk factors for homelessness among homeless adults, *American Journal of Public Health*, 85(12), 1642–9.

Kutza, E. (1987) *A Study of Undomiciled Elderly Persons in Chicago: A Final Report*. Chicago, Retirement Research Foundation.

Ladner, S. (1992) The elderly homeless. In M. Robertson and M. Greenblatt (eds), *Homelessness: A National Perspective*, New York, Plenum Press, pp. 221–6.

La Gory, M., Ferris, R. and Mullis, J. (1990) Depression among the homeless, *Journal of Health and Social Behaviour*, 31, 87–101.

Lally, M., Black, E., Thornock, M. and Hawkins, J. (1979) Older women in single room occupant (SRO) hotels: A Seattle profile, *The Gerontologist*, 19(1), 67–73.

Lamb, H. (1984) Deinstitutionalization and the homeless mentally ill, *Hospital and Community Psychiatry*, 35(9), 899–907.

Lamb, H. (1990) Will we save the homeless mentally ill? *American Journal of Psychiatry*, 147(5), 649–51.

Lamb, H. and Lamb, D. (1990) Factors contributing to homelessness among the chronically and severely mentally ill, *Hospital and Community Psychiatry*, 41, 301–4.

Lambert, C., Jeffers, S., Burton, P. and Bramley, G. (1992) *Homelessness in Rural Areas*. Rural Research Series No.12. Salisbury, Rural Development Commission.

Laufer, R. (1988) The serial self: war trauma, identity, and adult development. In J. Wilson, Z. Harel and B. Kahana (eds), *Human Adaptation to Extreme Stress: From the Holocaust to Vietnam*, New York, Plenum Press, pp. 33–53.

Lazarus, R. (1993) Coping theory and research: past, present, and future, *Psychosomatic Medicine*, 55, 234–47.

Leeds City Council (1997) Report on the Extent of Rough Sleeping in Leeds. Leeds, Homeless and Advisory Services Group, Department of Housing Services.

Leppard, D. (1994) Major wins street cred in fight against beggars. *Sunday Times*, 29 May, 2.

Liebow, E. (1967) *Tally's Corner: A Study of Negro Streetcorner Men*. Boston, Little, Brown and Co.

Liebow, E. (1993) *Tell Them Who I Am: The Lives of Homeless Women*. New York, Free Press.

Link, B., Phelan, J., Bresnahan, M. *et al.* (1995) Lifetime and five-year prevalence of homelessness in the United States: new evidence on an old debate, *American Journal of Orthopsychiatry*, 65(3), 347–54.

Lipmann, B. (1995) *The Elderly Homeless: An Investigation into the Provision of Services for Frail, Elderly Homeless Men and Women in the United States of America, Britain, Sweden and Denmark*, Flemington, Victoria, Wintringham Hostels.

Lishman, W. (1998) *Organic Psychiatry: the Psychological Consequences of Cerebral Disorder*, 3rd edn. Oxford, Blackwell Science.

Llewellin, S. and Murdoch, A. (1996) *Saving the Day: The Importance of Day Centres for Homeless People*. London, CHAR.

Lofland, J. and Lofland, L. (1984) *Analyzing Social Settings: A Guide to Qualitative Observation and Analysis*. Belmont, CA, Wadsworth.

London, J. (1903) *The People of the Abyss*. London, Isbister and Company.

Lowe, S. (1997) Homelessness and the law. In R. Burrows, N. Pleace and D. Quilgars (eds), *Homelessness and Social Policy*, London, Routledge, pp. 19–34.

Lund, B. (1996) *Housing Problems and Housing Policy*. London, Longman.

Macmillan, D. (1966) Senile breakdown in standards of personal and environmental cleanliness. *British Medical Journal*, 29 October 1966, 1032–7.

Maddox, G. (1964) Disengagement theory: a critical evaluation. *The Gerontologist*, 4, 80–3.

Maitra, A. (1982) Dealing with the disadvantaged: single homeless, are we doing enough? *Journal of Public Health, London*, 96, 141–4.

Malin, N. (1983) *Group Homes for Mentally Ill Handicapped People*. London, Her Majesty's Stationery Office.

Malpass, P. and Murie, A. (1994) *Housing Policy and Practice*, 4th edn. London, Macmillan Press.

Mann, K. (1992) *The Making of an English 'Underclass'? The Social Divisions of Welfare and Labour*. Buckingham, Open University Press.

Marcos, L., Cohen, N., Nardacci, D. and Brittain, J. (1990) Psychiatry takes to the streets: the New York City initiative for the homeless mentally ill, *American Journal of Psychiatry*, 147(11), 1557–61.

Mayhew, H. (1968) *London Labour and the London Poor*. Volume III. New York, Dover Publications. First published in 1861.

McCluskey, J. (1997) *Where There's a Will: A Guide to Developing Single Homelessness Strategies*. London, CHAR.

McCord, J. (1990) Long-term perspectives on parental absence. In L. Robins and M. Rutter (eds), *Straight and Devious Pathways from Childhood to Adulthood*, New York, Cambridge University Press, pp. 116–34.

McCord, W. and McCord, J. (1962) A longitudinal study of the personality of alcoholics. In D. Pittman and C. Snyder (eds), *Society, Culture, and Drinking Patterns*. New York, Wiley, pp. 413–30.

McLoughlin, D. and Farrell, M. (1997) Substance misuse in the elderly. In I. Norman and S. Refern (eds), *Mental Health Care for Elderly People*. New York, Churchill Livingstone, pp. 205–21.

McManners, H. (1993) *The Scars of War*. London, HarperCollins.

Meikle, P. (1992) Search for tramp's family, *City Post*, 20 February 3.

Merton, R. (1968) *Social Theory and Social Structure*. 3rd edn. Glencoe, IL, Free Press.

Middleton, A. (1994) Homeless are 'not there by choice' says Government report, *The Big Issue*, 82, 7.

Miller, S. and Miller, R. (1991) An exploration of daily hassles for persons with severe psychiatric disabilities. *Psychosocial Rehabilitation Journal*, 14(4), 39–51.

Ministry of Housing & Local Government (1969) *Council Housing Purposes, Procedures and Priorities*. Report of the Housing Management sub-committee. London, Her Majesty's Stationery Office.

Moore, J., Canter, D., Stockley, D. and Drake, M. (1995) *The Faces of Homelessness in London*. Aldershot, Dartmouth.

Morgan, R., Geffner, E., Kiernan, E. and Cowles, S. (1985) Alcoholism and the homeless. In P. Brickner, L. Scharer, B. Conanan, A. Elvy and M. Savarese (eds), *Health Care of Homeless People*. New York, Springer, pp. 131–50.

Morrish, P. (1996) *Preventing Homelessness: Supporting Tenants with Alcohol Problems*. London, Shelter.

Morse, G. (1992) Causes of homelessness. In M. Robertson and M. Greenblatt (eds), *Homelessness: A National Perspective*. New York, Plenum Press, pp. 3–17.

National Assistance Board (1966) *Homeless Single Persons*. London, Her Majesty's Stationery Office.

National Homeless Alliance (1997) *Towards Quality Report: On the 1997 Resettlement Conference, August 27th–28th*. London, National Homeless Alliance.

Nettler, G. (1957) A measure of alienation. *American Sociological Review*, 22, 670–7.

Neugarten, B. (1996) *The Meanings of Age: Selected Papers of Bernice L. Neugarten*. Chicago, University of Chicago Press.

Niner, P. (1989) *Homelessness in Nine Local Authorities: Case Studies of Policy and Practice*. London, Her Majesty's Stationery Office.

Niner, P. (1997) *The Early Impact of the Housing Act 1996 and Housing Benefit Changes*. London, Shelter.

Norris, F. and Murrell, F. (1984) Protective function of resources related to life events, global stress and depression in older adults, *Journal of Health and Social Behaviour*, 25, 424–37.

North, Carol and Smith, E. (1992) Posttraumatic stress disorder among homeless men and women, *Hospital and Community Psychiatry*, 43(10), 1010–16.

North, Carol, Pollio, D., Smith, E. and Spitznagel, E. (1998) Correlates of early onset and chronicity of homelessness in a large urban homeless population. *Journal of Nervous and Mental Disease*, 186(7), 393–400.

North, Christopher, Moore, H. and Owens, C. (1996) *Go Home and Rest? The Use of an Accident and Emergency Department by Homeless People*. London, Shelter.

O'Callaghan, B., Dominian, L., Evans, A. *et al.* (1996) *Study of Homeless Applicants*. London, Her Majesty's Stationery Office.

O'Connor, P. (1963) *Britain in the Sixties: Vagrancy*. London, Penguin.

Office of Population Censuses and Surveys (1991a) *Supplementary Monitor on People Sleeping Rough*. Preliminary Report for England and Wales. London, OPCS.

Office of Population Censuses and Surveys (1991b) *Census Officer Briefing of Enumerators for Persons Sleeping Rough*. Titchfield, Fareham, Hants, OPCS.

Office of Population Censuses and Surveys (1993a) *1991 Census: County Report 17/1: Inner London*. Part 1. London, Her Majesty's Stationery Office.

Office of Population Censuses and Surveys (1993b) *1991 Census: Report for Great Britain*. Part 1, Vol 1. London, Her Majesty's Stationery Office.

Office of Population Censuses and Surveys (1993c) *1991 Census: Ethnic Group and Country of Birth: Great Britain*. Vol 1. London, Her Majesty's Stationery Office.

Okely, J. (1983) *The Traveller-Gypsies*. Cambridge, Cambridge University Press.

Oldman, J. and Hooton, S. (1993) *The Numbers Game: Lessons from Birmingham*. London, CHAR.

O'Leary, J. (1997) *Beyond Help? Improving Service Provision for Street Homeless People with Mental Health and Alcohol or Drug Dependency Problems*. London, National Homeless Alliance.

Orwell, G. (1949) *Down and Out in Paris and London*. London, Penguin, in association with Seeker and Warburg. First published in 1933.

Park, P. (1962) Problem drinking and role deviation: a study in incipient alcoholism. In D. Pittman and C. Snyder (eds), *Society, Culture, and Drinking Patterns*. New York, Wiley, pp. 431–54.

Parkes, C.M. (1986) *Bereavement: Studies of Grief in Adult Life*, 2nd edn. Harmondsworth, Penguin.

Parsons, T. (1942) Age and sex in the social structure of the United States, *American Sociological Review*, 7, 604–16.

Parsons, T. (1951) *The Social System*. London, Routledge & Kegan Paul.

Paylor, I. (1992) *Homelessness and Ex-offenders: A Case of Reform*. Social Work Monographs. Norwich, Norfolk, University of East Anglia.

Pearlin, L. and Schooler, C. (1978) The structure of coping, *Journal of Health and Social Behaviour*, 19, 2–21.

Penhale, F. (1997) Homeless death could have been prevented, *The Big Issue*, 215, 4.

Peterson, W. and Maxwell, M. (1958) The Skid Row 'wino', *Social Problems*, 5, 308–16.

Pfohl, S. (1994) *Images of Deviance and Social Control: A Sociological History*, 2nd edn. New York, McGraw-Hill.

Pickard, L., Proudfoot, R. and Wolfson, P. (1991) *The Closure of Cane Hill Hospital: Report of the Cane Hill Evaluation Team*. London, Research and Development for Psychiatry.

Piliavin, I., Sosin, M., Westerfelt, A. and Matsueda, R. (1993) The duration of homeless careers: an exploratory study. *Social Service Review*, 65, 576–98.

Pittman, D. and Gordon, T. (1958) *Revolving Door: A Study of the Chronic Police Case Inebriate*. Glencoe, IL, Free Press.

Pleace, N. (1995) *Housing Vulnerable Single Homeless People*. York, Centre for Housing Policy, University of York.

Pleace, N. (1998) *The Open House Project for People Sleeping Rough: An Evaluation*. York, Centre for Housing Policy, University of York.

Pleace, N. and Quilgars, D. (1996) *Health and Homelessness in London: A Review*. London, King's Fund.

Plummer, K. (1983) *Documents of Life: An Introduction to the Problems and Literature of a Humanistic Method*. London, Unwin Hyman.

Porteous, J. (1976) Home: the territorial core, *Geographical Review*, 66, 383–90.

Pugh, R. (n.d.) *Service Delivery to Homeless Customers: A Guide to Issues about Homelessness and Good Practice in Service Provision*. Leeds, Benefits Agency Publishing Services.

Quilgars, D. (1998) *A Life in the Community: Home-link; Supporting People with Mental Health Problems in Ordinary Housing*. Bristol, Policy Press.

Rahimian, A., Wolch, J. and Koegel, P. (1992) A model of homeless migration: homeless men in Skid Row, Los Angeles, *Environment and Planning A*, 24, 1317–36.

Randall, G. (1992) *Counted Out: An Investigation into the Extent of Single Homelessness outside London*. London, Crisis and CHAR.

Randall, G. and Brown, S. (1993) *The Rough Sleepers Initiative: An Evaluation*. London, Her Majesty's Stationery Office.

Randall, G. and Brown, S. (1994a) *Falling Out: A Research Study of Homeless Ex-Service People*. London, Crisis.

Randall, G. and Brown, S. (1994b) *The Move In Experience: Research into Good Practice in Resettlement of Homeless People*. London, Crisis.

Randall, G. and Brown, S. (1995) *Outreach and Resettlement Work with People Sleeping Rough*. Ruislip, Department of the Environment.

Randall, G. and Brown, S. (1996) *From Street to Home: An Evaluation of Phase 2 of the Rough Sleepers Initiative*. London, The Stationery Office.

Reich, R. and Siegel, L. (1978) The emergence of the Bowery as a psychiatric dumping ground. *Psychiatric Quarterly*, 50(3), 191–201.

Ribton Turner, C.J. (1887) *A History of Vagrants and Vagrancy and Beggars and Begging*. London, Chapman and Hall.

Rich, T., Boucher, L. and Rich, D. (1995) Old and homeless in Tampa Bay: a survey. In D. Rich, T. Rich and L. Mullins (eds), *Old and Homeless – Double Jeopardy: An Overview of Current Practice and Policies*. Westport, CT, Auburn House, pp. 119–37.

Richardson, J. (1991) *Camden Town and Primrose Hill Past: A Visual History of Camden Town and Primrose Hill*. London, Historical Publications.

Robertson, M. (1987) Homeless veterans: an emerging problem? In R. Bingham, R. Green and S. White (eds), *The Homeless in Contemporary Society*. London, Sage.

Robins, L., Bates, W. and O'Neal, P. (1962) Adult drinking patterns of former problem children. In D. Pittman and C. Snyder (eds), *Society, Culture, and Drinking Patterns*. New York, Wiley, pp. 395–412.

Rogers, A. and Pilgrim, D. (1996) *Mental Health Policy in Britain: A Critical Introduction*. Basingstoke, Macmillan.

Ropers, R. (1988) *The Invisible Homeless: A New Urban Ecology*. New York, Insight, Human Sciences Press.

Rose, L. (1988) *Rogues and Vagabonds: The Vagrant Underworld in Britain 1815–1985*. London, Routledge.

Rosenheck, R. and Koegel, P. (1993) Characteristics of veterans and nonveterans in three samples of homeless men, *Hospital and Community Psychiatry*, 44(9), 858–63.

Rosenheck, R., Harkness, L., Johnson, B. *et al.* (1998) Intensive community-focused treatment of veterans with dual diagnosis. *American Journal of Psychiatry*, 155(10), 1429–33.

Rosenthal, R. (1994) *Homeless in Paradise: A Map of the Terrain*. Philadelphia, Temple University Press.

Rossi, P. (1989) *Without Shelter: Homelessness in the 1980s*. New York, Priority Press.

Rossi, P. (1990) The old homeless and the new homelessness in historical perspective, *American Psychologist*, 45(8), 954–9.

Rossi, P., Fisher, G. and Willis, G. (1986) *The Condition of the Homeless of Chicago*. Chicago, National Opinion Research Center, University of Chicago.

Roth, D., Bean, J., Lust, N. and Saveanu, T. (1985) *Homelessness in Ohio: A Study of People in Need*. Columbus, Ohio Department of Mental Health.

Roth, D., Toomey, B. and First, R. (1992) Gender, racial, and age variations among homeless people. In M. Robertson and M. Greenblatt (eds), *Homelessness: A National Perspective*. New York, Plenum Press, pp. 199–211.

Rowe, S. and Wolch, J. (1990) Social networks in time and space: homeless women in Skid Row, Los Angeles, *Annals of the Association of American Geographers*, 80(2), 184–204.

Rubington, E. and Weinberg, M. (1978) *Deviance: The Interactionist Perspective*. New York, Macmillan.

Russell, B. (1991) *Silent Sisters: A Study of Homeless Women*. New York, Hemisphere Publishing.

Rutter, M. (1971) Parent–child separation: psychological effects on the children, *Journal of Child Psychology and Psychiatry*, 12, 233–60.

Sahlin, I. (1997) Discipline and border control in Sweden: Strategies for tenant control and housing exclusions. In M. Huth and T. Wright (eds), *International Critical Perspectives on Homelessness*. Westport, CT, Praeger, pp. 139–52.

Schneider, J. (1984) Tramping workers, 1890–1920: a subcultural view. In E. Monkkonen (ed.), *Walking to Work: Tramps in America, 1790–1935*. Lincoln, University of Nebraska Press, pp. 212–34.

Schreuder, J. (1997) Post-traumatic re-experiencing in old aged: working through or covering up? In L. Hunt, M. Marshall and C. Rowlings (eds), *Past Trauma in Late Life: European Perspectives on Therapeutic Work with Older People*. London, Jessica Kingsley pp. 17–30.

Schur, E. (1979) *Interpreting Deviance: A Sociological Introduction*. New York, Harper & Row.

Schwam, K. (1979) *Shopping Bag Ladies: Homeless Women*. New York, Manhattan Bowery Corporation.

Scottish Office (1998) *Statistical Bulletin: Operation of the Homeless Persons Legislation in Scotland 1986–87 to 1996–97*. Edinburgh, Scottish Office Development Department.

Seeman, M. (1975) Alienation studies, *Annual Review of Sociology*, 1, 91–123.

Shanks, N. (1984) Mortality among inmates of a common lodging house, *Journal of the Royal College of General Practitioners*, 34, 38–40.

Shelter (1996) *Evaluations of the Extent of Rough Sleeping outside Central London*. Final Report for the Department of the Environment. London, Shelter.

Sheridan, M., Gowen, N. and Halpin, S. (1993) Developing a practice model for the homeless mentally ill, *Families in Society*, 74(7), 410–21.

Single Homelessness in London (1995) *Time to Move On: A Review of Policies and Provision for Single Homeless People in London*. Twickenham, SHiL, London Borough Grants Unit.

Snow, D. and Anderson, L. (1993) *Down on Their Luck: A Study of Homeless Street People*. Berkeley, University of California Press.

Snow, D., Baker, S. and Anderson, L. (1988) On the precariousness of measuring insanity in insane contexts, *Social Problems*, 35(2), 192–6.

Snyder, M., Tanke, E. and Bersheid, E. (1977) Social perception and interpersonal behavior: on the self-fulfilling nature of social stereotypes, *Journal of Personality and Social Psychology*, 35(9), 656–66.

Social Exclusion Unit (1998) *Rough Sleeping: Report by the Social Exclusion Unit*. London, The Stationery Office.

Solenberger, A. (1911) *One Thousand Homeless Men: A Study of Original Records*. New York, Russell Sage Foundation.

Sosin, M., Colson, P. and Grossman, S. (1988) *Homelessness in Chicago: Poverty and Pathology, Social Institutions and Social Change*. Chicago, School of Social Service Administration, University of Chicago.

Sosin, M., Piliavin, I. and Westerfelt, H. (1990) Toward a longitudinal analysis of homelessness, *Journal of Social Issues*, 46(4), 157–73.

Southerton, P. (1993) *Reading Gaol by Reading Town*. Stroud, Berkshire Books.
Spaull, S. and Rowe, S. (1992) *Silt-Up or Move-On? Housing London's Single Homeless*. London, SHiL.
Spradley, J. (1970) *You Owe Yourself A Drunk: An Ethnography of Urban Nomads*. Boston, Little, Brown and Co.
Steinbeck, J. (1995) *The Short Novels*. London, Minerva.
Stephens, J. (1976) *Loners, Losers, and Lovers: Elderly Tenants in a Slum Hotel*. Seattle, Univeristy of Washington Press.
Straus, M. (1978) Wife-beating: how common and why? In J. Eckelaar and S. Katz (eds), *Family Violence*. Toronto, Butterworths, pp. 34–49.
Straus, M., Gelles, R. and Steinmetz, S. (1980) *Behind Closed Doors: Violence in the American Family*. New York, Anchor.
Straus, R. (1946) Alcohol and the homeless man, *Quarterly Journal of Studies on Alcohol*, 7, 360–404.
Stroebe, M. and Stroebe, W. (1983) Who suffers more? Sex differences in health risks of the widowed, *Psychological Bulletin*, 93(2), 279–301.
Struening, E. and Padgett, D. (1990) Physical health status, substance use and abuse, and mental disorders among homeless adults, *Journal of Social Issues*, 46(4), 65–81.
Sudman, S., Sirken, M. and Cowan, C. (1988) Sampling rare and elusive populations, *Science*, 240, 991–6.
Sullivan, M. (1991) The homeless older woman in context: alienation, cutoff and reconnection, *Journal of Women and Aging*, 3(2), 3–24.
Susser, E., Conover, S. and Struening, E. (1989) Problems of epidemiologic method in assessing the type and extent of mental illness among homeless adults, *Hospital and Community Psychiatry*, 40, 261–5.
Susser, E., Goldfinger, S. and White, A. (1990) Some clinical approaches to the homeless mentally ill, *Community Mental Health Journal*, 26(5), 463–80.
Susser, E., Moore, R. and Link, B. (1993) Risk factors for homelessness, *American Journal of Epidemiology*, 15(2), 546–56.
Susser, E., Struening, E. and Conover, S. (1987) Childhood experiences of homeless men, *American Journal of Psychiatry*, 144(12), 1599–601.
Susser, E., Valencia, E., Conover, S. et al. (1997) Preventing recurrent homelessness among mentally ill men: a 'critical time' intervention after discharge from a shelter. *American Journal of Public Health*, 87(2), 256–62.
Sutherland, E. and Locke, H. (1936) *Twenty Thousand Homeless Men*. Chicago, J.B. Lippincott.
Swift, R. (1989) Crime and the Irish in nineteenth-century Britain. In R. Swift and S. Gilley (eds), *The Irish in Britain 1815–1939*. London, Pinter, pp. 163–82.
Sykes, A. (1969a) Navvies: their work attitudes, *Sociology*, 3, 21–35.
Sykes, A. (1969b) Navvies: their social relations, *Sociology*, 3, 157–72.
Talbot Association (1995) *25 Years of Caring Services to Destitute People in Glasgow: Annual Report 1995*. Glasgow, Talbot Association.
Taschner, S. and Rabinovich, E. (1997) The homeless in São Paulo: Spatial arrangements. In M. Huth and T. Wright (eds), *International Critical Perspectives on Homelessness*. Westport, CT, Praeger, pp. 13–29.
Thoits, P. (1982) Conceptual, methodological, and theoretical problems in studying social support as a buffer against life stress, *Journal of Health and Social Behaviour*, 23, 145–59.
Thompson, E. (1995) The 1991 Census of population in England and Wales, *Journal of the Royal Statistical Society A*, 158(2), 203–40.
Timms, P. (1993) Mental health and homelessness. In K. Fisher and J. Collins (eds), *Homelessness, Health Care and Welfare Provision*. London, Routledge, pp. 94–116.
Toth, J. (1993) *The Mole People: Life in the Tunnels beneath New York City*. Chicago, Chicago Review Press.

Trieman, N., Smith, H., Kendal, R. and Leff, J. (1998) The TAPS Project 41: Homes for life? Residential stability five years after hospital discharge. *Community Mental Health Journal*, 34(4), 407–17.

Underwood, J. (1993) *The Bridge People: Daily Life in a Camp of the Homeless*. Lanham, MD, University Press of America.

Veness, A. (1992) Home and homelessness in the United States: changing ideals and realities. *Environment and Planning D: Society and Space*, 10, 445–68.

Veness, A. (1993) Neither homed nor homeless: contested definitions and the personal worlds of the poor, *Political Geography*, 12(4), 319–40.

Vincent, J., Deacon, A. and Walker, R. (1995) *Homeless Single Men: Roads to Resettlement?* Aldershot, Avebury.

Wagner, D. (1993) *Checkerboard Square: Culture and Resistance in a Homeless Community*. Boulder, CO, Westview Press.

Walker, R., Brittain, K., Deacon, A. and Vincent, J. (1993) *Shelter for the Night, A Home for Life: The Dynamics and Functions of Alvaston Resettlement Unit*. Loughborough, Centre for Research in Social Policy, Department of Social Sciences, Loughborough University.

Wallace, S. (1965) *Skid Row as a Way of Life*. Totowa, NJ, Bedminster Press.

Wallace, S. (1968) The road to skid row, *Social Problems*, 16(1), 92–105.

Wasylenki, D., Goering, P., Lemire, D., Lindsey, S. and Lancee, W. (1993) The hostel outreach program: assertive case management for homeless mentally ill persons. *Hospital and Community Psychiatry*, 44(9), 848–53.

Waters, J. (1992) *Community or Ghetto? An Analysis of Day Centres for Single Homeless People in England and Wales*. London, CHAR.

Watson, S. and Austerberry, H. (1986) *Housing and Homelessness: A Feminist Perspective*. London, Routledge & Kegan Paul.

Weiner, L. (1984) Sisters of the road: women transients and tramps. In E. Monkkonen (ed.), *Walking to Work: Tramps in America, 1790–1935*. Lincoln, University of Nebraska Press, pp. 171–88.

Weitzman, B., Knickman, J. and Shinn, M. (1990) Pathways to homelessness among New York City families, *Journal of Social Issues* 46(4), 125–40.

Weller, M. (1989) Mental illness: who cares? *Nature*, 339, 249–52.

Welsh Office (1997) *Welsh Housing Statistics 1997*. Cardiff, Welsh Office.

Welte, J. and Barnes, G. (1992) Drinking among homeless and marginally housed adults in New York State. *Journal of Studies on Alcohol*, 53(4), 303–15.

Wenger, G. (1994) *Understanding Support Networks and Community Care*. Aldershot, Avebury.

Wilkinson, T. (1981) *Down and Out*. London, Quartet Books.

Williams, R. and Avebury, K. (1995) *A Place in Mind: Commissioning and Providing Mental Health Services for People Who Are Homeless*. N.H.S. Health Advisory Service. London, Her Majesty's Stationery Office.

Williams, S. and Allen, I. (1989) *Health Care for Single Homeless People*. London, Policy Studies Institute.

Williamson, K. (1993) Update on homelessness, *Housing Review*, 42(5), 75.

Wilson, D. (1995) *'We Will Need To Take You In': The Experience of Homelessness in Old Age*. Edinburgh, Scottish Council for Single Homeless.

Wilson, D. (1997a) *The First Two Years: Homeless Older People Revisited*. Edinburgh, Age Concern Scotland.

Wilson, D. (1997b) *Retirement from Tied Housing: A Review of Housing Providers' Policies*. Edinburgh, Age Concern Scotland and the Scottish Council for Single Homeless.

Winick, M. (1985) Nutritional and vitamin deficiency states. In P. Brickner, L. Scharer, B. Conanan, A. Elvy and M. Savarese (eds), *Health Care of Homeless People*. New York, Springer, pp. 103–8.

Winkleby, M. and White, R. (1992) Homeless adults without apparent medical and psychiatric impairment: onset of morbidity over time, *Hospital and Community Psychiatry*, 43(10), 1017–23.

Wintringham Hostels (1995–96) *Wintringham Hostels Annual Report 1995–96*. Flemington, Victoria, Wintringham.

Wolch, J. and Dear, M. (1993) *Malign Neglect: Homelessness in an American City*. San Francisco, Jossey-Bass.

Wolch, J., Dear, M. and Akita, A. (1988) Explaining homelessness, *Journal of American Planning Association*, 54, 443–53.

Wolch, J., Rahimian, A. and Koegel, P. (1993) Daily and periodic mobility patterns of the urban homeless, *Professional Geographer*, 45, 159–69.

Wright, J. (1989) *Address Unknown: The Homeless in America*. New York, Aldine de Gruyter.

Wright, J. (1990) Poor people, poor health: the health status of the homeless, *Journal of Social Issues*, 46(4), 49–64.

Wright, J. and Devine, J. (1995) Housing dynamics of the homeless: implications for a count, *American Journal of Orthopsychiatry*, 65(3), 320–9.

Wright, J. and Everitt, G. (1993) *Homelessness in Boston: A Shelter Lincolnshire Report*. Sleaford, Shelter Lincolnshire.

Zozus, R. and Zax, M. (1991) Perceptions of childhood: exploring possible etiological factors in homelessness, *Hospital and Community Psychiatry*, 42(5), 535–7.

Index

alcohol, 126–8
  and mental illness, 130–1
  drinking habits, 58, 106–7, 126–7
  preceding homelessness, 20–1, 50–1,
    52–3, 62, 67, 80–2, 90–1, 116, 126
  influence on resettlement, 177–8
alcohol services, *see* Services for special-
  needs, alcohol
alienation, 13, 17, 44, 61, 91, 113–16
  see also disaffiliation
Anderson, Nels, 10, 18, 25, 60, 61
anomie, 13, 45, 88
armed forces, 12, 19, 46–7, 69, 73, 80–2,
  86, 89, 92, 126
  see also merchant seamen

bag people, 3, 72, 107–9, 117, 128, 183
Bahr, Howard, 11, 12, 13, 44, 62, 113
begging, 102, 111
Bowery, New York City, 22, 80, 98, 105,
  118, 126, 134

casual wards, 26, 61, 98, 110, 147–148,
  152, 153, 166
  see also reception centres
Chicago, 22–3, 36, 39, 44, 60, 78–9, 98,
  107, 114, 118, 123, 124, 128, 133–4,
  137
Cohen, Carl, 5, 10, 19, 20, 22, 23, 24,
  60, 61, 69, 71, 73, 80, 98, 101, 114,
  118, 124, 126, 127, 128, 129, 130,
  132, 134, 136, 137, 162, 165, 183,
  184
cold-weather shelters, 99, 130, 150, 155,
  157, 183
Community support workers, 93, 173–4
coping skills, 72, 83, 90–1
  difficulties, 19, 45, 70, 72, 89, 91,
    120–1
  strategies used, 20

Craig, Tom, 3, 44, 71, 72, 83, 131, 150,
  151, 158, 159, 161, 169, 178, 179
Crime, victims of, 134

day centres, 99, 105–6, 159–60
deinstitutionalization, 71, 149, 150–1
demoralization, 4, 24, 99, 123–5
Department of the Environment,
  Transport and the Regions, (*also*
  Department of the Environment)
  30, 150, 151, 180
Department of Health, 150, 151
depression, 4, 24, 58, 110–11, 123–5,
  126–7, 128–30, 131
Detroit, 22–3, 105, 128, 134
Diogenes syndrome, 109
disaffiliation, 12, 17, 18, 89, 110, 119
  see also alienation
discharge
  from armed forces, 19
  from psychiatric hospitals, 74, 179
  from prisons, *see* prisons, discharge from
disengagement theory, 24
domestic violence, 52–4
Dromomania, 9–10
drug abuse, 131
Durkheim, Emile, 13

entrenched homelessness, 2–3, 17, 41,
  117, 140, 183
estrangement, *see* alienation
eviction, 22–3, 48, 50, 70, 74, 76–7, 81,
  91, 156

families
  absence/breakdown of relationships,
    11, 19, 43–5, 49, 57, 66–7, 72, 74,
    78, 89, 113–116
  childhood homes, 19, 20–1, 43–4,
    45–7, 80

contact with, 55, 56–7, 113–14,
115–116
see also parents
flop-houses, 98, 183
food, sources of, 105

Goffman, Erving, 12, 17, 108
Greve, John, 18, 68, 87

hoarding garbage, 16, 107–9
Hoboes, 10, 60–1
home
adjustment to, 111–12
creating a home in a doorway, 101,
120
creating a home in a hostel, 99
meaning of, 15
Homeless Mentally Ill Initiative (HMII),
130, 150–1, 161, 178, 183
homeless people
enumeration difficulties, 30–2
indigent, 14–15, 16, 183
priority need groups, 14–15, 149
statistics, 1, 29–31, 152
statutory, 13–14, 16, 184
homeless people (older)
assessing needs, 171–2
characteristics, 35–7, 103, 104,
113–15
circumstances preceding
homelessness, 37–8, 84–5
daily activities, 106–7
defining 'older', 5
diets, 105
enumeration difficulties, 30–2
in Chicago *see* Chicago
in Detroit *see* Detroit
in New York City *see* Bowery, New
York City; New York City
personal hygiene, 97–8
statistics, 30, 32–5
sub-groups, 140–5
use of services, 105–6, 113
use of health services, 136–8
women, 99, 101, 105, 107, 115, 123,
127, 128–9
homelessness
behaviours, 16, 111–13, 183
behaviours among housed people, 15,
16, 39, 109, 111–13, 143–4, 145
definitions of, 13–16, 148–9
entry into, 37–8
episodes of, 39–41, 124

indigent (unofficial) homelessness,
14–15
loss of roles and responsibilities, 2–3,
17
prevention, 91–3
statutory (official) homelessness,
14–15, 16
theories, reasons for, 4, 10–13, 17–23,
24–5, 43–5, 60–2, 71, 85–91, 93–4
hopelessness, 4, 123–5, 127
hostels, 32, 67, 98–9, 101, 103, 105,
149–50, 153–4, 155–7
Hostels Initiative, 149–50
housing
programmes, 149
shortage of, 18–19, 87
Housing Acts, 13–15, 149, 151, 163, 166
Housing Associations, 149, 154
see also St Anne's Shelter and Housing
Action, Leeds; St Mungo's, London
Housing Benefit *see* Social Security
benefits
housing departments *see* local
authorities, housing departments
housing, special-needs, 150, 154, 158–9
shared houses, 109, 154, 158, 184
high-care homes, 159, 183
other supported housing, 158

institutional-living, 11–12, 19, 149
Irish descent, 36–7, 64–5, 69
itinerant workers, 10–11, 60–2, 86,
109–10,

Keigher, Sharon, 22, 23, 36, 41, 72, 83
Koegel, Paul, 21, 73, 117, 123, 126, 130,
161
Kutza, Elizabeth, 22, 23, 36, 41, 71, 72,
79, 83, 114, 128, 129, 134, 137

labourers, 15, 61–2, 63–5
local authorities
housing departments, 14, 15, 32, 34,
149, 155, 158
social services departments, 149, 155,
158, 183
lodgings, 38, 64, 67–8, 85, 91
lodging-houses, 98, 149, 152, 153, 183

marital breakdown, 44–5, 52–7, 76, 110
mental health problems
among homeless people, 71, 128–30
among ex-homeless people, 15, 178

mental health problems *continued*
  and alcohol, 130–1
  difficulties of detecting illness, 122–3
  influence on resettlement, 177–8
  in old age, 20–1, 72, 109, 122
  preceding homelessness, 20–1, 72,
    73–9
  services for mentally-ill people, 138
  see also depression
merchant seamen, 15, 60, 62–3, 67, 86,
  104
Merton, Robert, 12, 13, 45, 88
migratory workers, *see* itinerant workers
mortality rates, 135–6

National Assistance Act, 148, 152–3
New York City, 22–3, 38, 80, 99, 101,
  124, 127, 128, 134, 136, 138
  see also Bowery, New York City
night-shelters, 98, 99, 105, 152, 155–6

Orwell, George, 98, 110, 147
out-reach work, 130, 150, 159, 162–3,
  169–70, 184

Parents
  death of, 19, 44, 47–9, 74
  problems experienced by, 20–1
  see also families
Parsons, Talcott, 11, 13, 23
physical health problems, 5, 131–6
  affected by lifestyle, 132
  linked to alcohol, 127, 132
Poor Law, 26, 147–8, 149
poverty, 18–19, 87–8, 104–5
prisons, 37–8
  discharge from, 86, 92
  use of, 40, 107, 153

Randall, Geoffrey, 19, 32, 33, 34, 35, 69,
  72, 92, 150, 155, 158, 159, 169,
  177, 180
reception centres, 67, 98, 152–3
  see also casual wards
rehabilitation programmes and services,
  157, 161, 163, 184
rehousing, 38–9
  see also resettlement
resettlement, 38–40, 168–79, 184
  adjusting to settled living, 174, 175
  advantages for older homeless people,
    174–5

non-homeless groups, 92, 93, 179
  preparation, programmes, 92, 157–8,
    163–4, 172–3, 178
  problems experienced by
    ex-homeless people, 111, 158, 169,
      175–7, 178
  stages of, 169–74
  services, 157–8, 163–4
  successes and failures, 69, 169,
    177–9
  support and monitoring at home, 93,
    163–4, 173–4, 179, 180
  units, 38, 149, 184
    see also reception centres
  workers, 150, 155, 157–8
retirement, 13, 69–70, 86
retreatism, 2–3, 13, 17, 20, 45, 88
  see also alienation
Rosenthal, Rob, 19, 21, 43, 47, 71, 72,
  116, 117, 123, 126, 131
Rossi, Peter, 15, 18, 20, 45, 98, 107, 112,
  114, 123, 124, 128
rough sleepers, *see* sleeping rough
Rough Sleepers Initiative, 30, 150–2,
  183, 184
Rowton Houses, 98, 152, 155

St Anne's Shelter and Housing Action,
  Leeds, 154, 158, 161–2, 163
St Mungo's, London, 154, 155, 160, 162,
  174
Salvation Army, The, 148, 152, 153, 154,
  155
seasonal workers, *see* itinerant workers
services for special-needs
  alcohol, 161
  detoxification units, 127, 161, 183
  mental health, 138, 161
  primary health-care, 136–7, 160–1
services specifically for older homeless
  people, 162–5
  Project Rescue, New York City, 164–5,
    169
  Grangetown PREP, Cardiff, 163
  Lancefield Street Centre, London, 6,
    33, 136, 163, 169, 171, 187–8
  Over 55s Accommodation Project,
    Leeds, 31, 163–4
  Valley Lodge, New York City, 165
  Wintringham Hostels, Melbourne,
    Australia, 165
shopping-bag ladies, *see* bag people

Skid rows, 10, 60–2, 98, 184
sleeping rough, 3, 4, 31, 32–3, 97–8,
    99–101, 105–7, 113, 119, 129, 130,
    132, 134, 150–1, 169–70, 184
  sites used, 3, 14–15, 99–101, 134
  mole people, 3
Snow, David, 18, 19, 20, 21, 43, 71, 72,
    109, 117, 122, 123, 140
social contacts
  integration with peers, 117–18, 126,
    140
  lack of, 11, 47, 58, 61, 66–7, 89, 140
social control, theories of, 88–9
Social Exclusion Unit, 92, 151, 166
Social Security benefits, 102–4, 150
  community care grants, 173
social services departments, *see* local
    authorities
socialization
  links to mental illness, 20
  theory of undersocialization, 11–12,
    19, 68–9, 90
  see also families, contact with; social
    contacts
Solenberger, Alice, 10, 11, 18, 44, 60, 61,
    62
Sosin, Michael, 19, 20, 21, 39, 41, 45,
    73
soup kitchens, 105–6, 152, 159–60
  see also day centres
spikes, *see* casual wards
SRO (Single Room Occupancy) hotels,
    98, 165, 184

stresses, 19, 20–1, 49, 51, 52, 54–7,
    72–3, 75, 77, 79–82, 89–91, 126
  psychological trauma, 72–3, 90–1

tramping system, 61
tramps, *see* vagrants and vagrancy
transience, 31, 50–1, 61–2, 66, 109–11,
    117, 184
  and depression, 110–11
  and mental illness, 109

vagrants and vagrancy, 9–10, 12–13, 16,
    109, 147–8, 152, 153, 184
  Vagrancy Acts, 10, 147, 153
  punishments for, 147–8, 153
voluntary organizations, 148, 151–2, 154
  CHAR (Campaign for the Homeless
    and Rootless), 149
  Crisis, 156, 165
  National Homeless Alliance, 149,
    180
vulnerability, 20, 36, 44, 45, 87, 89–90,
    92, 93

Wanderlust, 18
widowhood, 13, 44–5, 49–52, 79, 80, 81,
    110, 116
work, 10–11, 63–4
  casual jobs, 10, 61, 64, 101–2
  unemployment, 10–11, 18–19, 61, 68,
    87–8
Wright, James, 20, 21, 29, 31, 41, 45, 87,
    130, 131, 132, 133, 135, 161

Reviews of this book

'This is a remarkable book, based on Maureen Crane's many years of acquaintance with homeless older people. It throws light on the pathways which lead to homelessness, and should be required reading not only for policy makers in this field, but all those interested in the vicissitudes of the human life course.'

Peter G. Coleman, Professor of Psychogerontology, University of Southampton, UK

'Maureen Crane has undertaken research on older homeless people for a number of years. She has now brought together her own empirical studies with the work of others. This book presents a new perspective on an important neglected subject. In a clearly written account the complexity of the issues is shown. This book should be read not only by those interested in ageing but also by everyone concerned with social policy and with social exclusion.'

Anthea Tinker, Professor of Social Gerontology, Former Director of the Age Concern Institute of Gerontology, King's College, London, UK

'Drawing on 10 years experience of working with the elderly homeless, Maureen Crane, has produced a book that will be of immense value to those who wish to understand more about this growing social problem. Regardless of the many and varied reasons why some older men and women become homeless, Maureen Crane's book demonstrates that the pathways out of homelessness all involve basic concepts of social justice: namely that the elderly homeless are entitled to access the same levels of housing and aged care services that the rest of the community takes for granted.'

Bryan Lipmann, Victoria, Australia

'Although ageing persons are an important and growing segment of the homeless population, they have been largely ignored by service providers and policy makers. Maureen Crane's book will remedy this situation. Bringing together unique and long experience as a clinician, advocate, and researcher working with older homeless persons in London, Dr Crane offers a comprehensive, compassionate, and insightful look at this population that is rarely found in other texts on homelessness. This book is destined to become the standard reference for anyone interested in aging and homelessness.'

Carl I. Cohen, Professor, Department of Psychiatry, State University of New York, Health Science Center at Brooklyn, USA

'This definitive scholarly work on homelessness among the ageing will be of use to practitioners, planners and academics in the United States as well as United Kingdom. Synthesizing current literature on homelessness and homeless elders from America, Europe and Britain, the book complements available research on the poorest, most vulnerable, and marginalized among today's elders. Using dispassionate social science this ethnographic study argues for more compassionate treatment of a group of ageing people barely noticed in public policy.'

Sharon M. Keigher, Professor of Social Work, University of Wisconsin-Milwaukee, USA